MW00874338

U.S. WARS & DISEASES

Smallpox, Typhoid, Yellow Fever and others

Dr. Lee R. McDowell
2022

To my wife, Lorraine, three daughters (Suzannah, Joanna, Teresa and their husbands), thirteen grandchildren, and actual and expected great-grandchildren.

CONTENTS

INTRODUCTION

The author has published three books concerning history of the United States. As Americas we have much to be thankful for. We need to know our own history, the principles of our founding fathers and our government based on the Constitution. By studying the actions of our presidents, we learn more of the history of the United States. The first book (2018) "The Presidents, Humor, Events and Morality", tries to reach these objectives.

The second book, "The Presidents as Military Officers" emphasized each president in relation to military action prior to the presidency and as the Commander-in-Chief with military action and foreign policies. Of the 45 presidents, 31 were in the military, with 10 as Generals.

The present book, "Wartime Diseases" illustrates major battles and diseases in U.S. wars. Diseases have devastated humankind before written records. They have killed and crippled more persons than all wars ever fought.

The United States has been involved in Indian wars, international wars, the Civil War and two Worlds Wars. This book will show military activity for 13 major U.S. wars.

The major emphasis of this book is how diseases resulted in higher death loss than enemy action during these wars. During wars diseases became more severe due to the closeness of fighting troops. The most predominate diseases during the wars were smallpox, typhoid fever, malaria, yellow fever, venereal diseases, nutritional deficiencies (e.g., vitamins A, C and certain B vitamins). Childhood diseases such as measles, mumps, chicken pox and scarlet fever were often problems for adults. Diseases for particular wars were variable due to various control measures and other factors.

The disease rate was less for World War I than previous wars and further reduced in World War II. There were less diseases due to improved sanitation, insect controls various vaccines, and access to antibiotics including sulfonamides and penicillin.

Incidence of disease and severity of diseases will be noted. More of the armed forces died from infectious diseases than from combat during the early wars. It was not until World War II, that most deaths were from combat.

Some diseases were greatly influenced by sanitation and hygiene (e.g., typhoid and diarrhea/dysentery), while other diseases were due to insect infestation (e.g., malaria, yellow fever and typhus). Better control of sanitation and insect reduction greatly reduced many diseases. Disease is one of man's greatest enemies. It has killed and crippled more persons than all wars ever fought. During the French and Indian War yellow fever caused thousands of deaths and caused many people to flee the affected areas. The comment was made that the death rate was so high that people had to work day and night to bury the dead.

During the Revolutionary War Washington's army lost more troops to disease than to combat. For every soldier who fell to the British, ten died from disease. During this time the most dreaded disease was smallpox, a virus that killed one out of every three infected people. Smallpox threatened the destruction of the entire continental army. Washington decided on a crude mass inoculation for his continental forces. This was the first large-scale, state-sponsored immunization campaign in American History.

In the Mexican War nearly 13% of the entire U.S. force perished from diseases. Seven men died from disease for every man killed from battle.

There seems to be agreement that about two-thirds of Civil War deaths were from disease. The Civil War was the last large-scale war fought without knowledge of the germ theory of disease. Medicine in the United States was woefully behind Europe. For example, Harvard Medical School did not even own a single stethoscope or microscope until after the war.

Chapter 1 is a general discussion of world diseases. Fifteen major world epidemics, plaques and pandemics are discussed. Chapter 2 deals with European diseases in the Americas which resulted in a death rate of 90-95% of Native Americans. Chapters 3 through 14 deal with wars involving the colonies and then wars of the United States. The wars are as follows: King Philip's, French and Indian, American Revolution, War of 1812, Mexican-American, Civil War, Spanish-American, World War I, World War II, Korean, Vietnam, Iraq, and Afghanistan.

Chapters 3 through 14 are set up with two major sections of military events (including major battles) and diseases during wars. There will be references for each chapter and tables will summarize chronological events. Pictures with references to both war battles and diseases are provided.

I am grateful to the typing and proofing of this book by Teresa Ingley. Appreciation is expressed to Lorraine McDowell for her useful suggestions and assistance in proofing and editing of the entire book. Thanks to Joanna McDowell for proofing the entire book. In preparing this book I am grateful to Bert Ingley for his computer expertise and advice and preparation of the book cover.

CHAPTER 1

World Diseases

A. Introduction

Disease is one of man's greatest enemies. It has killed and crippled more persons than all wars ever fought. It has even influenced the course of history. Man has conquered many diseases. But millions of persons in all parts of the world still become ill from diseases each day. All living things can and do get diseases – plants and animals as well as humans.[1,2]

Human diseases include most conditions that interfere with the normal state of the body or of the mind. Diseases have many different causes. For example, some diseases, such as smallpox, typhus, measles, tuberculosis, cholera, pneumonia and scarlet fever are caused by germs. Other diseases, including kwashiorkor, beriberi, night blindness, pellagra, rickets, scurvy, pernicious anemia and iron deficiency anemia, result from poor diets. Still other disease conditions may be caused by allergies, harmful fumes in the air and conditions related to old age.[2-4]

Thousands of years ago man began to emerge from primitive self-contained communities and the chances of major disaster multiplied. This greater degree of civilization brought benefits, a higher standard of living and a fuller more intellectual life, but it also brought hazards. As human civilizations flourished, so did infectious disease. Large numbers of people living in close proximity to each other and to animals, often with poor sanitation and nutrition, provided fertile breeding grounds for disease. And new overseas trading routes spread the novel infections far and wide, creating the first global pandemics.[5]

Disease is a fundamental aspect of the human condition. Ancient bones tell us that pathological processes are older than humankind's written records and sickness still confounds our twenty-first century's technological pride. Disease is something men and women feel. It is something in our bodies – but also in our minds.[4]

Sickness can be linked to climatic and geographic factors. Ailments such as typhus, black death, malaria, dengue and yellow fever reflect specific environments that we share with insects that transmit disease to humans.

Some diseases originate with animals that are passed on to humans, sometimes after a disease mutation.

B. Diseases caused by Germs

Men once believed that evil spirits made people sick. It was not until the 1400's that scientists began to suspect that some diseases were caused by tiny, invisible particles called germs. Early researchers called these germs "living seeds of disease." They believed that germs developed out of nothing in the blood streams of man and of animals. In the 1500's, doctors began to suggest that some germs could be passed from one person to another and spread disease.

Bacteria and other germs were first seen under a microscope in the 1600's. But the germ theory of disease was not proved until the late 1800's. Robert Koch, a German physician, and Louis Pasteur, a French chemist, both experimented with anthrax, an infectious disease of man and animals. Koch showed that animals injected with anthrax germs soon got the disease. Pasteur developed a vaccine to slow down the multiplication of the germs. Alexander Fleming discovered the antibiotic penicillin from mold growth and by 1944 enough penicillin was available to treat wounded soldiers in World War II.

Today, scientists know that infectious diseases are caused by many kinds of germs, including bacteria, viruses, and protozoa. These microorganisms cause disease by attacking living tissue. Some germs live in the tissue and multiply so rapidly that the tissue dies. Others produce toxins (poisons) that kill tissue. Diseases have been shown to be reduced by better sanitation, with prevention of disease with vaccines and treatment with antibiotics.

C. Causes of Death

Cardiovascular diseases (heart disease and stroke) are the leading cause of death globally. The second biggest cause is cancer. For the industrialized developed countries, the leading diseases, in addition to cardiovascular disease and cancer, include diabetes, liver and kidney diseases, lung diseases, (e.g. TB, emphysema and pneumonia), drug disorders, Parkinson's disease and Alzheimer's/dementias.[6]

For the developing low-income countries cardiovascular disease and cancer are still leading causes of death, but a handful of deadly infectious diseases claim millions of lives worldwide each year. Respiratory tract infections (e.g. TB) and diarrhea diseases, HIV/AIDS, and malaria are killers; together these diseases account for more than one in eight deaths globally. As an example, the majority of TB deaths are in the developing world, half of all deaths occur in Asia. In an age of vaccines, antibiotics, and dramatic scientific progress, these diseases should have been brought under control. Yet they continue to kill at an alarming rate, particularly in the developing world. Worldwide pandemic diseases like the Spanish Flu (1918) and Corona virus (2019) have caused high death loss to both low- and high-income countries.[7]

D. World Epidemics, plaques and pandemics

Throughout the course of history, disease outbreaks have ravaged humanity, sometimes changing the course of history and, at times, signaling the end of entire civilizations. Some diseases have decimated populations with greater efficiency than wars.

Some diseases called contagious diseases, spread from one person to another. An epidemic takes place when a contagious disease, such as smallpox or typhoid fever, spreads widely through a community. When epidemics occur at the same time throughout the world, as did the influenzas epidemic (Spanish Flu) in 1918 and the corona virus (Covid 19) in 2019, then they are called pandemics. Notable world epidemics, plaques and pandemics are as follows:

a) Prehistoric epidemics in China – In Circa 3000 B.C. an epidemic wiped out a prehistoric village in China. The bodies of the dead were stuffed inside a house that was later burned down. No age group was spared, as the skeletons of juveniles, young adults and middle-aged people were found inside the house. The archaeological site is now called "Hamin Mangha" and is one of the best-preserved prehistoric sites in northeastern China. Archaeological and anthropological study indicates that the epidemic happened quickly enough that there was no time for proper burials, and the site was not inhabited again.

Even before the discovery of Hamin Mangha, another prehistoric mass burial that dates to roughly the same time period was found at a site called Miaozigou, in northeastern China. Together, these discoveries suggest that an epidemic raved the entire region.[8]

b) Plague of Athens – The Athenian plague is a historically documented event that occurred in 430-26 B.C. during the Peloponnesian War, fought between city-states of Athens and Sparta. The plague originated in Ethiopia, and from there it spread throughout Egypt and Greece. Initial symptoms of the plague included headaches, conjunctivitis, a rash covering the body, and fever. The victims would then cough up blood, and suffer from extremely painful stomach cramping, followed by vomiting and emitting an unnatural and fetid breath. Infected individuals would generally die by the seventh or eighth day.

The plague of Athens affected a majority of the inhabitants of the overcrowded city-state and claimed lives of more than 25% of the population. The cause of the Athenian plague of 430 B.C. has not been clearly determined, but many diseases have been put forward as possibilities, including smallpox, typhoid fever and Ebola. Many scholars believed that overcrowding caused by the war exacerbated the epidemic. Despite the epidemic, the war continued on, not ending until 404 B.C., when Athens was forced to capitulate to Sparta.[9]

c) **Antonine Plague** – The plague occurred in 165-180 A.D. in the Roman Empire, with the cause thought to be smallpox. It was brought into the Empire by returning soldiers and it affected Asia Minor, Egypt, Greece and Italy.

Unlike the plague of Athens, which affected a geographically limited region, the Antonine plague spread across the vast territory of the entire Roman Empire, because the Empire was an economically and politically integrated, cohesive society occupying wide swaths of the territory. The plague destroyed as much as one-third of the population in some areas, and decimated the Roman army, claiming the life of Emperor Marcus Aurelius.

The plague had impact on the Roman Empire supremacy. The plague may have killed over 5 million people in the Roman Empire. The plague affected ancient Roman traditions, leading to a renewal of spirituality and religiousness, creating the conditions for spreading of new religions, including Christianity. The Antonine Plague may well have created the conditions for the decline of the Roman Empire and, afterwards, for its fall in the West in the fifth century AD.[10]

d) **Plague of Cyprian** – 250 – 271 A.D. The plague was named after St. Cyprian, a bishop of Carthage (a city in Tunisia) who described the epidemic as signaling the end of the world, the Plague of Cyprian is estimated to have killed 5,000 people a day in Rome alone. A major symptom was a severe diarrhea, greatly reducing body strength. In 2014, archaeologists in Luxor (Egypt) found what appears to be a mass burial site of plague victims. Their bodies were covered with a thick layer of lime (historically used as a disinfectant). Archaeologists found three kilns used to manufacture lime and the remains of plague victims burned in a giant bonfire. Experts aren't sure what disease caused the epidemic.[8]

e) **Justinian Plague** – The plague is named after Byzantine Emperor Justin and is considered the bubonic plague. This was one of the deadliest pandemics in recorded history that broke out in the sixth century (541-542 A.D.) in Egypt and spread fast to Constantinople, which was the capital of the Eastern Roman (Byzantine) Empire. The outbreak, which spread from Constantinople to both the West and East, had killed up to 25 to 100 million people. Staple foods became scarce, and people died of starvation as well as of the disease itself. The Justinian plague generally followed trading routes providing an "exchange of infections as well as of goods," and, therefore, was especially brutal to coastal cities. Military movement at the time also contributed to spreading the disease. During the plague victims experienced hallucinations followed by fever and fatigue with lesions appearing in the groin area or armpits. Infected individuals then died within days, often vomiting blood.

Prior to the disease the Byzantine Empire had conquered much of the historical Roman Mediterranean coast, including Italy, Rome and North Africa. The pandemic weakened the empire. As the Byzantine Army failed to recruit new soldiers and ensure military supplies to battlegrounds in the wake of the spread of the illness, their provinces came under attack. By the time the pandemic had disappeared the Empire had lost territories in Europe to the Germanic – speaking Franks and Egypt and Syria to the Arabs.[9]

f) Leprosy – The oldest documented evidence for leprosy has been traced to 2000 B.C. Leprosy grew into a pandemic in Europe in the 11th century during the Middle Ages. Leprosy is a slow-developing bacterial disease that causes sores and deformities. Leprosy was believed to be a punishment from God that ran in families. This belief led to moral judgements and ostracization of victims. Now known as Hansen's disease, it still afflicts tens of thousands of people a year and can be fatal if not treated with antibiotics. In the 1980s, there were nearly 5.2 million cases worldwide. Leprosy rates have declined and now cases are rare.[11]

g) The Black Death (Bubonic Plague) 1347 – The Justinian Plague never went away, and then it returned 800 years later with reckless abandon. The Black Death, which hit Europe in 1347, claimed an astonishing 200 million lives in just four years (Fig.1.1). Within 50 years of its reign, by 1400, it reduced the global population from 450 million to below 350 million, possibly below 300 million, with the pandemic killing as many as 150 million. Some estimates claim that the Black Death claimed up to 60% of lives in Europe at that time. It would take 200 years for the population of Europe to recover to the level seen prior to the Black Death. The. Black Death, or pestilence, that hit Europe and Asia in the 14th century was the deadliest pandemic recorded in human history. Excellent reviews on the history of the Black Death are available.[5,8,9,12] The disease, caused by a bacillus bacterium is carried by fleas on rodents (Fig.1.2). Such infected hosts then transmit the disease further and can infect humans – bubonic plague. Humans can transmit the disease by droplets, leading to pneumonic plague.

The plague originated in central Asia and was taken from there to the

Crimea by Mongol warriors and traders. The plague entered Europe via Italy, carried by rats on Genoese trading ships sailing from the Black Sea. It was known as the Black Death because it could turn the skin and sores black while other symptoms included fever and joint pain. With up to two-thirds of sufferers dying from the disease, it is estimated that between 30% and 50% of the population of those places affected died from the Black Death. In the early 1340s, the disease had previously struck China, India, Persia and Egypt.

The mortality of the Black Death varied between regions, sometimes skipping sparely populated rural areas, but then exacting its toll from the densely populated urban areas, where population perished in excess of 50, sometimes 60%. London never really caught a break after the Black Death. The plague resurfaced roughly every 20 years from 1348 to 1665 – 40 outbreaks in 300 years. And with each new plague epidemic, 20% of the men, women and children living in the British capital were killed.

The plague had arrived in Europe in October 1347, when 12 ships from the Black Sea docked at the Sicilian port of Messina. People gathered on the docks were met with a horrifying surprise: Most sailors aboard the ships were dead, and those still alive were gravely ill and covered in black boils that oozed blood and pus. Sicilian authorities hastily ordered the fleet of "death ships" out of the harbor, but it was too late. Even before the "death ships" pulled into port at Messina, many Europeans had heard rumors about a "Great Pestilence" that was carving a deadly path across the trade routes of the Near and Far East.

In a panic, healthy people did all they could to avoid the sick. Doctors refused to see patients; priests refused to administer last rites; and shopkeepers closed their stores. Dead bodies became so prevalent that many remained rotting on the ground and created a constant stench in cities. Many people fled the cities for the countryside, but even there they could not escape the disease: It affected cows, sheep, goats, pigs and chickens as well as people. In fact, so many sheep died that one of the consequences of the Black Death was a European wool shortage. Many people, desperate to save themselves, even abandoned their sick and dying loved ones.

Entire neighborhoods, sometimes entire towns, were wiped out or settlements abandoned. Crops could not be harvested, traveling and trade became curtailed, and food and manufactured goods became short. The plague changed the course of Europe's history. With so many dead, labor became harder to find, bringing about better pay for workers and the end of Europe's system of serfdom. The plague broke down the normal divisions between the upper and lower classes and led to the emergence of a new middle class.

The immediate effect of the Black Death for affected countries was a general paralysis, with trade largely ceasing. The military of many countries was affected. England and France were so incapacitated by the plague that the countries called a truce to their war. The war was halted by a truce on May 2, 1349 and did not break out again generally until September 1355. In 1350, with the death of so many able-bodied men, the defense of the realm became a matter of grave concern, and towns were required to supply men-at-arms, ships and sailors from their depleted resources. With raging populations in Greenland, Vikings lost the strength to wage battle against native populations, and their exploration of North America halted.

The Black Death epidemic had run its course by the early 1350s, but the plague reappeared every few generations for centuries. Modern sanitation and public-health practices have greatly reduced the impact of the disease but have not eliminated it. While antibiotics are available to treat the Black Death, according to the World Health Organization, there are still 1,000 to 3,000 cases of plague every year.

h) Typhus epidemic, 1482-1492 – Typhus is an infectious disease caused by rickettsia, characterized by a purple rash, headaches, fever, gangrenous sores and finally smell of rotting flesh. Historically a cause of high mortality during wars and famines, there are several forms, transmitted by vectors such as lice, ticks, mites and rat fleas.[13]

The first reliable description of the disease was in 1489 during the Spanish siege of Baza against the Moors during the War of Granada (1482-1492). During the siege, the Spaniards lost 3,000 men to enemy action, but an additional 17,000 died of typhus.[14]

In historical times terms such as "jail fever" was common in English prisons and is believed to have been typhus. It often occurred when prisoners were crowded together into dark, filthy rooms where lice spread easily. Thus, "imprisonment until the next term of court" was often equivalent to a death sentence. In 1759, an English authority estimated that each year, a quarter of the prisoners had died from what was later known as typhus.

Prevention of typhus is by reducing exposure to organisms that spread the disease and by a vaccine. Treatment is use of antibiotics.

i) Smallpox of Latin America, 15th-17th century – The history of smallpox extends into pre-history, with the disease probably emerging in human populations about 10,000 B.C. The earliest credible evidence of smallpox is found in the Egyptian mummies of people who died some 3,000 years ago. Smallpox has had a major impact on world history. The Japanese smallpox epidemic of 735-737 is believed to have killed as much as one-third of Japan's population. Smallpox was a leading cause of death in the 18th century. Every seventh child born in Russia died from smallpox. It killed an estimated 400,000 Europeans each year in the 18th century, including five reigning European monarchs. Most people became infected during their lifetimes, and about 30% of people infected with smallpox died from the disease.

Smallpox was endemic to Europe and Asia for centuries, a persistent menace that killed three out of ten people it infected and left the rest with pockmarked scars. But the death rate in the Old World paled in comparison to the devastation wrought on native populations in the New World when the smallpox virus arrived in the 15th century with the first European explorers. Chapter 2 illustrates the massive death rates due to introduction of smallpox and other European diseases.

The indigenous peoples of the Americas had no natural immunity to smallpox and the virus cut them down by the tens of millions. Following the arrival of the Spanish in the Caribbean, diseases such as smallpox, measles and bubonic plague were passed along to the native populations by the Europeans. With no previous exposure, these diseases devastated indigenous people, with the exception of Noah and the biblical flood, there hasn't been a kill off in human history to match what happened in the Americas – 90 to 95 percent of the indigenous population wiped out over a century.[11,13,16]

Upon arrival on the island of Hispaniola, Christopher Columbus encountered the Taino people, population 60,000. By 1548, the population stood at less than 500. This scenario repeated itself throughout the Americans. In 1520, the Aztec Empire was destroyed by a smallpox infection and in 1532 the Inca Empire had been destroyed by the disease. The Spaniards Hernan Cortes and Francisco Pizarro would probably not have been able to defeat these empires without the aid of smallpox. For the Aztecs, Mexico goes from 11 million people pre-conquest to one million, after defeat by Cortes.

Smallpox eventually killed between 300 and 500 million people worldwide, during the 20th century alone. After vaccination programs, smallpox was eradicated by 1979 and is credited for creating the medical science of vaccination.

j) Cocoliztli epidemic - 1545 – 1549 – This Cocoliztli Epidemic was a form of viral hemorrhagic fever that killed 15 million inhabitants of Mexico and Central America. Among a population already weakened by extreme drought, the disease proved to be utterly catastrophic. A recent study that examined DNA from the skeletons of victims found that they were infected with a subspecies of *Salmonella* known as *S. paratyphi C*, which causes enteric fever, a category of fever that includes typhoid. Enteric fever can cause high fever, dehydration and gastrointestinal problems and is still a major health threat today.[8]

k) Philadelphia Yellow Fever epidemic - 1793 – Yellow fever, which is transmitted by the *Aedes aegypti* mosquito had long been known as one of the most lethal and feared diseases. Symptoms of yellow fever include fever, chills, headaches, abdominal pain and liver damage causing yellow skin. In 1793 there was a yellow fever epidemic in Philadelphia, the United States capital at the time. It wasn't until winter arrived – and the mosquitoes died out – that the epidemic finally stopped. By then, more than 5,000 people had died.

No one knows for sure, but scientists believe that yellow fever has plagued the world for at least 3,000 years. Yellow fever virus originated in Africa and was brought to the western hemisphere during the slave trade era with the first epidemic reported in 1648 in the Yucatan (Mexico). Over the ensuing 200 years outbreaks occurred widely in tropical America, the North American coastal cities and Europe.

Between 1839 and 1860, some 26,000 people in New Orleans contracted yellow fever, with thousands dying. In the brief Spanish-American war at the end of the 19th century, for every soldier who died in battle, 13 died of yellow fever. Major Walter Reed proved that mosquitoes transmitted the disease. With mosquito control measures, work on the Panama Canal could continue. By 1906, roughly 85 percent of canal workers had been hospitalized with either yellow fever or malaria.[17]

l) Typhoid Fever, before 1800s – Typhoid fever is a bacterial disease caused by *Salmonella typhi*. While rare in industrialized countries, typhoid fever is a significant threat in some low-income countries.[18,19] Symptoms of typhoid fever range from mild to serious and usually develop one to three weeks after exposure to the bacteria. Symptoms include fever, headache, nausea, constipation or diarrhea, loss of appetite, and a rose-colored rash on the body.

Typhoid fever spreads from person to person via contaminated food and water. Transmission is via the fecal-oral route, meaning that contaminated feces may enter water supplies or food supplies, which may then be consumed. Infected individuals can then infect others.

Typhoid fever has been documented throughout history and during the American Civil War. Nearly 80,000 Union soldiers died of the disease. Many historians believe Alexander the Great perished from typhoid fever.

Typhoid fever is found more commonly in densely populated areas in developing countries where water supplies are vulnerable to contamination. About 21 million cases of typhoid fever and 220,000 deaths occurred annually worldwide. Antibiotics are the only effective treatment for typhoid fever, with vaccination available.

m) First Cholera pandemic - 1817 – Cholera likely has its origins in the

Indian subcontinent as evidenced by its prevalence in the region for centuries. In 1817 was the first of seven cholera pandemics over the next 150 years. The disease first spread by trade routes (land and sea) to Russia in 1817, later to the rest of Europe, and from Europe to North America and the rest of the world. In Russia one million people died. The reach of the British Empire and its navy spread cholera to Spain, Africa, Indonesia, China, Japan, Italy, Germany and America, where it killed 150,000 people.

Since it became widespread in the 19th century, cholera has killed tens of millions of people. The cholera bacterium (*vibrio cholerae*) is spread through feces-infected water and food. A vaccine was created in 1885. Cholera is now no longer considered a pressing health threat in Europe and North America due to filtering and chlorination of water supplies, but still heavily affects populations in developing countries.[20]

n) American Polio epidemic - 1916 – Polio, also known as infantile paralysis, was known in ancient times. The disease is caused by a virus that attacks the gray matter of the brain and spinal cord. A polio epidemic that started in New York City caused 27,000 cases and 6,000 deaths in the United States. The disease mainly affects children and often leaves survivors with permanent disabilities.

Polio epidemics occurred sporadically in the United States until the Salk vaccine was developed in 1954. Cases in the United States declined as the vaccine became available. The last polio case in the United States was reported in 1979. Worldwide vaccination efforts have greatly reduced the disease, although it is not yet completely eradicated.[8]

o) Influenza – The flu, or influenza, is a highly contagious viral infection that mainly affects the respiratory system. It's usually a seasonal illness, with yearly outbreaks killing hundreds of thousands of people around the world. Symptoms of the flu include sudden onset fever, coughing, sneezing, a runny nose, and severe malaise, though it can also include vomiting, diarrhea and nausea.

Completely new versions of the virus may infect people and spread quickly, resulting in pandemics. Influenza pandemics would be defined as infections that spread throughout the world, with death tolls in the millions. In addition to specific year influenzas, there's the seasonal flu that kills between 250,000 and 500,000 people every year and has claimed between 340 million and one billion human lives throughout history.[21]

There are thought to have been 31 known pandemics which were in 1510, 1557, 1580, 1729, 1878 (Avian Flu), 1889 (Russian pandemic), 1918 (Spanish Flu), 2009 (Swine Flu) and 2019 (Coronavirus, COVID-19).

The 1918 Spanish flu pandemic was the deadliest in history, affecting one-third of the world's population and killing up to 50 million people. Spanish flu had an immense influence on our civilization. The flu was recorded in Europe and then spread fast to America and Asia. India, one of the worst-hit by the pandemic, lost between 17 and 18 million people, roughly 6% of its population.[12] The virus came in several waves and killed its victims quickly, often within a matter of hours or days. More U.S. soldiers in World War I died from the flu than from battle. Some authors even point out that it may have tipped the outcome of World War I, as it affected armies of Germany and the Austrian-Hungarian Empire earlier and more virulently than their Allied opponents.[22]

An outbreak of the coronavirus (COVID-19) was detected in mainland China in December 2019. Every continent in the world, except Antarctica, has been affected by this highly contagious virus. Researchers believe the new virus mutated from a coronavirus in bats.

The virus may be transmitted through expelled droplets, from when an infected person coughs or sneezes. The virus is stable for several hours to days, so may be picked up by touching surfaces. Strategies to reduce the spread of the virus is to regularly wash hands, wear a face mask and avoid close contact with others.[23]

The COVID-19 outbreak that has already infected about 2 million and killed over 126,000 people would change the world. But the outbreak has seen countries imposing drastic restrictions on people's movements. Unemployment rate in the U.S. has shot up to the levels not seen since the end of Second World War. Governments across the world, including the U.S. administration, are beefing up spending to stimulate an economy that shows signs of depression. Radical changes, good or bad, are already unfolding.

E. Deadly infectious diseases as global killers

A handful of deadly infectious diseases, especially in low-income countries, claim millions of lives worldwide each year - lower respiratory tract infections (e.g. pneumonia, bronchitis), diarrheal diseases, HIV/AIDS, tuberculosis, and malaria. Together, they account for more than one in eight deaths globally. Several of these diseases have plagued humankind throughout history, often decimating populations with greater efficiency than wars.[7]

a) Malaria – Malaria is an ancient disease. About 10,000 years ago, malaria started having a major impact on human survival and is found published in ancient Chinese, Mesopotamia, Egyptian and Hindu texts. Malaria is caused by infection with protozoan parasites belonging to the genus *Plasmodium* transmitted by female *Anopheles* species mosquitoes. The parasite from the mosquito first goes to the liver and then invades red blood cells. The danger is increased for those also suffering with sickle cell anemia. The symptoms of malaria are intense attacks of chills, sweats and great weakness.

In the 20th century alone malaria claimed between 150 to 300 million lives, accounting for 2 to 5 percent of all deaths. Similar to the other global killers, malaria occurs mostly in poor, tropical, and subtropical areas of the world. In 2014, an estimated 214 million people were infected with malaria worldwide, leading to the death of about 438,000 people, most of whom were young children in sub-Saharan Africa. Malaria, both epidemic and endemic, continued to plague the United States until the early 20th century. It struck presidents from Washington to Lincoln, weakened Civil War soldiers by the hundreds of thousands (in 1862, Washington, D.C., and its surroundings were so malarious that General McClellan's Army en route to Yorktown was stopped in its tracks). During World War II more soldiers fell to malaria than to enemy forces. Sixty thousand American soldiers died of malaria during the African and South Pacific campaigns.

Malaria can be controlled and prevented by destroying Anopheles mosquitoes and use of antimalaria drugs (e.g. quinine). There is a problem with drug-resistant malaria.[24]

b) Tuberculosis (TB) – TB is a serious infectious disease that attacks primary the lungs but can affect almost any part of the body. TB is a contagious, infectious disease, due to Mycobacterium tuberculosis that has always been a permanent challenge over the course of human history. TB for many years was known as consumption. The symptoms of TB include fever, sweating, coughing and blood-stained sputum.

TB has very ancient origins; it has survived over 70,000 years. Three million years ago, an early progenitor of the bacteria might have infected early hominids in East Africa and 15,000-20,000 years ago, for the first time, the common ancestor of modern strains of mycobacterium tuberculosis might have appeared. The first written documents describing TB, dating back to 2,300 and 3,300 years ago, were found in India and in China, respectively. Egyptian mummies, dating back to 2400 B.C., reveal skeletal deformities typical of tuberculosis.[5,25] TB currently infects nearly 2 billion people worldwide; with around 10.4 million new cases of TB each year, almost one third of the world's population are carriers of the TB bacillus and are at risk for developing active disease.[26] According to the United Nations, TB is the world's deadliest infectious disease. In 2018 around 1.5 million people died from the bacterial infection. Patients with corona virus represent a significant danger because their lungs are already weakened by TB.

TB is a great problem in developing countries. The vast majority of TB deaths are in the developing world and more than half of all deaths occur in Asia. Today, almost all TB patients can be treated successfully with drugs. Isoniazid is one of the most effective TB drugs. There has been a problem with rise of drug resistant strains of the disease.

c) Pneumonia – Pneumonia and other lower respiratory infections account for more than 4 million deaths worldwide each year – the greatest global killer among infectious diseases. Pneumonia is also the leading cause of death of the very young, often striking children with low birthweight or those whose immune system is weakened by malnutrition or other diseases. The majority of deaths occur in developing countries.[7]

d) Diarrheal disease – Diarrhea is one of the top 10 leading causes of infectious disease deaths worldwide, accounting for 1.5 million deaths annually. Children under age 5 account for more than half of those deaths. These infections are so widespread in developing countries that parents often fail to recognize when symptoms become critical. Children die simply because their bodies are weakened – often through rapid loss of fluids and undernourishment. The burden of diarrheal diseases is highest in deprived areas where there is poor sanitation, inadequate hygiene, and unsafe drinking water.[7]

e) HIV/AIDS – HIV stands for human immunodeficiency virus, the virus that causes acquired immunodeficiency syndrome (AIDS), the final stage of HIV infection. HIV appears to have jumped to humans early in the 20th century from a subspecies of chimpanzee in West Africa – most likely when humans hunted these animals for meat and came into contact with their infected blood. The virus slowly spread across Africa and later to other parts of the world.

Unlike most other viruses, HIV attacks the immune system destroying a type of white blood cells (e.g., T cells) that the immune system needs to fight disease. HIV is transmitted by having sex with someone infected with HIV, by sharing needles and syringes with an infected person, through blood or blood product transfusions, or by being exposed as a fetus or an infant to the virus before or during birth or through breastfeeding.

At the end of 2015, more than 36 million people worldwide were infected with HIV. More than 2 million were newly infected in 2015 and an estimated 1.1 million died.[7]

F. Effects of disease on U.S. wars

Wartime epidemics of infectious diseases have decimated the fighting strength of armies, caused the suspension and cancellation of military operations, and brought havoc to the civil populations of belligerent and nonbelligerent states. Throughout American's first 145 years of war, far more of the country's military personnel perished from infectious diseases than from enemy action (Table 1.1). This enduring feature of war was finally reversed in World War II, chiefly as a result of major medical advances in prevention (vaccines) and treatment (antibiotics). Safeguarding the health of a command is indispensable for the success of any campaign. Wars are lost by disease, which causes an enormous drain on the military's resources and affects both strategy and tactics. Disease and combat mortality data from America's principal wars (1775-present) fall into two clearly defined time periods: the Disease Era (1775-1918), during which infectious diseases were the major killer of American's armed forces, and the Trauma Era (1941-present), in which combat-related fatalities predominated. The trend established in World War II continues to the present day. Although there are currently more than 3,400 U.S. military fatalities in Iraq, the disease-death toll is so low that it is exceeded by the number of suicides.[3,27]

G. Summary

Throughout history disease had killed many at a young age. It has killed and crippled more persons than all wars every fought. Diseases have many different causes such as germs resulting in diseases, such as smallpox, measles, typhoid fever and cholera. Malaria and yellow fever were brought about by mosquitoes, typhus by lice and the black death resulted from fleas on rats. Some diseases, such as kwashiorkor, beriberi, scurvy and rickets, and iron deficiency anemia are caused by nutrient deficiencies. Diseases may be caused by allergies, harmful fumes and conditions related to old age.

More people die from cardiovascular diseases and cancers. However, low-income individuals in developing countries often succumb to deadly infectious diseases: respiratory tract infections (e.g., TB), diarrheal diseases, HIV/AIDS, and malaria. In early history there were epidemics, plagues and pandemics (worldwide distribution of a disease).

Some of the earliest plagues were in Circa China, (3,000 B.C.), Athens Greece (430-426 B.C.), Antonine plague, Roman Empire (165-180 A.D.), plague of Cyprian, Tunisia (250-271 A.D.) and Justinian Plague, Eastern Roman Empire (541-542 A.D.). The causes of these plagues are unknown with thoughts of possibly smallpox, typhoid fever or Ebola. For the Antonine and Justinian plagues the causes were suggested as smallpox and bubonic plague, respectively.

Some diseases were prehistory. Smallpox was active 10,000 B.C. with best evidence of smallpox found in Egyptian mummies of people who had died some 3,000 years ago. Yellow fever is believed to have plagued the world for at least 3,000 years. TB has had very ancient origins, as it has survived over 70,000 years. About 10,000 years ago malaria had a major impact on humans. Leprosy was known 2,000 B.C. Influenza has been around throughout history with 33 known pandemics since 1510. Cholera is believed to have been in India for centuries.

Smallpox in Europe was a disease that routinely killed about 30% of children; if they survived, they would be immune to the disease. When smallpox was introduced to native Americans there were 90-95% death rates from this and other European introduced diseases.

One of the worst plagues was the Black Death (Bubonic Plague) which killed 200 million in just four years. Influenza, usually a seasonal illness with yearly outbreaks kills hundreds of thousands of people around the world. The 1918 Spanish flu pandemic was the deadliest in history, killing 50 million people.

Infectious diseases during wars have decimated the fighting strength of armies and have resulted in suspensions and cancellation of military operations. The Aztec and Inca Empires were conquered by the Spanish conquistadors in the 1500s. Many believe that both the Aztecs and Incas would have been victorious had it not been for the massive deaths caused by smallpox. During the early American wars infectious diseases were the major killer of armed forces. Starting with World War II combat – related fatalities predominated over diseases.

Table 1.1 United States Military Casualties of War[27]

War or Conflict	Date	Total U.S. Deaths			Wounded	Total U.S. casualties	Missing	Deaths as percentage of Total Population
		Combat	Other[a]	Total				
American Revolutionary War	1775-1783	8,000	17,000	25,000	25,000	50,000		1%
War of 1812	1812-1815	2,260	12,740	5,000	4,505	20,000		0.207%
Black Hawk War	1832	47	25i8	305	85	390		
Second Seminole War	1835-1842	328	1,207	1,535		1,535		
Mexican-American War	1846-1848	1,733	11,550	13,283	4,152	17,435		0.057%
Civil War: total	1861-1865	214,938	450,000	☐655,000				
Spanish-American War	1898	385	2,061	2,446	1,622	4,068		
Philippine-American War	1898-1913	1,020	3,176	4,196	2,930	7,126		
World War I	1917-1918	53,402	63,114	116,516	204,002	320,518	3,350	0.11%
World War II	1941-1945	291,557	113,842	405,399	670,846	1,076,245	30,314	0.39%
Korean War	1950-1953	33,686	2,830	36,516	92,134	128,650	4,759	
Vietnam War	1955-1975	47,424	10,785	58,209	153,303	211,454	1,603	
Gulf War	1990-1991	149	145	294	849	1,143	0	
War in Afghanistan	2001-present	1,833	383	2,216	20,050	22,266	0	
Iraq War	2003-2011	3,836	961	4,497	32,222	36,710	2	

[a] Deaths- "other" includes all non-combat deaths including, those from disease, accidents, suicide and murder. The overwhelming cause of death in "other" is from contagious disease.

Fig. 1.1 The Black Death was a devastating global epidemic of bubonic plaque that struck Europe and Asia in the mid-1300s.

Fig 1.2 Bubonic Plaque caused by a bacillus bacterium carried by fleas on rodents.

CHAPTER 2

Early Diseases in the Americas

A. Introduction

There was a great loss of life for Native Americans due to lack of disease immunity. The population just prior to the arrival of Columbus was estimated to be between 90-112 million - more people lived in the Americas then Europe. Disease claimed the lives of 80 to 100 million Indians by the first of the 17th century. Europeans (starting with Columbus) introduced diseases that resulted in a death rate of 90-95% of Native Americans.[1]

Old World European bacteria and viruses turned the New World into an abettor. So, too, did African diseases like malaria and yellow fever when they arrived. There existed vast, super-deadly pandemics, the speed and scale of the projected losses "boggle the mind". Historically Calloway (2003) noted, how can one understand losses of such unparalleled scope?[2]

B. Death from European Diseases

a) Smallpox in Caribbean regions visited by Columbus – The early introduction of European diseases would have been by Columbus with his visits to the Caribbean Islands. Most likely the smallpox virus was introduced to the Caribbean by Columbus' Spanish crew (Fig. 2.1). This was recorded in Hispaniola (Dominican Republic and Haiti) in 1518. It had killed 1/3 of the native population, then the disease moved on to other parts of the Americas.[1]

b) Smallpox in Mexico – In 1519 Hernan Cortes began conquest of the Aztecs of Mexico. According to several Spanish accounts the invading Spaniards included an African slave named Francisco Eguia, who had smallpox. Also, the smallpox brought by the Columbus crew was affecting other American sites. A different theory was that the carriers of smallpox were Cuban Indians. The disease reached to Tenochtitlan (Mexico City) and devastated the Aztecs. Smallpox laid waste to the metropolis and the rest of the empire.

When Columbus landed the central Mexican plateau had a population of over 25 million. By contrast Spain and Portugal together had a population of less than ten million. Central Mexico was the most densely populated location on earth, with more than twice as many people per square mile than China or India.[3] With large numbers of people together the disease had a great killing opportunity.

In their battle with the Aztecs, Cortez's army won most battles thanks to their guns, horses and steel blades despite being outnumbered. Cortez was wise in using the enemies of the Aztecs to join in battle allied with the Spanish. In one brutal night battle, three quarters of Cortez's men were killed. The Aztecs made a bad mistake by not hunting down and killing the last Spaniards. The Spaniards regrouped and joined with other Indian allies and won the war in 1521. The last battle had been costly as casualty estimates range up to 100,000.

During this time period the great city lost at least a third of its population. In the absence of smallpox, it seems likely that Cortez would have lost the war with the Aztecs. After Cortez, the population collapsed by 1625 to about 700,000, approximately 3 percent of its size at the time that he first landed.[3]

c) **Smallpox in the Inca Empire of South America** – Dobyns (1963) correctly concluded that smallpox had invaded South America prior to the arrival of any Europeans.[4] Taken as a whole, Dobyns thought, that smallpox had killed nine out of ten living in the Inca empire. In 1491 the Incas ruled the greatest empire on earth. The Inca Empire extended over a staggering thirty-two degrees of latitude. The empire was greater than the Ming Dynasty in China, Ivan the Great's Russian empire, the Ottoman Empire, the Aztec Empire and bigger by far than any European state.

Dobyns (1963) had concluded that the smallpox virus had arrived originally from Hispaniola as a result of the Columbus visits.[4] The disease was established in Hispaniola in 1518. The disease organism jumped from Hispaniola to Puerto Rico and Cuba. From here only a short distance to Central America and Colombia. Going through Colombia the virus ravished Indian tribes.

Next the virus moved to the Inca Empire, a few hundred miles from Panama. The smallpox epidemic moved to every corner of the hemisphere, causing destruction in places that never saw Europeans. Smallpox has an incubation period of about 12 days, during which time infected individuals, who may not know they are sick, will infect anyone they meet. With good roads and great population movements, the Incan empire was positioned for a major epidemic.

The head Inca, Wayna Qhapaq, died when "a great plaque of smallpox" broke out in 1524 or 1525. The outbreak was so severe that more than 200,000 died of it, for it spread to all parts of the Kingdom.[5] In addition to killing Wayna Qhapaq, it also killed his son and designated heir – and his brother, uncle and sister-wife. The main generals and much of the officer corps died as well, "all faces covered with scabs."

Wayna Qhapaq had died in the first smallpox epidemic, but the virus struck the Inca empire again in 1533, 1535, 1558 and 1565. The Incas died by the scores and hundreds. Villages were depopulated. Corpses were scattered over the fields or piled up in huts. The fields were uncultivated; the herds were untended resulting in the price of food increasing so that many persons could not afford it; they escaped the disease only to die from famine.[4]

After smallpox killed the head Inca, there was a civil war between two brothers who wanted to replace Wayna Qhapaq. The winning brother was Atawallpa. After the horrific battle, estimated dead was 35,000. After the final battle the victors stopped outside the small city of Cajamarca, Peru where they learned that pale, hairy people who sat on enormous animals had landed on the coast. The Spaniard Francisco Pizarro in 1532 ambushed Atawallpa's five or six thousand troops, with a Spanish force of only 168. The Spaniards had the surprise plus horses, cannons, superior broadswords and were wearing armor.[5]

The Incas had been decimated by smallpox about eight years before the Spanish arrived. Had it not been for the Civil War and smallpox, Pizarro and the Spanish army would likely have been defeated by the armies of Atawallpa.

The Incas and other Indian groups were susceptible to other European diseases:

- 1546 Typhus (probably)
- 1558 Influenza (along with smallpox)
- 1614 Diphtheria
- 1618 Measles
- 1616 Viral Hepatitis

d) Death in southern United States from Spanish expedition – Hernando DeSoto's Spanish exploration in southern U.S. was looking for gold but resulted in diseases and death to Native Americans. In late 1539 DeSoto sailed to Florida, U.S.A., with 600 soldiers, 200 horses and 300 pigs. For four years the expedition wandered through what are now the states of Florida, Georgia, North and South Carolina, Tennessee, Alabama, Mississippi, Arkansas, Texas and Louisiana. The Native Americas fought back unsuccessfully and were in awe of the Spaniards' horses and guns.

In their travels in and around the Mississippi (via barges), several thousand Indian soldiers approached in canoes and mocked the Spanish. Without fear De Soto marched right into cities and demanded food. Along the way they managed to rape, torture, enslave, and kill countless Native Americans.[1]

During these four years the Spanish report a land "thickly set with great towns and cities". Each city protected itself with earthen walls, sizeable moats, and dead eye archers. After De Soto departed, no Europeans visited this part of the Mississippi Valley for more than 100 years. In 1682, 139 years after De Soto, Frenchman (Robert De LaSalle) visited much the same area and found cities and towns deserted. De Soto found 50 settlements in one strip of the Mississippi, by LaSalle's time the number had shrunk to perhaps 10, some probably inhabited by recent immigrants.[7]

What had happened was a civilization had crumbled from De Soto's earlier visitation. Most historians and anthropologists believe the culprit was disease, smallpox and perhaps measles? Perhaps it was due to De Soto's pigs.[8] When humans and domesticated animals share quarters, they are exposed to each other's microbes. Over time animal diseases jump to human's: avian influenza becomes human influenza, bovine rinderpest becomes human measles, and horsepox becomes human smallpox.

Measles and smallpox would have burned out through the 600 men long before they reached the Mississippi. Swine, mainstays of European agriculture, transmit anthrax, brucellosis, leptospirosis, and tuberculosis. Pigs can pass diseases to deer and turkeys, which can affect people. Therefore, perhaps the pigs were involved in the death loss.

The idea that pigs were responsible for the deaths is speculation. After the Spanish departed, mass graves became more common in the Southeast. However, proof is lacking that a single Indian in a grave died of a pig transmitted disease.

The societies of Caddo (Texas-Arkansas border) and Coosa (western Georgia) both disintegrated soon after De Soto's visit. Caddo had monumental architecture, public plazas, ceremonial platforms, etc.; after De Soto, the Caddo began digging community cemeteries. Pettula (1993) concluded that the Caddon population fell from 300,000 to 8,500; a drop of 96%. In the 18th century, the population shrank to 1,400.[9]

e) Deaths in New England (U.S.A.) – More evidence of death from European diseases was seen from a British ship in 1619. From southern Maine to Narragansett Bay, the coast was empty – "utterly void". What had once been a line of busy communities was now a mass of tumble-down homes and untended fields overrun with blackberries. Among the homes and fields were skeletons bleached by the sun – "and the bones and skulls upon the several places of their habitations made such a spectacle".

The crew of a British ship realized they were sailing along the border of a cemetery 200 miles long and 40 miles deep. The settlements they passed lay empty to the sky, but full of untended dead.[1]

The many deaths had begun between 1616-1619, a few years before the Plymouth colony and Pilgrims in 1620. This event had resulted from a French ship wreaked at Cape Cod, with the Wampanoag Indians killing all but five of the ships crew. The five captured crew members were taken to the Wampanoag settlements; unfortunately, the Europeans carried a disease that decimated the Indians. Based on accounts of symptoms, the epidemic was probably from viral hepatitis. It is also suggested that the disease was leptospirosis, so rats from European ships would have been the culprits.[10] The Indians died in heaps as they lay in their houses. In their panic, the healthy fled from the sick, carrying the disease with them to other communities.[11]

Beginning in 1616, the pestilence took at least three years to exhaust itself and killed as much as 90% of Wampanoag Indians in coastal New England. Groups like the Narragansett, which had been spared by the epidemic of 1616, were crushed by a smallpox epidemic in 1633.

The Pilgrims, in 1620 had few problems with the Wampanoag as they were greatly weakened by their high death loss. The Pilgrims were not prepared for living in New England without food or shelter, arriving six weeks before winter. Most of the Pilgrims were not knowledgeable in agriculture. The Wampanoag were very helpful in providing food and beneficial agricultural practices. The Wampanoags permitted the Pilgrims to remain among them since they had formally allied with them against their mortal enemies the Narragansett.

C. Lack of Disease Resistance in Native Americans

Indians died at extremely high rates from European diseases, evidence suggests that the Native Americans were somehow uniquely vulnerable. An example of lack of disease resistance in Native Americans is with the disease measles. Normally measles is a childhood disease that is uncomfortable, but not deadly. It was, however, deadly to the Native Americans. An example of this was in 1967, a missionary's 2-year-old daughter came down with measles in a village on the Toototobi River in Brazil. She was checked by Brazilian doctors before departure. The Yanomami Indians had never encountered the measles virus. Many died and the virus spread, carried by exposed people. Several thousand doses of vaccine helped but the death rate was 8.8% for affected villages.[12]

There are two types of immunity or susceptibility to disease; acquired immunity and genetic resistance.[1] Acquired immunity is immunity gained from a previous exposure to a pathogen; as an example, people never exposed to chicken pox are readily infected by the virus. However, after the disease, the immune system is trained to recognize the virus and never catch it again.

Native Americans were genetically unusually susceptible to foreign microbes and viruses. As a group Native Americans' immune system has less ability to defend against disease. Essential parts of the immune system are human leukocyte antigens (HLA) and leukocytes. The HLA in cells recognize foreign invaders and make also available for destruction by leukocytes (white blood cells). Native and non-Native Americans were given a measles vaccine. There was limited immune response from Indians, but robust response from non-Indians.[13,14]

All people have multiple types of HLA; however, overall, Indians have fewer HLA types. Populations from Europe, Asia and Africa have at least 35 main HLA classes, while Indian groups have no more than 17. Indians' closest genetic relatives are indigenous Siberians. They too suffered from smallpox in 1768. In 1797 Captain James Cook visited the shoreline; it was a cemetery. It is believed the single epidemic killed more than three of four Siberians.

Europeans know the horrors of the Black Death in 1347 which killed 1/3 of its victims. However, a much higher death rate for disease, 90-95% was found for smallpox in Native Americans. Old-world bacteria and viruses turned the new world into an abattoir.

In Europe, Africa and Asia smallpox was a constant, terrible disease, infecting almost every child, killing many and leaving others with the characteristic pock marks. The survivors were now immune to the disease. The European adults, including the Conquistadors, were immune and would not develop the disease again. Smallpox and other European diseases didn't exist in the Americas, so all Indians were susceptible (Table 2.1). There were many interactions between Europe, Asia and Africa for many years; therefore, there was exposure to many diseases.

For the Spanish, the depopulation of the New World was an unintended tragedy. The Spanish had wanted Native peoples for forced labor. Indian deaths were a financial blow. To resupply themselves with labor, the Spaniards began the slave trade from Africa.[15]

Table 2.1 illustrates Diseases in early America.

D. Summary

In the late 1400s Europeans, starting with Columbus, introduced diseases that resulted in a death rate of 90-95% of Native Americans. European bacteria and viruses turned the New World into abattoirs. So too did African diseases like malaria and yellow fever when they arrived.

Smallpox devastated both the Aztec and Inca empires, which gave the Spanish a great advantage in conquering both of these great empires. In addition to smallpox other killing diseases at this time included typhus, influenza, diphtheria, measles and viral hepatitis.

The Spanish under Hernando DeSoto visited in 1539 10 southern states in the U.S. over four years. As a result of the visit, civilizations crumbled due to disease. A British ship observed a cemetery 200 miles long and 40 miles deep from Maine to Narragansett Bay, resulting from European diseases. Many deaths from disease had occurred prior to landing of the Pilgrims in the Plymouth Colony in 1620. The Pilgrims had little problems with the Wampanoag Indians as they had been greatly weakened from their high death losses.

Native Americans were found to lack disease resistance compared to Europeans, Asians and Africans. Native Americans were found to be unusually susceptible to foreign microbes and viruses. Essential parts of the immune system are human leukocyte antigens (HLA) and leukocytes. The HLA in cells recognize foreign invaders and leukocytes destroy them. Native Americas have much fewer HLA classes, resulting in reduced resistance to disease.

Table 2.1 Early American Diseases[1,6,10,13]

Late 1400s	Columbus's Spanish crew introduces smallpox virus to Dominican Republic and Haiti killing 1/3 of native population.
1519	In Hernan Cortes's conquest of Aztecs of Mexico, a crewmember introduced smallpox resulting in many deaths.
1524 or 1525	A severe outbreak of smallpox in the Inca Empire, killing more than 200,000.
1539-1543	Hernando DeSoto's four-year Spanish exploration of southern U.S. introduced European diseases to the region.
1619	Evidence of death from European diseases was observed by a British ship. From southern Maine to Narragansett Bay, the coast was empty. The crew of the British ship realized they were sailing along the border of a cemetery 200 miles long and 40 miles deep. The deaths had resulted from a French shipwreck around 1616. Captured crew members were taken to Wampanoag settlements, unfortunately the Europeans carried a disease that decimated the Indians. As many as 90% of Wampanoag Indians died probably from viral hepatitis.
1682	Frenchman Robert De LaSalle visited the same southern region DeSoto had visited 139 years earlier. The region was found to have a greatly reduced population due to European diseases introduced previously by the DeSoto visit. The societies of Caddo (Texas-Arkansas) and Coosa (Western Georgia) had both disintegrated after DeSoto's visit.
1768	Indians' closest genetic relatives are indigenous Siberians. They too suffered from smallpox in 1768. It is believed that the single epidemic killed more than three of four Siberians.
1967	Evidence suggests that Native Americans are uniquely vulnerable to European diseases. As an example, a missionary's 2-year-old daughter came down with measles in a village on the Toototobi River in Brazil. Normally measles, a childhood disease, is not deadly. However, Yanomami Indians had never encountered the measles virus, and many died from the disease.

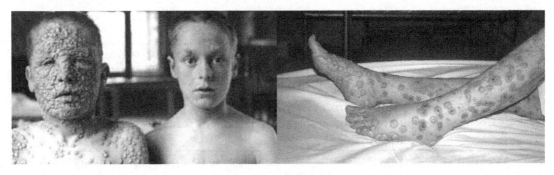

Fig. 2.1 Smallpox was one of the deadliest and most contagious disease known to humankind. Smallpox killed over half a billion people in the 20th century alone. This resulted in an even greater loss of life to Native Americans with the arrival of Europeans in the late 1400s.

CHAPTER 3

King Philip's War

A. Introduction

Native Americans, including Wampanoag Indians, had resided in present day New England as early as 9000 B.C. The Pilgrims arrived for settlement in 1620. The early Pilgrims had little problems with the Wampanoag Indians as evidenced by the first Thanksgiving in 1621. The leader of the Wampanoag, Massasoit and son Metacom had helped the Plymouth Pilgrims survive their first winter in the New World. For 55 years there was peace between the colonists and the Wampanoag. The early Pilgrims and Puritans had arrived in America to escape persecution and had established good relations with the natives. However, the later settlers that arrived only saw the Indians as an obstacle to overcome.[1]

During the 55-year span between the arrival of the Mayflower and the outbreak of King Philip's War, the English had prospered, multiplied and expanded their settlements while the natives were in a slow state of decline from diseases introduced by the Europeans and loss of tribal lands to the whites.[2] The natives had become increasingly dependent on English goods, weapons and food while their own resources dried up as the fur trade slowed, their tribal lands were sold, and Native-American leaders were forced to recognize English authority.

King Philip's War, also known as Metacom's War or the First Indian War, was an armed conflict between English colonists and the American Indians of New England from 1675 to 1676 (Fig. 3.1). It has been called American's forgotten war; most Americans have never heard of King Philip. The Wampanoag name of Metacom was the son of Massasoit, who had greeted the first colonists of New England at Plymouth in 1620.

King Philip was the English name of Metacom (Metacomet) a Wampanoag chief. The name "King Philip" was derived from his peaceful relationship with English settlers. However, he felt betrayed by Plymouth colony's continual encroachment of Wampanoag land, and eventually led the Wampanoag and other Native American bands in New England in the conflict with English settlers.[3]

B. Military Activity

The war was the Native American's last-ditch effort to avoid recognizing English authority and stop English settlement on native lands. Metacom (or King Philip) led the 14 month (1675-1676) bloody rebellion (Table 3.1). The battles were led by the Indian tribe Wampanoag, and joined by Nipmuck, Pocumtuck and Narragansett Indians. The Mohegan and Mohawk Indians fought for the English.

Reasons for the hostilities were twofold: 1) Philip's brother Alexander had been arrested on suspicion of plotting war in 1662, and mysteriously died during questioning and 2) In January 1675, Christian Indian John Sossamon warned Plymouth Colony that Philip planned to attack English settlements. The English ignored the warning and soon found Sossamon's murdered body in an icy pond. A jury of colonists found three Wampanoag men guilty of the murder and executed them. Tensions between the Wampanoag and the colonists set the stage for war.[4]

The war began after Wampanoag braves killed some English owned cattle. Cattle were always a source of friction as they repeatedly trampled Indian corn. A Wampanoag Indian was killed by the farmer. This set-in motion a native uprising that threaten to wipe out the Massachusetts Bay and Plymouth Bay colonies.

In June 1675, the Wampanoag carried out raids in Massachusetts, killing many colonists and pillaging and destroying property. The English response was destroying Philip's home village in Rhode Island. In the Battle of Bloody Brooks (September 1675) almost all the colonists and militia were killed. In December 1675 the colonial militia attacked a massive Narragansell and Wampanoag fortication in Western Rhode Island known as the Great Swamp Fight, 300 Indians estimated killed.[3]

During the winter campaign of 1676. King Philip's confederacy continued to assault English colonies throughout Massachusetts, Rhode Island, Connecticut and Maine, proving there was no safe place for colonists to hide. In one ambush 60 colonists and 20 Christian Indians were all killed, with nine men captured and gruesomely tortured to death.

Throughout the spring of 1676, the tide begun to turn for the English. In May, the militia attacked and killed up to 200 Indians at the Battle of Turner Falls. By late summer, King Philip and his allies were weakened and on the run. Benjamin Church, using friendly Indians as scouts, tracked Philip throughout the summer while Philip made hit and run attacks on isolated farms in the region. But Church eventually caught up with him. An Indian who was guiding Church fired his musket and sent a musket ball through Philip's heart. The death of Philip effectively ended Native American resistance in New England.[2]

Benjamin Church was arguably the most effective leader in the colonial militia against Philip. He had deep respect for his Indian friends and their successful fighting tactics. He sought their advice and took it. The war was the beginning of American Army Rangers, Church was the first leader of the army Rangers.

Benjamin Church, referred to as the "First Ranger", was the grandson of Mayflower passenger Richard Warren.[5] On a personal note, I am the 13th direct descendant of Richard Warren and 11th direct descendant of Benjamin Church.

The effects of war, on both the colonists and the natives, were disastrous. This war was one of the bloodiest conflicts (per capita) in U.S. history. In percentage of population killed, it was the bloodiest war ever fought on American soil.[6] Total casualties for King Phillip's War was 10 times that of the civil War. The population of New England was 52,000, with the death toll of 600 to 800.

Over 1,000 colonists died with Plymouth Colony suffering the most. The losses were far worse for the natives though. Out of the total population of 20,000 Native-Americans in southern New England at the time, an estimated 2,000 were killed, another 3,000 had died of sickness and starvation, around 1,000 were captured and sold into slavery, and transported to other areas. As a result of King Philip's War, the Indian population of southern New England was reduced by about 40 to 80 percent. One-third of New England's 100 or so colonial towns and villages were either burned to the ground and abandoned or substantially destroyed.[5] An estimated 1,200 homes had been burned. The war also ruined New England's economy by nearly halting the fur trade, killing 8,000 head of cattle, interrupting the importing and exporting of goods and causing a decline in the fishing industry.

Many of the Indians who escaped execution or enslavement fled northward. The refugees from southern New England and their descendants continued to fight the English throughout the French and Indian War; in effect King Philip's war never came to a definitive end.[6]

C. Diseases of Native Americans prior to the Pilgrims

Disease devastated the Indian populations in New England. Native American health had declined even before Columbus came to the New World. It is thought that Indians' health got worse because they depended on corn. Also, they began to live in denser communities allowing infectious disease to spread quickly. However, the population declined rapidly when Europeans arrived in the 16th century. Perhaps about 80,000 Indians lived in New England. A century later New England's population began to disappear, some tribes were already extinct. By 1506 both French and Portuguese fishing ships showed up and by 1519 a hundred European ships made round trips to North America. European visitors brought with them diseases to which the Indians had no immunity, including smallpox, typhus, measles, tuberculosis, cholera and bubonic plague.

In North America Maine's Passamaquoddy Indians were among the first to have contact with the Europeans. They were devastated by a typhus epidemic in 1586. Typhus and other diseases reduced the Passamaquoddy population from 20,000 down to 4,000.[7]

From 1616-1619 a severe plague swept the Massachusetts coast. The epidemic swept through Indian country with a horrible ferocity and wrought changes in Indian societies. The explorers and fisherman had brought disease to the Native Americans.

There was uncertainty of the cause of the plague, perhaps smallpox, yellow fever or bubonic plague. Other thoughts based on symptoms suggest the plague was from viral hepatitis or leptospirosis.[8] (see also Chapter 2, Section Be) Leptospirosis would suggest that rats from European ships would have been the culprits. Most of the Indian population died, with not enough survivors to bury the dead. It was estimated that as many was 90% of the 4,500 Indians of the Massachusetts tribe perished in the epidemic between 1616-1619.

Disease conveniently cleared coastal New England of Native Americans just prior to the Pilgrims arrival, as the previous tenants had died of a gruesome infectious disease. The pilgrims in 1620 chose an abandoned Wampanoag village for their new home. Arrival of the pilgrims continued introduction of Eurasian diseases including smallpox, diphtheria, cholera, measles, and typhoid. Even worse, later some English purposely distributed diseased blankets to the unsuspecting Wampanoags, thus wiping out entire villages.

The English settlers met the Wampanoag Chief Massasoit, whose weakened position due to disease left him in search of allies. He used this opportunity to strengthen himself against his enemies, the Narragansett. The Wampanoags, decimated by Eurasian diseases, and the sickly pilgrims having no knowledge or wherewithal to survive in a hostile world became in many ways dependent on one another. During King Philip's War there were diseases among the Indians, but no reliable records.

D. Diseases Affecting the Colonist

There is lack of information on specific diseases affecting immigrant settlers or the fighting force during King Philip's War. Prior and during this time period Malaria was deadly to many new arrivals, especially in the Southern colonies. Epidemics of many diseases were reported during colonial times particularly smallpox epidemics during 1675 to 1676 would have been affecting the general population as well as the fighting troops.

In addition to malaria and smallpox, disease epidemics included yellow fever, cholera, measles, diphtheria, scarlet fever, chicken pox, typhus, typhoid, mumps and dysentery. Likewise, there were respiratory diseases of colds, influenza and pneumonia. There were also sexually transmitted diseases. There was one disease, apparently of American origin, syphilis.[8] A particularly virulent sequence of smallpox outbreaks took place in Boston, Massachusetts from 1636 to 1698. Yellow Fever was a disease that caused thousands of deaths and caused many people to flee the afflicted areas. Both diarrhea/dysentery and typhoid can be deadly, but when a person has both at the same time it is almost impossible to recover.[1]

Two vitamin deficiencies were a problem for colonists, beriberi (deficiency of thiamin or vitamin B_1) and scurvy (vitamin C deficiency). Scurvy had been most devastating during the first winter for the Pilgrims in Plymouth, Massachusetts (1620-1621). The Mayflower sailed with 102 emigrants and of the 102, only 57 survived. Some of the deaths were as a direct result of scurvy while other deaths may have resulted from an indirect effect of scurvy, with the lack of vitamin C resulting in a lower resistance and greater susceptibility to disease organisms. (e.g. pneumonia).[10]

E. Summary

King Philip's War, from 1675 to 1676, was a conflict between English Pilgrim colonists and American Indians of New England. (Table 3.1) The early Pilgrims had few problems with the Wampanoag Indians as illustrated by the first Thanksgiving in 1621. However, 55 years later was the outbreak of King Philip's War. The basis for the war was that the English had prospered, multiplied and expanded their settlements, while the Indians were in a slow state of decline from European diseases and loss of tribal lands to the whites. King Philip was the English name of Metacom, a Wampanoag chief.

The war was known as the First Indian War. This 14-month war was one of the bloodiest conflicts (per capita) in U.S. history. With the death of King Philip, the war ended with a colonist victory.

During this time period epidemics of many diseases brought death to colonists. The diseases included smallpox, yellow fever, diphtheria, typhus, malaria, measles, scarlet fever, influenza and dysentery. Disease also devastated the Indian populations in New England. There was great loss of life as the Native Americans lacked disease immunity. The explorers and fishermen had brought disease to the Indians, even before the Pilgrims arrived. It is estimated the European diseases had killed between 85 to 95% of Native Americans.

Table 3.1 Highlights of King Philip's War[5,6]

December 1620	English Pilgrims arrive in Massachusetts and establish Plymouth colony. The Wampanoag Indian leader Massasoit and So Metacom (later named King Philip) helped Plymouth Pilgrims survive their first winter in the New World. There was peace for 55 years.
1662	King Philip (Metacom) became chief of the Wampanoags. He began plotting against the colonists, as he felt betrayed by Plymouth colony's encroachment of Wampanoag land. He concluded that his people could survive only by driving the Whites out. Philip's brother Alexander had been arrested on suspicion of plotting war and mysteriously died.
January 1675	Christian Indian john Sossamon warned the Plymouth colony that Philip planned to attack English settlement. Sossamon was murdered and three Wampanoag were executed. Tensions between the Wampanoag and colonists set the stage for war. The bloody rebellion lasted 14 months (1675-1676).
June 1675	The Wampanoag carried out raids in Massachusetts, killing many colonists and pillaging and destroying property. The English responded, destroying Philip's home village in Rhode Island.
September 1675	In the Battle of Bloody Brooks many colonists and militia were killed.
December 1675	In the Great Swamp Fight 300 Indians were killed by the colonial militia.
Winter 1676	King Philip's confederacy continued to assault colonists and destroy property. In one ambush 60 colonists and 20 Christian Indians were killed with nine men captured and gruesomely tortured to death.
May 1676	The militia attacked and killed up to 200 Indians at the Battle of Turner Falls.
Summer 1676	By late summer, King Philip and his allies were wakened and on the run. Benjamin Church, who was referred to as American's "First Ranger", tracked Philip throughout the summer. During this time Philip made hit and run attacks on isolated farms. Church eventually caught up to Philip and he was killed. The death of Philip effectively ended Native American resistance in New England. The war was one of the bloodiest conflicts (per capita) in U.S. history. In percentage of population killed, it was the bloodiest war ever fought on American soil.

Fig. 3.1 King Phillip's War was an armed conflict between English Colonists and American Indians of New England from 1675 to 1676.

CHAPTER 4

French and Indian War

A. Introduction

The French and Indian War starting in 1754 was a conflict between the empires of Great Britain and France for control of the North American continent (Fig. 4.1). This pitted the colonies of Britain against those of New France, each side supported by military units from the parent country and by American Indian allies. At the start of the war, the French colonies had a population of roughly 60,000 settlers, compared with 2 million in British colonies. The outnumbered French particularly depended on the Indians.[1]

European nations had declared a wider war upon one another overseas in 1756. This global war, in addition to Great Britain and France, also included Austria, Prussia, Russia and Sweden. The worldwide event was the seven-year war of 1756-1763. The larger scale war began two years into the French and Indian War.

The Indians supporting the French were the Wabanaki Confederacy member tribes Abenaki and Mi'kmaq, and the Algonquin, Lenape, Ojibwa, Ottawa, Shawnee, and Wyandot tribes. The British colonists were supported at various times by the Iroquois, Catawba, and Cherokee tribes. The Battles took place primarily along the frontiers between New France and British colonies, from the Province of Virginia in the south to Newfoundland in the north.[1]

B. Military activity

In 1753 the French had expanded and built forts into an area that is now western Pennsylvania. The young 21-year-old Virginia militia captain, George Washington, gave the French warning that they would have to leave or face the consequences. In 1754 Washington and his men fired on a small French scouting party killing 14 French soldiers (Battle of Jumonville Glen). The French were outraged, and from this point forward, battles between the French and British escalated. Most consider this early battle, led by Washington, to be the unofficial beginning of the war. Fearing reprisal from the French, Washington ordered the construct of Fort Necessity. A month after the victory of the small skirmish that began the war, Washington found himself outnumbered and was forced to surrender to the French.[2]

In 1755, British General Edward Braddock, accompanied by George Washington led a force of 1,500 regulars and provincials, who were badly beaten at the Battle of Monongahela, where over 900 men were killed, wounded or captured by the French. Braddock had ignored the warning of the unconventional fighting style of the French and Indians, which involved surprise attacks from behind trees, rocks and other concealed spots. Braddock failed to take advice from his experienced American officers which included Washington. Washington succeeded in leading some of the men to safety.[3]

The initial armed conflicts did not go well for Great Britain; the French built Fort Duquesne and alongside their Native American allies, repeatedly defeated the British. During 1755 and 1756 the French had won a string of victories, defeating in quick succession the young George Washington, General Edward Braddock, and Governor William Shirley. It is interesting that it was not until 1756 that the British formally declared war (marking the official beginning of the seven-year war), but the new commander in America, Lord Loudoun, met with little success against the French and their Indian allies.

The tide turned in 1757, because William Pitt was the new British leader. In July 1758, the British won their first great victory at Louisbourg, near the mouth of the St. Lawrence River. A month later, they took Fort Frontenac at the Western end of the river. In November 1758 Fort Duquesne was captured. In 1759 the British won a spectacular victory in the Battle of Quebec. In 1760, with the fall of Montreal, the French lost their last foothold in Canada.

In late 1760 Spain joined France against the British. From then on, the British concentrated on seizing French and Spanish territories in other parts of the world. It was not until February 1763 that the French and Indian War officially ended with signing of the Treaty of Paris. The British received Canada from France and Florida from Spain; Louisiana was given to Spain. With these events the American colonies no longer had European rivals to the north or south, and now there was an opening of the Mississippi Valley to westward expansion.[4]

The French and Indian War was the bloodiest American war in the 18th century, it took more lives than the American Revolution. Death estimates for France and First Nations allies was 3,000 killed, wounded or captured, while for Britain, the American colonies and Iroquois Confederacy there were 10,400 killed, wounded or captured. Other death estimates range from 3,000 to 15,000 for the war.

C. Diseases affecting colonists

Epidemics of many diseases were reported during colonial times including during the French and Indian War. From the epidemics in the colonies, mortality was high for infants and small children especially from diphtheria, smallpox, yellow fever, and malaria. In port cities many colonies had outbreaks of typhus due to lice and the many rats and fleas in the holds of ships which spread the disease.

In the colonies, smallpox and malaria were an endemic. Malaria incidence was particularly high and deadly in the southern colonies. Most everyone could be expected to be infected. George Washington was reported to have had malaria, which he contracted at age 17. Due to malaria and other diseases of newly arrived able-bodied young men, over ¼ of the Anglican missionaries died within five years of their arrival in the Carolinas.[5]

The epidemics of smallpox were recurrent, devastating and frequent. Colonists tried to prevent the spread of smallpox by isolation and inoculation. The inoculation caused a mild form of the disease but sometimes it was fatal.[6] In Europe and Great Britain children would contract smallpox, most would survive but some would die. However, the survivors would now be immune to the disease. Most of the second-generation colonists would not have been exposed to the disease as children. Colonists in the French and Indian War were less susceptible to smallpox because of a less dense population. Therefore, colonists often reached adulthood without coming into contact with the smallpox virus, but since they had no immunity incidence for the disease was high.

Yellow fever was a disease that caused thousands of deaths, and many people to flee the affected areas. At the end of one week, an afflicted person was either dead or recovering.[6] The death rate was so high the people had to workday and night to bury the dead.

Numerous diseases had been brought to the Americans, see Chapter 2 (Section D). After importation of slaves, more serious parasitic diseases came to colonial America (e.g., Hookworm). The slaves were carriers of hookworm, polluting the soil that they worked, depositing the parasitic eggs.

By the 18th century, colonial physicians, following the models in Great Britain, introduced modern medicine to cities, and made some advances in vaccination, pathology, anatomy and pharmacology. However, there seemed no knowledge of sanitation and hygiene. It still would be many years before doctors realized the importance of hygiene (e.g., disinfecting surgical instruments in medicine). Due to lack of sanitation, dysentery and severe diarrhea were major problems in the French and Indian War. George Washington had dysentery many, many times. He was in such agony during one battle that he put a pillow underneath him in the saddle of his horse.[7]

D. Diseases affecting Native Americans

Most of the major diseases we are familiar with today originated in the Old World. For the Native Americans the era of limited diseases ended with the arrival of Europeans to the Americas. The major effect of disease for Native Americans occurred prior to the French and Indian War. The greatest genocide in the history of many resulted from introduction of European diseases to Native Americans. Many Native Americans had died from contact. A large number of deaths has resulted with Europeans arriving in the 16th century. By 1506 both French and Portuguese fishing ships made trips to the New World, unknowingly bringing death to Native Americans. As an example, in the state of Florida alone, there were 700,000 Native Americans in 1520 but by 1700 the number was around 2,000.[8]

Large populations of Native Americans were wiped out later during the colonial period when they contracted illnesses including smallpox. Epidemics of European – introduced diseases (e.g., smallpox, influenza and measles) reduced the population of Native Americans in New England by 90 percent between 1615 and 1633. The diseases brought by Europeans are not easily tracked, since there were numerous outbreaks, and all were not equally recorded.

It is suggested that in the 18th century smallpox outbreaks during the French and Indian and American Revolutionary wars killed more than 100,000 Native Americans.[9] British leaders in the French and Indian War in 1756 were very concerned with smallpox outbreaks in the military. They hoped that the smallpox would abate with the arrival of winter. The threat of the disease breaking out among troops had caused some of both the New England troops and the Indians to leave the war effort and go home.[10]

In August 1757 French and Indian troops besieged the British Fort William Henry which capitulated with an agreement to withdraw. During the withdrawal the Indian allies attacked the British column. The aftermath of the siege may have contributed to the transmission of smallpox into remote Indian populations, as some Indians were reported to have traveled from beyond the Mississippi to participate in the campaign and returned afterward. A massive outbreak of smallpox among western Indian tribes led many of them to stay away from trading in 1758. The disease probably spread through the crowded conditions at Fort William Henry after the battle.[11]

Anderson and Wetmore (2006) summarized the history of smallpox with the Cherokee Indians.[12] Smallpox and other diseases brought by Europeans and enslaved Africans were more devastating to the Cherokee and other southeastern Indians than war. The Cherokee had been exposed to smallpox for a period of three centuries. Likely their first exposure was in 1698, which decreased their population measurably. The tribe had its worst epidemic in 1738-1739, when the disease was brought by traders or was brought back from an expedition where the Cherokees aided the British against the Spanish in Florida. For this epidemic, between 7,000 and 10,000 Cherokees died, representing about one-half of the tribe's population. Smallpox struck the Cherokee people again in 1759-1760 during the French and Indian War, resulting in devastating death loss.

Smallpox as a weapon in America can be traced to the British during the French and Indian War and during the Pontiac Rebellion which broke out after the war. Smallpox was the weapon behind one of the first known cases of biological warfare. Sir Jeffrey Amherst, the commander of the British army in North America had suggested contaminating the native tribes who were hostile to British forces with the virus during the French and Indian War. The British army used smallpox, contaminated blankets to spread the virus among natives, resulting in an epidemic with an estimated 50% mortality rate. Also, sometimes the illnesses spread after direct contact with European settlers, often resulting in deadly outbreaks that decimated entire villages.[13]

Table 4.1 illustrates highlights of the French and Indian War.

E. Summary

The French and Indian War was part of a larger war mostly between Great Britain and France. The war in North America began in 1754 between these countries and their colonies. Indians were on both sides during the war. In February 1763 the war officially ended with France losing their North American colonies.

This had been the bloodiest American war in the 18th century. Death estimates for France and their allies were 3,000 killed, wounded or captured, while more than three times this number for the British side. Many more deaths were from disease versus enemy combat. Epidemics of many diseases were reported during the French and Indian War. Smallpox and Malaria were endemic, killing many. There were high death rates from yellow fever, Typhus, influenza, measles and typhoid fever. Other diseases included parasites, dysentery and scurvy. Much disease in the military was due to lack of sanitation (e.g. dysentery and typhoid fever). Native Americans suffered from many diseases due to arrival of Europeans. Between 1615 and 1633 introduced European diseases had reduced the Indians in New England by 90%.

Table 4.1
French and Indian War[1,2]

1754	The French and Indian War began for control of the North American continent. This was between the colonies of Britain and France, supported by the parent country and Indian allies.
1754	Virginia militia captain, George Washington, warned the French to leave forts they had built, but they refused.
1754	The first battle was when Washington and his men fired on a French scouting party. Fearing reprisal Washington ordered the construction of Fort necessity.
1754	At Fort necessity Washington was outnumbered and was forced to surrender to the French.
1755	British General Edward Braddock, accompanied by Washington with 1500 troops were badly beaten at the Battle of Monongahela.
1755-56	The French won a string of victories against the British.
1758	The tide turned against the French; the British won their first great victory at Louisburg.
1758	Next the British took Fort Frontenac and in November captured Fort Duquesne.
1759	The British won a great victory at the Battle of Quebec.
1760	With the fall of Montreal, France lost their last foothold in Canada.
1763	The French and Indian War officially ended with the Treaty of Paris, with France losing their North American colonies.
1754-1763	The casualties were 3,000 killed, wounded, or captured for the French and allies with three times this number for the British side.
1754-1763	Diseases of children of colonist with high mortality included diphtheria, smallpox, yellow fever, malaria and typhus.
1754-1763	Epidemics of smallpox and malaria were frequent and devastating.
1754-1763	Yellow fever caused thousands of deaths, with many people fleeing from the area.
1754-1763	Many native Americans died during and prior to the war of European introduced diseases.
1754-1763	It is suggested that smallpox outbreaks during the French and Indian and American Revolutionary Wars killed more than 100,000 Native Americans.

Fig. 4.1 The French and Indian War was a conflict between Great Britain and France for control of North America.

CHAPTER 5

American Revolutionary War

A. Introduction

Unfortunately for the British, the fruits of victory from the French and Indian War (1754-1763) brought seeds of future trouble with Great Britain's American colonists. Great Britain had borrowed heavily form British and Dutch bankers to bankroll the war, doubling British national debt.

King George III argued that since the French and Indian War benefited the colonists by securing their borders, they should contribute to paying down the war debt. Also, to defend his newly won territory from future attacks, King George III also decided to install permanent British army units in the Americas, which required additional sources of revenue. Therefore, in 1765, parliament passed the Stamp Act to help pay down the war debt and finance the British army's presence in the Americas. It was the first internal tax directly levied on American colonists by parliament and was met with strong resistance.[1]

Since the "Stamp Act" did not raise enough money, it was followed by the unpopular "Townshend Acts" and "Tea Act", which further incensed colonists who believed there should be no taxation without representation. The colonists showed their resistance to the Tea Act by dumping British tea in the harbor, with the event known as the "Boston Tea Party". Theses taxing attempts were met with increasingly stiff resistance, until troops were called in to enforce the Crown's authority. In 1776 Thomas Jefferson drafted the Declaration of Independence which noted rights that were demanded by the colonists. Britain's increasingly militaristic response to colonial unrest would ultimately spur colonial rebellion that eventually developed into a full-scale Revolutionary War.[2] The Revolutionary War was a war unlike any other – one of ideas that shaped "the course of human events". With 165 principal engagements from 1775-1783, the Revolutionary War was the catalyst for American independence. Disease was important in the war, more deaths resulted from disease compared to enemy combat.

B. Military activity

The war started following skirmishes at Lexington and Concord in April 1775. When the Second Continental Congress assembled in Philadelphia in May 1775, George Washington was elected Commander in Chief of the Continental army. He took command of his ill-trained troops and embarked upon a war that was to last six grueling years. His army lost more battles than it won. But it was never destroyed. Washington believed that as long as the Americans could keep an army in the field, the British could not win. Washington kept his army in the field as he had an unusual ability to inspire men.[1] Excellent comprehensive reviews of the war are provided.[3-7] The following is an overview of some major battles and events during the war:

a) Battles on Long Island and New York City – In August 1776, the British launched their campaign to capture New York City. The. British own the battle at Brooklyn Heights. Then General Howe assaulted Washington's flank on August 27 and inflicted 1,500 Patriot casualties, while the British suffered 400 casualties.[5] By mid-November the British had taken almost 3,000 prisoners and captured Fort Lee and Fort Washington. In the face of a siege he seemed certain to lose, Washington then decided to withdraw.

During the campaign a general lack of organization, shortages of supplies, fatigue, sickness, and above all, lack of confidence in the American leadership resulted in a melting away of untrained regulars and frightened militia. Washington had been fortunate that General Howe was more focused on gaining control of New York than on destroying Washington's army.[8]

b) The Battle of Trenton – At this time the enlistments of Washington's army were about to expire. Washington decided that only a bold step could see the army and the revolutionary cause from oblivion.

By October 1776 Washington and his troops, who had been greatly outnumbered, were constantly retreating from the superior British forces. He desperately needed a victory to boost morale. On Christmas Day, Washington and his troops crossed the Delaware and attacked Hessian soldiers and Prussian mercenaries fighting for the British at Trenton, New Jersey (Fig. 5.1). By forging ahead through a raging snowstorm, Washington and his troops surprised the enemy and won a remarkable victory. Future President James Monroe was with Washington at the battle. Prior to the actual battle, Monroe led a company to knock out two Hessian cannons. During the skirmish Monroe was shot, he would have bled to death, but a doctor who volunteered to go with him at the last moment, saved his life.[1]

c) Battles at Princeton, Brandywine Creek, Germantown and Philadelphia – On January 3, 1777, Washington attacked at Princeton and for the first time caused a British line to break. The redcoats, however, triumphed again in September 1777 at Brandywine Creek in Pennsylvania and the following month at Germantown. Then they captured Philadelphia, the seat of the U.S. government, and sent the Continental Congress fleeing.[9]

d) Battles of Saratoga – Fought eighteen days apart in the fall of 1777, the two Battles of Saratoga were a turning point in the American Revolution. The British invasion from Canada captured Fort Ticonderoga with ease. However, Burgoyne moved slowly which gave the Americans time to regroup under General Horatio Gates. To support Gates Washington sent Benedict Arnold, his best infantry commander, and others to raise Gates' strength to about sixty-five hundred men. After a furious struggle Burgoyne surrendered.[3]

e) Valley Forge – In December 1977 Washington led his poorly fed and weary army to their winter quarters at Valley Forge, Pennsylvania. They suffered thousands of deaths over the next six months. Most were from disease, compounded by lack of food and proper clothing, poor shelter, and the extreme cold. Historians' estimates range from 2,000 to more than 3,000 men lost. The British, by contrast, were comfortably quartered in Philadelphia; they paid for their supplies in pounds sterling, while Washington had difficulty procuring supplies with depreciating American paper currency.[4]

f) French entry into the war – The Americans received a boost in 1778 when France, long Britain's archenemy and buoyed by Gate's victory at Saratoga, recognized the United States as an independent nation. Perhaps some of this was revenge for loss of the French and Indian War. French entry into the war changed its dynamics, for the British were no longer sure of command of the seas and had to worry about an invasion of their home islands and other colonial territories across the globe.

g) Southern Strategy – In late 1778, General Clinton sent 3,000 troops by ship from New York to Georgia and launched a Southern invasion. He seized Savannah, reinforced by 2,000 British and loyalist troops, and repelled an attack by Patriots and French naval forces. The success bolstered the British War effort. General Clinton marshaled a force of more than 10,000 men that in the first half of 1780 successfully besieged Charleston, South Carolina. In June 1780 he captured over 5,000 Continental soldiers and militia in the single worst defeat of the war for the Americans.[4] This turned out to not be so successful for the British as their army was weakened by disease, malaria and probably yellow fever and/or typhus.

General Cornwallis attempted to extend British authority into North Carolina but was defeated in the October 1780 Battle of Kings Mountain, and also was defeated in the January 1781 Battle of Cowpens. Kings Mountain in particular proved a decisive blow to further attempts to win and control North Carolina.

Nathanael Green, as head of the southern Continental forces, had waged an effective partisan campaign against Cornwallis at Hillsboro, North Carolina in March of 1781. Although he lost the Battle of Guilford Court House, Greene inflicted significant casualties on Cornwallis while retaining his own army intact.[10] Cornwallis made a decision to move out of the Carolinas to avoid disease and depressing hot weather, the main disease was malaria. He moved the troops to Virginia and his fateful encounter at Yorktown.

h) Removing Indian British allies from the war – In the summer of 1779, Washington and Congress decided to strike the Iroquois warriors of the "Six Nations" in a campaign to force Britain's Indian allies out of New York, which they had used as a base to attack American settlements around New England. The Indian warriors joined with Tory rangers and slew more than 200 frontiersmen in June, using barbarities normally shunned, and they laid waste to the Wyoming Valley in Pennsylvania.[11] General John Sullivan defeated and dispersed the Iroquois, ending their threat to the region.

i) Battle of Yorktown and end of war – In early September 1780 the French and Continental armies marched to Yorktown, while the British and French fleets met in the Battle of the Chesapeake (Fig.5.2). The French victory was strategically vital, for it denied the British control of the Chesapeake and set the stage for the encirclement of Cornwallis at Yorktown.[6] With the French and American troops blocking Cornwallis on land and pounding him and the French navy blocking his ocean exit, he capitulated in October 1781. It was not until April 1783 that the peace treaty was finalized.

Washington bade farewell to his officers and resigned his commission on December 1783. Washington gave a brief statement: "I consider it an indispensable duty to close this last solemn act of my official life, by commending the interests of our dearest country to the protection of Almighty God." [11]

Washington was referred to as being "First in war, first in peace and first in the hearts of his countrymen". The official records indicated the importance of disease during the war. The U.S. military casualties for the Revolutionary War were: 8,000 deaths from combat, 17,000 for other deaths (mostly disease) with an additional 25,000 wounded.[12]

C. Diseases during the Revolutionary War

Explorers, fisherman and European colonization introduced smallpox and other diseases to the Americas in the 16th century. Over the course of a little more than three centuries, outbreaks of disease appeared sporadically. Epidemic diseases became an increasingly serious problem during the period of rebellion in America. New England had the country's highest population density experiencing many outbreaks of smallpox, diphtheria, scarlet fever, measles, influenza, and whooping cough.

A Philadelphia hospital compiled an extensive report about diseases during the Revolutionary War period. Aside from mental disorders which affected nearly one fifth of all patients, half of the hospital's cases concerned seven disorders: scurvy – 15%, fevers – 9%, venereal disease – 9%, dropsy (edema) – 6%, eye disease – 4%, and respiratory disease – 4%. Cities and urban centers did not fare as well as the countryside, poor sanitation and close proximity of dwellers allowed contagion to spread rapidly among the concentrated populations.[13]

a) Smallpox – One of the greatest threats to the army came not from enemy bullets but from disease. Perhaps the most dreaded disease was smallpox, caused by a virus that kills one out of every three infected people. The American colonists, however, might have gone for years without any exposure to smallpox. It is difficult to track smallpox deaths during the Revolutionary War, but estimates indicated that Washington's army lost more troops to disease in general than in combat. One study suggests that for every soldier who fell to the British, ten died from some sort of disease. Washington himself was no stranger to smallpox; while traveling in Barbados in 1751, he contracted the disease. However, Washington's case was mild leaving him with scarring on his nose.[14]

The Continental Army was severely susceptible to smallpox because of the close proximity of its soldiers' living quarters. Early in the war smallpox struck the northern army at Quebec. According to General Benedict Arnold, some 1,200 of the approximately 3,200 Continentals in the Montreal area were unfit for duty, most of them sick with smallpox.

Smallpox threatened the destruction of the entire army. Major General John Thomas, the commander of the army in Quebec, died of smallpox, "The smallpox", mourned John Adams, "is 10 times more terrible than the British, Canadians and Indians together." By mid-July 1776 an estimated 3,000 men of the northern army were sick, mostly from smallpox. In 1777 alone, more than one hundred thousand people in North America died as the result of virulent smallpox epidemics. Washington wrote that smallpox "is more destructive to an army than the Enemy's Sword".

In Europe, smallpox had become an endemic disease by the 18th century. Generally, exposure often happened during childhood, therefore, virtually the entire adult population was immune. Also, during the war the British took quickly to inoculating fresh troops.

Colonies dealt with smallpox in two different ways: quarantine and inoculation. Each colony had its own quarantine laws which took different forms and were often enforced at the local level. Some colonials, particularly the wealthy, chose to be inoculated. Inoculation involved deliberate exposure to smallpox, usually through an incision made on the arm. This still resulted in a case of smallpox, but frequently one with milder symptoms and a greater chance of survival, with immunity as the end goal.[15]

Washington struggled with the question of inoculation. Washington faced a difficult choice: whether or not to inoculate his army. Inoculated soldiers would develop a mild case of the disease, which most would survive. They would then be immune. His other option was to do nothing other than insolate and treat the sick and hope the army avoided a major outbreak. There was danger that inoculated soldiers could transmit smallpox until fully recovered, so an inoculation program could trigger an uncontrollable epidemic. Also, the inoculated soldiers would be unfit for duty for weeks while recovering and as many as 2% of his soldiers could die. If the British attacked while the men were out of commission the army could be destroyed.

After weeks of indecision and after heavy losses in Boston and Quebec, Washington issued the order to have all troops inoculated on February 5, 1777. The practice was soon implemented across the colonies. Army physicians also inoculated veteran soldiers who had yet to be exposed. Washington needed the process to be done in secret. He feared that the British would learn of the army's temporary weakness and use it to their advantage. Washington's unheralded and little-recognized resolution to inoculate the Continental forces must surely rank among his most important decisions of the war. Moreover, Washington's decision for mass inoculation within the army reflects the first large-scale, state-sponsored immunization campaign in American History, making Washington a key player in early American public health endeavors.[15]

Towards the last stages of Yorktown, it was reported that a desperate General Cornwallis purposely infected a good number of African Americans with smallpox. Under cover of darkness, the infected former slaves were forced past the British lines and left where rebel and French forces would find them with the hope of spreading the disease throughout the camps surrounding the English forces. Likewise, during the Canadian invasion by American forces, several prostitutes in Quebec were intentionally infected with smallpox, then sent out among besieging American troops.[16]

b) Other Diseases – Epidemic diseases, besides smallpox, during the American Revolutionary War included outbreaks of scarlet fever, diphtheria, measles, malaria, influenza, ague (fever disease), typhoid fever and typhus. Other disease conditions such as parasites (e.g., hookworm) and dysentery were periodical problems. The nutritional deficiency scurvy was found in those not consuming vitamin C adequate diets. Diseases were common during colonial times. George Washington was plagued with smallpox, tuberculosis, malaria, dysentery and diphtheria. Sometimes there was no specific name given to a disease condition. For example, prior to the victory of the Battle of Trenton, sickness left 500 of Lieutenant James Monroe's (future president) 700 Virginians unfit for duty.

Most of the diseases in the Americas originated in Europe. There has been a worldwide distribution of influenza. The earliest English settlers introduced diseases such as tuberculosis, typhoid fever, typhus, diphtheria, scarlet fever and measles. Some parasites such as hookworm and the disease of yaws are believed imported into the American colonies on slave ships.[17]

Typhus was a disease related to fleas of rats and typhoid fever was associated with sewage. Typhus was transmitted by the bites of lice that had also infested rats. This was endemic among colonists in port cities when ships contained many rats in the holds. Typhoid fever was a high component of military operations with close proximity of soldiers with unsanitary sewage handling. In the war more men died from typhoid fever than in military deaths or from wounds.[18] Typhoid has been called a disease of civilization. There was a rise of typhoid fever as newly constructed sewers poured their contents into the rivers and lakes from which towns drew their drinking water. Likewise, in military encampments latrines were mistakenly placed upstream, resulting in fecal contaminated water.

In Oxford Massachusetts, between 1766 and 1769, 10% of its community members died from diphtheria. Rural colonies in the mid-Atlantic experienced relatively few epidemics.

The rural south was mostly spared from epidemics. However, malaria was most prevalent in the south in coastal regions and years with greater incidence of mosquitoes. Malaria was endemic, and especially in the southern colonies everyone could be expected to become infected. Malaria was a factor for Cornwallis surrounded at Yorktown. Cornwallis's army left the Carolinas because of extreme heat and malaria. At Yorktown historians J.R. McNeal notes that Cornwallis's army was simply melting away from Malaria. He noted a critical role was played by "revolutionary mosquitoes".[19] Also, yellow fever was frequently encountered in coastal settlements, especially where mosquitoes were found in abundance. The more affluent families moved to higher ground during mosquito season.

Like typhoid fever, dysentery was due to unsanitary conditions related to sewage. In the 1700s-1800s, dysentery was a disease causing many deaths. Dysentery was very epidemic in nature. The disease struck communities extremely hard at times. It flared up quite irregularly and the patterns of transmission differed from one outbreak to the next. The same previous results point to complex links between possible explanations such as sanitary conditions and population concentrations for example in connection with wars. Soldiers were in the habit of relieving themselves wherever they wished, including outside their own tents, turning encampments into mucky breeding grounds for dysentery.[20] During the French and Indian War and American Revolutionary War there were many deaths due to dysentery. This would be true for future wars until sanitation and disease pathogens were understood.

There were many scurvy deaths until diets were improved with vitamin C rich fruits and vegetables. British forces (both the Navy and Army) during the revolutionary war experienced scurvy during the late winter and early spring months. Sir Gilbert Blane stated that of 175,990 British men in war at sea, only 1,234 were killed in action, but deaths from disease (mostly scurvy) claimed 18,545 men. British land troops observed that a concoction prepared from spruce or hemlock trees was of benefit for scorbutic soldiers. The Continental army avoided scurvy with some lime juice and spruce beer. A liquid concoction derived from the tips of spruce trees added to beer was used by George Washington as a regular antiscorbutic ration for American soldiers in the Revolutionary War. Also, during the time period of the Revolution, a cruise of the British Channel fleet in 1780 was obliged to return to England as 2,400 men were afflicted with scurvy.[21]

c) Disease influenced by climate – During the Revolution, leaders on both sides recognized the perils of warm weather campaigning in the feverish low country of South Carolina and Georgia. The British suffered the most significant losses from the region's fevers. Sickness played a large role in the war in the Lower South. Malaria and other fevers killed and incapacitated large numbers of soldiers and felled key commanders at critical moments. British Lt. Col. Aured Clark reported in early July that the heat and sickness in Savannah, Georgia was "beyond anything you can conceive." "Our suffering from sickness in this vile climate is terrible and continues to a very great degree." He had been "extremely ill" himself. A Hessian regiment had lost "many men and some officers, and at present had not above sixty men fit for duty."

For all their blundering, the British might well have succeeded in their southern strategy had it not been for the diseases that weakened their army. The diseases were largely fevers from malaria and probably yellow fever and/or typhus. General Cornwallis cited that saving his army from another Carolina fever season as one of the main reasons for his decision to move north to Virginia and his fateful encounter at Yorktown that October, which ended the war.[14]

Table 5.1 Illustrates highlights of the American Revolutionary War.[22,23]

D. Summary

The American Revolutionary War between the Colonists and the British resulted from rigid control of the colonies by Britain. They taxed the Colonists, in part to help pay for the French and Indian War. The Colonists resisted taxation without representation. Taxing attempts were enforced by militaristic response to colonial unrest. Colonial rebellion eventually developed into the Revolutionary War of 1775-1783. The Americans were led by General George Washington.

There were 165 principal engagements in the war. The colonist had to fight Indians as well as Hessian soldiers. The American received a boost in 1778 when France joined the war against the British. The American victory in October 1781 was at the Battle of Yorktown. The Americans and French troops had blocked General Cornwallis on land and the French navy blocked his ocean retreat thus ending the war.

Epidemic diseases were a serious problem with many outbreaks of smallpox, diphtheria, tuberculosis, scarlet fever, measles, influenza, whooping cough, scurvy and dysentery. Smallpox was the disease causing the most deaths. In February 1777 General Washington ordered all troops to be inoculated for smallpox. Diseases were common during colonial times. George Washington was plagued with smallpox, tuberculosis, malaria, dysentery and diphtheria. Death from disease was greater than military action. The U.S. military casualties for the war were: 8,000 deaths from combat and 17,000 from other causes (mostly diseases).

Table 5.1
American Revolutionary War[22,23]

1763
After French and Indian War, the British expected the 13 colonies to help pay for war expenses.
1765
To raise revenue the British parliament passed the "Stamp Act", then the "Townshend Acts" and "Tea Act". For the colonists this was taxation without representation.
1773
Colonists showed resistance by dumping British tea into the ocean. This event is known as "Boston Tea Party".
1775
The Revolutionary War began with skirmishes at Lexington and Concord.
The Second Continental Congress elected George Washington as Commander of the Continental Arms.
1776
Thomas Jefferson drafted the Declaration of Independence which noted inalienable rights for the colonists, that include life, liberty and the pursuit of happiness.
The British won the Battle of Brooklyn and captured Fort Lee and Fort Washington. Washington and his troops won a remarkable victory at the Battle of Trenton; future president James Monroe was wounded in the engagement.
1777
In the Fall the Continental army won the Battle of Saratoga but suffered hardships at their winter quarters at Valley Forge.
Smallpox struck the Continental army at Quebec; 1,200 of 3,200 troops were unfit for duty due to smallpox.
Washington ordered all troops to be inoculated against smallpox.
1778
France entered the war to join the Continental army.
The British were successful in capturing Savannah, Georgia and Charleston, South Carolina. However, their army was weakened by the diseases malaria, yellow fever and / or typhus.
1779
General John Sullivan defeated the Iroquois Indians to remove them as British allies.
Anthony Wayne's troops stormed Stony Point.
John Paul Jones' *Bonhomme Richard* captured the British ship *Serapis*.
1780
Charleston fell after a British siege.
The British defeated the Americans at Camden.
American frontiersmen stormed the Loyalist positions on Kings Mountain.

British General Cornwallis left the Carolina due to extreme heat and malaria for Yorktown.
1781
Patriots won a victory at Cowpens, S.C.
The French fleet drove a British Naval force from Chesapeake Bay.
Cornwallis' forces surrendered at Yorktown.
1783
The United States and Great Britain signed the final peace treaty in Paris.
The Peace Treaty was finalized in Paris.
1775-1781
Diseases during the war included malaria, yellow fever, smallpox, typhoid, typhus, diphtheria, measles, influenza, scarlet fever, dysentery and scurvy.
Continental army casualties from the war were 8,000 deaths from combat and 17,000 mostly from disease.

Fig. 5.1 Washington crossing the Delaware for a surprise at Battle of Trenton.

Fig. 5.2 American Revolution, Battle of Yorktown.

CHAPTER 6

War of 1812

A. Introduction

The War of 1812 is sometimes referred to as the "Second War of Independence". This was the first large scale test of the American republic on the world stage. The conflict was between the new nation of the United States against Great Britain and its North American colonies in Canada.

Britain since the 1790s was also at war with Napoleon's France during the War of 1812. Due to the war with France, Britain had enforced a naval blockade to choke off neutral trade to France, which the U.S. contested as illegal under international law. To man the blockade, Britain pressed American merchant sailors into the Royal Navy. The British impressments of American seamen and the seizure of cargos were unacceptable. The British were also supplying arms to American Indians who raided and killed American settlers on the frontier. Also fueling the desire for war with Britain was a feeling that Britain never truly gave up thinking of America as a "lost" colony that should be punished. Many felt that the British had not yet come to respect the United States as a legitimate country. On June 18, 1812, President James Madison signed into law the American Declaration of War, after heavy pressure from the War Hawks in Congress.[1]

The war lasted two years and eight months. With most of its army in Europe fighting Napoleon, Britain adopted a defensive strategy, with offensive operations initially limited to the border and the western frontier along with help from Indian allies. Later after the defeat of Napoleon, in the spring of 1814, the British intensified military action in America.[2]

American prosecution of the war effort suffered from its unpopularity, especially in New England, where it was referred to as "Mr. Madison's War". In addition to President Madison, three future presidents were heavily involved in the War of 1812. During the war, James Monroe was Secretary of State and War under Madison. Both William Henry Harrison and Andrew Jackson were generals, winning important battles for America.

It was also a war of stunning spectacle, with British and American warships battling on the Great Lakes. On the land, the Americans were for the most part unprepared and inept. But on the lakes, they were often formidable, and gave the British a preview of what was to come on the high seas in the next century. The war became a bitter war of retribution. The Americans burned the capitol of upper Canada, the British burned Buffalo, the White House the Capital, and the Library of Congress.[3]

Over 1600 British and 2,260 American soldiers, marines and sailors died during the war. These figures do not include deaths among Canadian militia forces or losses among native tribes. For both sides, diseases played a major role in the war. More soldiers and sailors died from disease than from enemy battle.

B. Major battles of the War of 1812

There were numerous battles, skirmishes and raids during the War of 1812. Battles were fought in four major theaters: the Atlantic Coast, the Canada – U.S. border, the Gulf Coast, and the American West. Likewise, there were many naval battles at sea, most in the Atlantic. There were many Indian raids, many of these supported by the British. A chronological order of major battles and events (Table 6.1) are as follows:

a) **Capture of Detroit (August 16, 1812)** – Only weeks after the war began, American General William Hull surrendered Detroit, along with a sizable army, without resistance to a smaller British force. This was a humiliating defeat for Americans.

b) **Capture of the HMS *Java*, HMS *Guerriere*, the HMS *Macedonian* (August-December 1812)** – The new U.S. frigates *Constitution* and *United States* started the war with a bang, performing well in a series of Atlantic engagements that boosted American morale after a disappointing beginning to land battles.[3]

c) **Battle of Queenston Heights (October 13, 1812)** – In a dramatic battle, British and Canadian troops turned back an American incursion into Canada. This was a major American defeat.[3]

d) **Battle of York (April 27, 1813)** – American capture of Fort York and the adjacent town of York (at the location of present-day Toronto), achieved by an amphibious assault of troops from Sackets Harbor. The entire American force withdrew by May 8, but only after vandalizing and looting much of the town and burning the buildings of the provincial legislature. The burning of the Capitol building during the British raid on Washington was retribution for the American actions in York, Canada.[1]

e) **Battle of Lake Erie (September 10, 1813)** – Oliver Hazard Perry won fame for his heroic deeds in this victory, which secured Lake Erie for the rest of the war and paved the way for the liberation of Detroit. A squadron under the command of Captain Perry defeated a British squadron. After the victory, the famous words of Perry were "we have met the enemy and they are ours". This was a great moral victory for the Americans. With their supply line cut, the British in southwestern Lower Canada were forced to abandon Detroit and Fort Amherstburg and retreat eastward toward the Niagara Peninsula.[4]

f) Battle of the Thames, Ontario (October 5, 1813) – The victory at the Battle of Lake Erie forced the British to retreat form the Detroit region. They were pursued and overtaken by General William Harrison's army. British General Procter was forced to retreat north up the Thames River to Moraviantown, where his allies, the tribal confederacy under Shawnee leader Tecumseh and war chief Roundhead of the Wyandot tribe, had no choice but to follow. They led about 500 Native American warriors. The British retreat was badly managed, the soldiers had been reduced to half rations.

Harrison's forces made a frontal attack on the British. The exhausted, dispirited and half-starved British regulars fired once before retreating. Procter and about 250 of his men fled from the battlefield, while the rest of his soldiers threw down their weapons and surrendered. From the battle both Shawnee leader Tecumseh and Chief Roundhead were killed. Harrison's army had defeated a force of seventeen hundred British and 500 Indian troops and secured the Northwest for the United States. This had resulted in the destruction of the Native American coalition. The pivotal battle is considered to be one of the great American victories in the war, second only to the Battle of New Orleans.[5]

g) Battle of Horseshoe Bend (March 27, 1814) – General Jackson led his troops against Creek Indians known as Red Sticks (sticks with sharp iron secured at the end) who were responsible for continued slaughter of white settlers' families. On August 30, 1813, Creek Indians attacked Fort Mims on the Alabama River. A thousand of the Red Sticks attacked and killed nearly 300 people, including many women and children. This Creek Civil War was now part of the War of 1812.[6]

Several battles between the Red Sticks and Jackson's troops took place. The decisive battle was at Horseshoe Bend in March 1814. With support from the mounted infantry, Jackson ordered his men over the high, compact Indian fortification resulting in a highly destructive conflict. Men and boys with fixed bayonets besieged the earth and log rampart toward the whooping, taunting sounds of a determined enemy.

Jackson's men, with a three-to-one numerical advantage exacted a great toll at Horseshoe Bend. This battle gave a deathblow to the Creek's hopes for defeating the White man. In this action, the best and bravest of their warriors were destroyed – 557 left dead on the ground. Of Jackson's army, one-tenth of that number was lost. The Battle of Horseshoe Bend was certainly one of the most destructive encounters between Whites and Indians in North American history. As a result, the Red Sticks were no longer a force of significance. With the defeat, Jackson forced the tribe to cede their claim to 23 million acres of what is now Alabama and Georgia.[6]

h) Battle of Lundy's Lane (July 25, 1814) – In one of the bloodiest battles of the war, one marked by extensive hand-to-hand fighting, the Americans were forced out of Canada for good.

i) Battle of Bladensburg, Maryland (August 24, 1814) – The Americans' worst battle of the war during which a British force of less than five thousand troops routed an American force of nearly seven thousand, leaving Washington undefended. The Americans were defended manly by state militias of Maryland and Virginia. The U.S. troops were poorly organized with inadequate discipline, retreating from the battle. Although the British had suffered heavier casualties than the Americans, they had completely routed the defenders. Some of the British dead "died without sustaining a scratch. They collapsed from heat exhaustion and the strain of punishing in forced marches over the five days since landing at Benedict."[7]

When it became clear that Bladensburg was the British target, President Madison and James Monroe (later to become both Secretaries of State and of War) moved to the scene. The president had gone to the camp to encourage, by his presence, the army defending the capital. President Madison left just before the heavy fighting began. Some suggest that the battle was "the greatest disgrace ever dealt to American arms."

j) Burning of Washington, D.C. (August 24-25, 1814) – After easily defeating the American defenders at Bladensburg, The British headed for Washington, D.C. The British burned the Capital Building, the Library of Congress, the White House and buildings housing the Treasury and War Departments (Fig.6.1).[4]

k) Battle of Plattsburgh, New York (September 11, 1814) - The British had launched a poorly coordinated campaign, which they lost. The. American victory brought an end to the British invasion of New York. Captain George Downie's squadron, supported by three of Sir George Prevost's divisions, was defeated on Lake Champlain, New York, by Master Commodore Thomas MacDonough's squadron.[1]

l) Attack on Baltimore and Fort McHenry, Maryland (September 12-13,

1814) – After having inflicted a severe embarrassment on the Americans with the burning of Washington, D. C., the British next turned their attention to Baltimore. There was a combined sea and land assault on the important port city of Baltimore. The Americans repulsed both the bombardment of Fort McHenry and the land invasion. At Fort McHenry, American gunners kept the enemy far enough away that the assault caused little damage, but the battle's exploding bombs were witnessed by Francis Scott Key, who memorialized the scene in "The Star-Spangled Banner".[8]

m) Battle of New Orleans (January 8, 1815) – On December 1, 1814 General Andrew Jackson arrived in New Orleans to prepare the vulnerable city for the major assault that was bound to come (Fig.6.2). Jackson put together a truly unique American Army. Regular U.S. troops, volunteer militia from Tennessee, Kentucky, Louisiana and the Mississippi Territory, free blacks, Creoles, Native Americans and even a band of pirates comprised Jackson's new force. However, Jackson's army was greatly outnumbered and inexperienced compared to the superior British troops that threatened New Orleans.[4]

Jackson ordered a night attack, which caught the British by surprise and set them back on their heels. Without waiting for the British to coordinate their forces, Jackson attacked. A combined naval and ground assault resulted in dozens of casualties on both sides and served to announce Jackson's resolve. The British commander, Sir Edward Pakenham, was a man of daring who had distinguished himself against Napoleon and had every reason for confidence in opposing Jackson.[9]

Two hours before daylight on January 8, 1815, the British troops began their final assault. Their failure to capture several American batteries left them exposed, and from behind fortifications fronted by a canal and flanked by the Mississippi River, woods, and swamps, Jackson's men annihilated them.

Across that foggy field, British commander Pakenham's orderly columns advanced. At the center of the American position, the Stars and Stripes flew from a high staff. The American batteries roared as Jackson is said to have called out, "Give it to them boys; let us finish the business to-day." The Tennesseans fired at a distance of two hundred yards. In the recollections of those who were there, a thunderous fire poured forth for several minutes, along with cannon blasts and screaming rockets. Pakenham himself charged at the head of the mostly Irish 44th Regiment, riding through a storm of bullets, his horse shot out from under him. He mounted another, and a short time later one of the American artillery pieces showered its lead and the British commander fell mortally wounded. Others of his field officers died as well in that charge; the lead column eventually crumbled and turned in retreat. It took no more than twenty-five minutes for the main assault to be repelled.[9,10]

New Orleans was saved, and in the process the proud British lost their best field officers: three major generals, eight colonels and lieutenant colonels, six majors, and eighteen captains. British casualties exceeded 2,000, with nearly 300 killed, while the Americans lost only 13 dead and 39 wounded. Although the death loss was low for the American side, some 500 of Jackson's men would die of fevers and dysentery in the weeks following the battle.

The battle of New Orleans should never have taken place. Prior to the battle, on December 24 negotiators from Britain and the United States, meeting in Europe, had signed the Treaty of Ghent to end the war. News of its signing, however, would not reach Jackson for weeks after the battle was over.

C. Diseases during the War of 1812

a) Organization of military medicine – When the War of 1812 began there was no central organization of the Medical Department for the U.S. Army. For many years the medical personnel had only consisted of a few regimental surgeons and their mates, scattered at isolated posts, with no official medical chief. Since army medicine suffered from basic organizational shortcomings, the War Department was ill prepared when the war broke out. Officials had no standardized system of accounting for or replenishing its medical supplies, or for evaluating the competency and training of its medical staff.[11]

During the war, physicians and surgeons often had neglected to record and transmit their experiences and observations. Uninterested in military medicine, the civilian physicians and surgeons of the day were ignorant of the disease incidence to armies, unfamiliar with hygiene of camps, and inexperienced in the operation of military hospitals.

On June 11, 1813, the venerable, respected, and forceful Dr. James Tilton was recalled from retirement and appointed Physician and Surgeon General of the United States Army. In February of that year, he had published his informative and forthright book "Economical Observations on Military Hospitals and Cure of Diseases Incident to an Army." The opinions expressed in this helped reorganize the medial department and an issuance of "Rules and Regulations for the Army", which defined the duties of the Physician and Surgeon General. This was the starting point in the establishment of the definitive Medical Department of the Army. The Burlington, Vermont hospital during the war included in the broad concepts of cleanliness, ventilation, isolation of febrile patients, attention to diet, and the location of the hospital on high grounds, 60 or 70 feet above the nearby water. At Burlington during the first 4 months of 1814, there were 2,412 admissions and 75 deaths. The record made by this model hospital was a demonstration that infectious diseases could be considerably controlled, and lives saved, by application of sanitary measures devised without the benefit of microbiology long before the bacteriological era.[11]

b) Medical Knowledge of the Day – In the pre-Pasteur age there was no understanding of the microbial etiology of infectious disease, and there were only a few preventive measures that were useful and many that were actually detrimental. The big advances in military medicine were decades away. William Morton would develop ether anesthesia for surgery, but not before 1846. Florence nightingale would create the professional nurse and reform the British hospital, but not until 1857. Robert Koch would put forth his germ theory in 1890. The notion that infection could spread through organism's invisible to the naked eye, for instance, did not gain widespread acceptance until the latter half of the nineteenth century. Although the War of 1812 took place well before these advances, there were many skilled military surgeons, most of them aware of the salutary effects of cleanliness.[12]

As usual, there was a general neglect of sanitation and as much sickness among the troops in the north and in the south. The chief diseases were typhus (called "Lake Fever" along the northern border), diarrhea/dysentery, and pneumonia, especially a form known as "peripneumonia notha." Although no new principles were introduced, some remarkable achievements significant for preventive medicine, were attained.

Even with their limited understanding of the science of germs, however, military doctors appreciated certain risk factors. Most had observed the deleterious effects of poor camp sanitation. Unfortunately, an army surgeon could usually only advise his commander to enact practices thought to reduce disease – separating latrines from cooking areas and water sources, enforcing cleanliness through routine bathing with soap, and restricting alcohol abuse, a major cause of sickness among soldiers.

Military surgeons sometimes did treatments that would be considered barbaric and often would make the patient's condition worse. Bleeding was thought to reduce blood volume and reduce fever and infection. This procedure was believed to be the treatment of choice – thanks to the efforts of Declaration of Independence signer and physician Dr. Benjamin Rush. He frequently practiced bleeding which is now known to have increased the death rate. Blistering, the practice of creating a skin infection on the patient, was thought to lead to pus that would carry away infection. Other physicians deliberately induced vomiting in an attempt to combat disease. Such practices were seldom helpful and often made the patients' condition worse. Some drugs provided no benefit and were unhelpful, as in the treatment of syphilis with the toxic element mercury.[13]

c) General cause of deaths – The typical soldier in the War of 1812 did not die from the effects of bullets or cannonballs, but instead from the effect of germs. In fact, fully three-quarters of the war deaths resulted from disease, most commonly typhoid fever, pneumonia, malaria, measles, typhus, smallpox and diarrhea. Of the estimated twenty thousand soldiers, militiamen and Native warriors who died in the war, nearly three-quarters succumbed to something other than a battle wound.[13]

d) Mosquito diseases – Mosquito born infectious diseases had plagued the colonists and was highly in evidence during the time period of the War of 1812. The viral disease yellow fever had caused repeated epidemics in seaports from New Orleans, Louisiana to Halifax, Nova Scotia.

Yellow fever epidemics were seasonal, later learned due to season of mosquitoes. People learned to move to areas that did not seem to suffer from the disease. This of course was because high-dry locations did not suffer from the epidemics. Only affluent families could afford to move seasonally to safer areas. During mosquito season soldiers suffered from the yellow fever epidemics. President Thomas Jefferson noted in 1800 that the U.S. would never have cities on the scale of those in Europe because population centers were doomed to periodic yellow fever epidemics causing high death rates.[14]

The other common mosquito-borne disease was protozoal malaria. Malaria was most common in the warmer southern colonies. Malaria was actually one of the few infections for which there was an effective treatment. When the Spanish conquered the Peruvian Incan Empire, they were introduced to cinchona bark and its effectiveness in treating fever in general and malaria in particular, and the bark had become a staple of the physician's medicine chest for more than a century.[14] However, many physicians at the time of the war lacked this medication.

e) Smallpox – Smallpox is a viral disease that carried an approximate 30% mortality rate and an almost universal morbidity, with scarring and blindness being the most significant results. During the American Revolutionary War smallpox was prevented in the Continental Army by inoculation. This was an intentional induction of the disease, transmitting the virus from a patient with a mild case of smallpox to healthy individuals. The success of this procedure is based on two concepts. First, once a person has smallpox, immunity is permanent. Second, mortality from the inoculation was much less than the disease naturally acquired. The mortality for the soldiers was reduced to 1-2% as a result of mandatory inoculation. George Washington was responsible for mandatory inoculation of the entire continental army in 1777. Thus, for the War of 1812, smallpox was less of an issue (see Chapter 5,

Section C).

f) Typhus and Typhoid – Typhus was a disease related to lice or to fleas of rats. This was most common in port cities where ships had transported rats. It was the bites of lice from the rats that caused the disease. Typhoid was common in the military operations of the War of 1812 due to unsanitary sewage handling. Sewage near food and water brought about the disease.

g) Diarrhea/Dysentery – Like typhoid fever, diarrhea/dysentery was due to unsanitary conditions related to sewage. Dysentery had accompanied soldiers on campaigns with dismal regularity since the earliest recorded wars. The term "Flux" was an inclusive term for all types of diarrheas, rendering a soldier's life miserable and in many cases short. Although yellow fever epidemics were more dramatic, dysentery and other diarrheas were far more common and almost certainly a greater cause of disability in the War of 1812, as it had been in the Revolutionary War. In the Revolutionary War Washington had cited the biblical book of Deuteronomy as a justification for requiring that latrines be located at a distance from campsites. Dysentery generally results from infection with *Escheria* or *Salmonella*, *Shigella*, or *Camphlobactor* species. An American army surgeon noted: "Among soldiers in the field, filth and bad provisions abound." It is among that class of men that dysentery appears with all its hideous forms."

A surgeon's writing from Buffalo in November 1812 reported that three or four soldiers of the U.S. Army there were dying each day, and that more than 100 of those wounded in an October attack on Queenston had died. The most common diseases afflicting men at Buffalo, he said, were dysentery and measles. At Lewiston, some units reported one-third to one-half of their men sick that autumn.[12]

Although it is usually not fatal, dysentery markedly impairs an army's effectiveness. In August 1813 fully one-third of the American army was on sick report, and virtually all of those suffered from dysentery.[14] In the last battle of the War of 1812 General Jackson had remained physically weak from his long bout with dysentery. He looked "very badly," wrote one of the fighting men, "and has broken very much." The ailing general had sent a letter to Secretary of War Monroe on January 3, saying that it would be wise for Washington to appoint someone to succeed him, "When my want of health, which I find to be greatly impaired, shall oblige me to retire" from command.

h) Respiratory diseases – The respiratory diseases of influenza and pneumonia caused many deaths, particularly in the crowded conditions of makeshift hospitals for the military. Infection spread; in one month, a pneumonia epidemic killed seventy-five residents in the Burlington hospital.

i) Alcohol – The addiction of alcohol was a serious problem for some soldiers. However, soldiers sometimes knew for days in advance that they were facing an amputation. A soldier might hoard his daily ration of alcohol, and consume it shorty before the surgery, in attempt to deal with the pain.

j) Venereal disease – In both the American Revolution and the War of 1812 venereal disease was epidemic. There was no effective treatment, although mercury was regularly employed. In general, punishment was used in lieu of therapy. During the Revolution, officers were fined $10 and enlisted men $4 if they were diagnosed with venereal infection. The proceeds were used to buy dressings and bedclothes for the military hospitals.[12]

k) Battle wounds – Finally, wound infection was depressingly common. In fact, it was universally accepted that wounds would not heal until they had begun to drain so-called laudable pus, a situation that we now understand to be the result of staphylococcal infection. During the war, often 25 percent of the wounded who were admitted to hospitals died, and the vast majority of those succumbed to unrelated infections. Infections were due to unsanitary treatment of wounded personnel and lack of sanitation of operating equipment. When the weather was intensely hot, flies were seen in myriads and lighting on the wounds, depositing their eggs, so that maggots were bred in a few hours.[2]

l) Foods – Food poisoning was also common as well as nutritional deficiencies. A common deficiency was scurvy when vitamin C rich green vegetable or fruits were unavailable. Lack of vitamin C foods were most likely during winter and early spring.[15]

Table 6.1 illustrates War of 1812 highlights.

D. Summary

President Madison declared war in 1812 due to illegal activity under international law by Britain. The British used blockades, impressments of American seaman and seizure of cargos. They also supported Indians to kill American settlers. The war lasted 2 years and 8 months and ended with the Treaty of Ghent in late December 1814. News of the peace did not reach America in time to prevent the Battle of New Orleans.

The long-term results of the war were generally satisfactory to both sides. In the end of the war, neither side won any new territory. The war helped to secure America's unfettered access to the sea, which played a large role in the post-war economic boom. The Canadians showed their resistance to being controlled by the U.S. Native Americans were the big losers in the war; lacking

British support the Indians barrier to westward expansion was removed. A nationalistic value for the U.S. was that Francis Scott Key wrote what became our national anthem during the attack on Ft. McHenry in Baltimore.

Over 1,600 British and 2,260 American soldiers, marines, and sailors perished in this war on both land and water. The greatest death loss was from disease as more fatalities were due to various diseases compared to enemy combat.

Three-quarters of the war deaths resulted from disease, most commonly typhoid fever, pneumonia, malaria, measles, typhus, smallpox, yellow fever, diphtheria, and diarrhea/dysentery. Lack of sanitation was directly related to diarrhea and typhoid fever. Mosquito related diseases were yellow fever and malaria. Often 25 percent of wounded who were admitted to hospitals died with the majority succumbing to unrelated infections, mostly due to unsanitary treatment and unsanitary operating equipment.

Table 6.1 Highlights of War of 1812[4]

1812 (June 18)	President Madison signed into law declaring war on Great Britain.
1812 (August 16)	A humiliating defeat for U.S. as Detroit is captured.
1812 (Aug. – Dec.)	U.S. frigates Constitution and United States perform well in a series of Atlantic engagements.
1812 (October 13)	In Battle of Queenston Heights, British and Canadian troops turn back U.S. incursion into Canada.
1813 (April 27)	Americans capture York (now Toronto).
1813 (September 10)	American forces under Oliver Perry won the Battle of Lake Erie.
1813 (October 5)	Troops under General William Harrison win the important Battle of the Thames against British and Indian forces.
1814 (March 27)	General Jackson led his troops to victory over Creek Indians in the Battle of Horseshoe Bend. The battle was a deathblow to the Creek's hopes for defeating the white man.
1814 (July 25)	The British won the Battle of Lundy's Lane, forcing Americans out of Canada. This was one of the bloodiest battles of the war.
1814 (August 24)	The Battle of Bladensburg was a poor showing for American troops. After the British won the battle, they invaded Washington, D.C. and burned the Capital and White House.
1814 (September 11)	At the Battle of Plattsburgh on Lake Chaplain, the British lost due to a poorly coordinated campaign.
1814 (September 11)	The British combined a sea and land assault on Fort McHenry and Baltimore. Americans repulsed both the bombardment of Fort McHenry and the land invasion. Observing the battle's exploding bombs, Francis Scott Key memorialized the scene in "The Star-Spangled Banner."
1815 (January 8)	In the Battle of New Orleans forces under General Jackson annihilated British troops. The war had officially ended 15 days earlier, but the peace settlement had not reached New Orleans.

Fig. 6.1 British troops burn Washington D.C.

Fig. 6.2 On January 8, 1815, The Battle of New Orleans was a decision victory for Andrew Jackson's troops.

CHAPTER 7

Mexican - American War

A. Introduction

In the 1844 U.S. presidential election, Democrat James K. Polk was elected on a platform of expanding U.S. territory in Oregon and Texas. Polk, like many other Americans, fervently believed in the idea of Manifest Destiny, the country stretching from the Atlantic to the Pacific.

Oregon was the name given to all the land between Alaska and California, west of the Rocky Mountains. Both Great Britain and the U.S. claimed the territory but compromised by splitting the territory with a boundary at the 49th parallel.[1]

Perhaps the most important event of Polk's presidency was the Mexican - American War. The troubled Mexico-United States relations were inflamed by the possibility of the annexation of Texas, as Mexico still viewed Texas as an integral part of Mexico. The annexation occurred during the last few days of President John Tyler's presidency, offering to admit Texas to statehood. The Mexican envoy to the U.S. resigned two days after Polk became president, knowing Polk was in favor of Texas statehood. Not only had the United States made Texas a state, but it had also set the Rio Grande as its southern boundary. Mexico insisted the boundary ended further north at the Nueces River.[2]

The Mexican War involved more than just making Texas a state; there had been attempts to purchase California and New Mexico as well. Polk sent an envoy to offer Mexico up to $20,000,000 in return for California and the New Mexico country. In California Captain John C. Fremont was fermenting rebellion among American settlers. To bring pressure, Polk sent General Zachary Taylor (and later president) to the disputed area on the Rio Grande. Mexico had every reason to be suspicious given Taylor's army in Texas and Fremont's aggression in California. Since no Mexican leader could cede half his country and still stay in power, Polk's envoy was not received.

Taylor's army of 4,000 troops was sent to build a fort along the Rio Grande within the disputed terrain. Polk, not wanting to appear as the bad guy, looked for a pretense to declare war on Mexico. The Texas-Mexico border gave him the issue he was looking for. To Mexican troops this was aggression, and they attacked Taylor's forces, killing 11 soldiers. The attack was enough for Polk. Addressing Congress, Polk loudly proclaimed that Mexico had invaded U.S. territory and shed American blood. The war was on (Fig.7.1).[3]

Support for the war was high in the Southern states and the American West. Whigs and Northern Democrats rejected the war because they saw it was another attempt by Polk to expand slavery. They also felt that the president deceived them by inciting a war and that the war itself was not only unjust but also illegal.[4]

B. Military Activity

The two major generals of the war were Zachary Taylor and Winfield Scott. Numerous future Civil War generals and leaders – including Ulysses Grant, William Sherman, George Meade, Franklin Pierce, James Buchanan, Robert E. Lee, Stonewall Jackson, James Longstreet and future Confederate President Jefferson Davis – fought in the war as either regular officers or volunteers.[3] Three war participants became U.S. presidents, Zachary Taylor, Ulysses Grant and Franklin Pierce.

President Polk devised a strategy to conquer California, New Mexico, and northern Mexico using a volunteer army of 70,000. A portion of this force was assigned from each state and territory in the Union, to make each feel an interest in the war."[1]

James Polk was the first U.S president to truly function as Commander-in-Chief of the armed forces. This is unlike modern-day presidents who call on generals to mastermind wars for them, Polk ran the war himself, working 18-hour days and clashing with his generals. After arguing with Whig generals, Polk became so paranoid that he trusted only himself to do the job.[4]

The Mexican American War (1846-1848) was fought from California to Mexico City and many points in between. There were several main engagements: the American army won all of them. Here are some of the more important battles fought during that bloody conflict. The two major generals Zachary Taylor and Winfield Scott fighting in Mexico and John Fremont in California. Major engagements were as follows:[5]

a) Battles of Palo Alto and Resaca de la Palma (May 8-9, 1846) – The battle near the Rio Grande was where Mexican General Mariano Arista laid siege to Fort Texas, knowing Zachary Taylor would have to come to break the siege. During the same time, General Taylor cooperates with U.S. naval ships stationed in the Gulf of Mexico to block the mouth of the Rio Grande. The U.S. easily won the battle, though outnumbered. Taylor's victory resulted in 92 Mexicans killed and 116 wounded versus nine Americans killed and 44 wounded.[1]

The day after Palo Alto General Arista planned a type of ambush only five miles from Palo Alto. General Arista had already received sufficient reinforcements to replace the losses at Palo Alto, and so for the coming contest, as before, about 6,000 men.[6] Taylor's smaller army of 1,700 troops set out and were prepared to meet force with force, in hand-to-hand combat. Taylor unleashed infantry attacks that eventually sent the hard-fighting Mexican army in flight across the Rio Grande, with some soldiers panicking and drowning in the river's current. Arista admitted he left behind 160 dead,

228 wounded and 159 missing. For the Americans 33 had been killed and 89 wounded. There could not be the slightest doubt that Taylor had gained a sweeping victory in the battle of Resarade al Palma.

During the battle Taylor sat on his horse, Old Whitey, in the thickest of the fight, with his sword drawn, while the balls were rattling around him. Unknown to Taylor his victories elevated him to heroic status in the United States. In June 1946 he was promoted to the full rank of major general and had received a formal commendation from Congress.

b) Battle of Monterey (September 21-23, 1846) – General Taylor continued his slow March into the Mexican north, to the most important city, Monterrey. General Arista after his disastrous campaigns against the intruders had been replaced by General Pedro de Ampudia for the defense of Monterrey. He had between 7,000 and 8,000 regular Mexican troops and probably 3,000 militia. His forces were well armed and well supplied. His artillery numbered 42 cannon and was excellently distributed for a stubborn resistance. Taylor had a well-disciplined, well-organized, well-commanded little army, full of confidence, and an unswerving trust in the skill of its officers and commander Taylor.

Taylor decided to approach the city from the plains along the eastern end of the city and have part of his army attack the heights in the west. Forces under General William Worth attacked Federation, a fortified Mexican post in the heights. After winning there they attacked a second post, Independencia, where they clawed their way up a steep hillside and engaged in hand-to-hand combat before subduing the enemy. The Americans now controlled the eastern heights. In the meantime, Taylor launched a diversion against eastern Monterrey, which required house-to-house combat. The hard-fought urban combat led to heavy casualties on both sides. The triumph of General Taylor's soldiers had successfully stormed "impregnable" Monterrey in three short days. In the fighting for Monterrey, Taylor lost 120 killed, 389 wounded and 43 missing. On the Mexican side, 367 men died.[2]

During the fighting "Old Rough and Ready", a name given to Taylor, was oblivious to danger. He set his men a splendid example of physical bravery by participating personally in the carnage, battling on foot in their very midst. Taylor's success at the battle of Monterrey gave to the American people an acute sense of American military courage such as they had not experienced since Andrew Jackson's victory at New Orleans.[4]

c) The war in the west – There were many battles, none of which were very large scale, to win the west, mostly in California and New Mexico. These were all won by U.S. forces. On June 10, 1846, Frémont leads a group of Californians against the local authorities and declared the establishment of the Bear Flag Republic in northern California. Later, on July 7, 1846, a contingent of U.S. marines raised the American flag claiming that California was annexed to the United States.[5]

d) Battle at Buena Vista (February 22-23, 1847) – After the battle at Monterrey, relations between President Polk and Zachary Taylor soured because he feared enthusiasm for Taylor would damage his own Democratic Party's prospects. Being vindictive and playing politics in January 1847, Polk removed most of Taylor's unit to the Mexican coast to serve under General Winfield Scott, a Whig much less popular than Taylor. Taylor was incensed. Polk's maneuver was aimed at pressuring him to quit, but resigning would make it look like he was deserting his men.

Taylor disobeyed orders and went forward with the 5,000 remaining troops. Mexican General Santa Anna had learned that Taylor had lost most of his troops so moved to first defeat Taylor prior to battling General Scott. Outnumbered by more than four to one, made up almost entirely of volunteer troops and green volunteers at that, and containing only between 450 and 500 regulars, the force which faced the legions of Anta Anna was scarily impressive. Hearing of the Mexican movement upon his position, Taylor deployed his outnumbered command in a mountain pass near the Hacienda Buena Vista, where his small numbers might do the best.[4]

As Taylor's forces were greatly outnumbered, Mexican General Santa Anna told Taylor: "You are surrounded by twenty thousand men and cannot in any human probability avoid suffering a rout. ...I wish to save you from a catastrophe, and for that purpose give you this notice, in order that you may surrender at discretion."

Taylor went against all odds and won the Battle of Buena Vista, defeating the Mexican army. At the end of the battle more than 3,400 of Santa Anna's men lay dead or wounded. Taylor lost 650. The Battle of Buena Vista was the largest battle of the war.[7] Because of Taylor's military victories the Whig Party was very interested in considering him as presidential candidate. With his other victories this made him a national hero. President Polk's plan to prevent Zachary Taylor from becoming a hero to challenge the Democrat Party in the next election was a failure. By reducing Taylor's troop strength, the victory at the Battle of Buena Vista with overwhelming odds ensured Taylor's hero status. Americans were gratified that General Santa Anna had been defeated, since he was the general responsible for killing all the defenders of the "Alamo" in the Texas battle for independence.

e) Siege of Veracruz (March 9-29, 1847) – General Scott oversaw the landing of thousands of American troops near Vera Cruz on Mexico's Atlantic coast to begin a siege. He used his cannons and some massive guns borrowed from the navy. The surrender was twenty days later.[8]

f) Battle of Cerru Gordo ("Fat Hill") (April 17-18, 1847) – Mexican General Antonia López de Santa Anna had regrouped after his defeat at Buena Vista and marched with thousands of determined troops. Santa Anna allowed Scott's army to march inland, counting on yellow fever and other tropical diseases to take their toll before Santa Anna chose the place to engage the enemy. In the battle Santa Anna's left flank was vulnerable and General Scott exploited this weakness and avoided Santa Anna's artillery. The battle was a rout and the Mexican army retreated in disarray to Mexico City.

g) Battle of Contreras (August 19, 1847) The American Army under Scott made its way inland towards Mexico City. In the battle Santa Anna fails to support the Mexican line at a critical moment turning victory into rout.

h) Battle of Chapultepec (September 12-15, 1847) – The army under Scott broke through the walls of Mexico City with fierce fighting and captured the capital. Ulysses Grant and his men hoisted a howitzer into a church belfry that had a commanding view of the San Cosme gate. The action brought him the honorary rank of brevet captain, for "gallant and meritorious conduct in the Battle of Chapultepec." Mexico City belonged to the invaders and Mexican authorities were ready to negotiate.

Due to the American victories, the president's representative in Mexico negotiated the Treaty of Guadalupe Hidalgo. Under the treaty's terms, the Texas border was fixed at Rio Grande and Mexico ceded New Mexico and California to the United States for $15 million. As a result, the U.S. gained a great deal of territory, the states of California, Nevada, Colorado, Oklahoma, and Wyoming were all included in the Mexican cession. The losses to Mexico amounted to one-third of its original territory from its 1812 independence. With the previous loss of Texas this would be closer to one half of its original territory lost. Acquisition of the territory precipitated a bitter quarrel between the North and South over expansion of slavery.[7]

The Mexican war was the second costliest war in American history in terms of the percentage of soldiers who died. Of the 78,718 American soldiers who served, 13,283 died, constituting a casualty rate of 16.87 percent. To put this in perspective, for the U.S. more than one-tenth of men in the war did not survive their term of service. By comparison, the casualty rate was 2.5 percent in World War I and World War II, 0.1 percent in Korea and Vietnam, and 21 percent for the Civil War. Of the casualties, 11,562 died of illness, disease, and accidents. Most historians estimate as many as 25,000 Mexican troops and civilians died.[9] Personal recollections of President Grant were that 39 men he had known at West Point died. Four members of his 1843 class lost their lives."[10]

The statement of the Mexican War being the second costliest war is only true if King Phillips War (1675-1676) is not considered. Total casualties for King Phillips War based on percent of population was 10X that of the Civil War. The New England population at that time was 52,000. The death rate was 600 to 800, by far the highest toll of any American War.

C. Diseases during Mexican-American War

In terms of deaths due to disease, the Mexican War was the deadliest of all American wars. A higher percentage of U.S. troops died from sickness during the Mexican invasion than any war in American history."[10] Nearly 13% of the entire U.S. force perished from disease. Of the total 12,535 war deaths, 10,986 (88%) were due to infectious diseases; seven men died from disease for every man killed from battle. An excellent review of the health and disease conditions during the Mexican - American War was published by Richard Winders in 1997. Much had been made of the ease with which Americans marched across Mexico, scoring victory after victory on their way to the Halls of Montezuma. A trail of bodies, however, marked their path.

Detrimental causes leading to disease included: poor or lack of tents, bad water, impure air, unsanitary privies, variable and extreme temperatures, scarcity of fuel, poor diets, hard marching and lack of adequate medical treatment.[11] Factors leading to disease and specific diseases were:

a) **Disease residence** – Volunteers suffered a much higher rate of infectious disease than regulars. One regular officer remarked on the disproportionate amount of illness in volunteer regiments, "They cannot take care of themselves; the hospitals are crowded with them. Most of these were young farmers of temperate habits. It was likely that farm boys lacked the well-developed immune systems of city dwellers whose constant exposure to disease had made them more resistant.

b) **Shelter** – Sheltering the army against the elements was inadequate during the early part of the war. There had been lack of tents and many tents could not keep out rain nor wind and blown dust, making them practically useless. Some reports noted men sleeping in water and mud while many others were sleeping on dirt floors. Throughout the war, constant exposure to the weather helped to break down some men's resistance to disease. The conclusion was that barracks where men lay were filthy. Disease would inevitably follow, leaving the army weak and vulnerable to bacteria and viruses.[11]

c) **Water** – Inadequate and contaminated drinking water resulted in widespread illness. Sometimes water was contaminated with sea salt as well as being brackish tasting. At times river water that was consumed, contained dead cows and horses. Thirsty men were ready to drink anything, even muddy water. One report noted soldiers drinking water from buffalo wallows and ruts in the road, muddy, filthy and water covered with scum, which the horses of the mounted men refused to drink. With water sources as these, it is little wonder that dysentery and diarrhea ran rampant in the army. To add to the water problem, diets of salt pork intensified thirst.[11]

d) **Marches** – Hard marches created health problems. With the musket and supplies, the load was at least 40 pounds. After marching in the July heat and high humidity, many men were sick, lame and exhausted. Soldiers along the Rio Grande had to deal with dust drawing it into their lungs. Danger existed for those unable to keep up during marches. Stragglers were easy prey for the guerrillas and bandits who shadowed the lines of march. Some died along the way, victims of sunstroke.

e) **Diets** – Poor diets resulted in diseases and laid the foundation for the discharge of many soldiers from the army. It was suggested that poorly cooked rations as a cause of dysentery and diarrhea. Scurvy was reported at two different locations within the army. Scurvy could result from lack of vegetables and fruits or overcooking vegetables which destroys the Vitamin C needed to prevent scurvy.[12]

f) **Medical Treatment** – During the war in hospitals there were many dedicated doctors as well as their staff. However, not all medical attention in the field and in hospitals was of high standards. Unable to care for themselves, patients were at the mercy of the medical staff. Overworked doctors and an uncaring staff sometimes committed acts of cruelty and neglect. In one instance, a surgeon in Vera Cruz ordered attendants to gag a dying man whose screams disturbed the ward.[11]

Overcrowding led to poor conditions that hampered treatment and resulted in criticism of the Medical Department. Unsanitary conditions and the lack of antiseptics undoubtedly resulted in numerous infections, which slowed recovery and even killed some patients. The very size of the hospital at Vera Cruz led to some needless deaths; too many patients were massed together to be properly cared for at one place. It was observed that many men had no beds but simply were lying on the brick floor with only a blanket beneath them. Some patients laid on the bricks in the same vermin-infested clothes they had worn for weeks.

One complaint called several surgeons as "insolent ruffians." The notation was "a man in the states would be ashamed to speak to his dog in a way these men addressed the sick." One uncaring doctor reportedly told a man to "go to hell" when he asked for medicine to give a dying friend.

Hospital staff also came in for their share of criticism with patients exposed to the carelessness of nurses and attendants with daily insults by ruffians. Some hospital stewards were thieves, "The breath is scarcely out of the body of the deceased before the 'stewards' are rifling his pockets." With the sick seen by the staff mainly as a source of revenue, "many died from the want of proper attention."

g) **Major diseases during the war** – The vast majority of American forces were victims of diseases such as dysentery, yellow fever, malaria and smallpox. Dysentery (both bacterial and amebic) and yellow fever resulted in the highest death rates. Diseases such as smallpox, influenza, measles, malaria, cholera, and mumps took their toll too, especially on troops from rural environments whose immunities were less developed than those of their urban compatriots. Poor sanitation contributed to the spread of illness, with volunteers – who were less disciplined in their sanitary practices than regular troops were – dying in greater numbers than the regulars. Disease was spread as a result of crowded camps, resulting in outbreaks to reach epidemic proportions of influenza, smallpox and measles.[13]

The disease of yellow fever affected the strategy of General Winfield Scott in the Mexican War. Scott's entire plan was based on striking Vera Cruz during the winter and marching west of the "Yellow Fever Line" into the Sierra Madres before the yellow fever season started (Fig.7.2). Yellow fever frightened Scott more than the Mexicans. Yellow fever began to occur in small numbers almost as soon as the forces landed, though not at epidemic strength. On April 18, Scott's forces won a crushing victory at Cerro Gordo. Now Scott could breathe a sigh of relief as he crossed the Sierra Madres range and had passed the Yellow Fever Line.[8]

Although yellow fever was greatly feared and did cause deaths, the real killers were diarrhea and dysentery. Generally, cases of yellow fever were diagnosed quickly, and the victim taken to the hospital, where they received timely treatment. Men with diarrhea and dysentery, on the other hand, often stayed in camp untreated and were taken to the hospital only after their condition had deteriorated too far for them to recover. Camp pollution was the greatest error committed by U.S. troops in the Mexican War. The indifference of line officers and recruits to the need for proper sanitation and military hygiene fueled the dysentery outbreaks, and the poor conditions in military hospitals contributed further to the spread of disease.[13]

Venereal disease both syphilis and gonorrhea, constituted a serious health problem in some areas of Mexico. Infected prostitutes evidently had conducted a substantial business with American soldiers to create a serious health problem. The treatment for venereal disease called for doses of mercury and cauterization of ulcers with an acid solution. By regulation, all recruits entering the army were vaccinated for smallpox. During the Revolutionary War George Washington began a tradition of smallpox vaccination for the troops (see Chapter 5). One surgeon found that the Mexican heat had spoiled his stock of smallpox vaccine, making it impossible to prevent the disease. An outbreak of smallpox caused the entire 2nd Pennsylvania Regiment to be quarantined and unavailable to General Scott.[8] Untold suffering and death could have been prevented, had the practice of vaccination been extended to all army personnel, regular and volunteer.

Table 7.1 illustrates the highlights of the Mexican-American.

D. Summary

The Mexican – American War (1846-1848) was fought from California to Mexico City with many points in between. The war began with a dispute as to the U.S. – Mexican border, the Rio Grande or Nueces River. President James Polk functioned as Commander-in-Chief of the U.S. forces. The two major generals were Zachary Taylor and Winfield Scott. President Polk ordered General Tayler to build a fort near the Rio Grande, which resulted in an attack by the Mexicans and the beginning of the war. All major battles were won by the U.S.

As the result of the war, the Mexico - U.S. border was fixed at the Rio Grande and Mexico ceded large amounts of territory to the U.S., gaining the states of California, Nevada, Utah, most of Arizona and parts of other states. The idea of Manifest Destiny was completed with the country stretching from the Atlantic to the Pacific.

The war was costly, with a U.S. casualty of rate of 16.87 percent. Of the total deaths, 88% were due to infectious diseases. Seven men died from disease for every man killed from battle. Detrimental causes leading to disease included poor tents, overcrowded camps, bad water, poor diets, hard marching, lack of sanitation and adequate medical treatment. The vast majority of American forces were victims of diseases such as dysentery, yellow fever, malaria and smallpox. Camp pollution and lack of proper sanitation fueled dysentery outbreaks.

Table 7.1
Mexican American War[5,10,13,14]

1844	
In the presidential election James K. Poke had advocated expanding U.S. territory for the idea of Manifest Destiny, the country stretching from the Atlantic to the Pacific.	
1846	
The war with Mexico was started over disagreements over the Texas border with Mexico. President Poke ordered General Zachary Taylor to build a fort along the disputed border of the Rio Grande. To Mexico this was aggression and they attacked Taylor's forces, killing 11 soldiers. Polk proclaimed that Mexico had invaded U.S. and the war was on.	
May 8-9	Battles of Palo Alto and Resaca de la Palma – In both battles Taylor's troops prevailed despite being outnumbered. Now Taylor crossed the Rio Grande and proceeded to invade Mexico.
June-July	War in the West – many battles, but most in California and New Mexico. General Frémont leads a group of Californian an American flag was raised claiming California annexed to the U.S.
Sept. 21-23	Battle of Monterey – Some of the battle involved house to house combat. General Taylor's soldiers successfully won what was thought to be "impregnable Monterrey" in three days. The Americans lost 120 killed and 367 died on the Mexican side. Taylor was becoming a great hero to America.
1847	
February 22-23	Battle Buena Vista – President Poke did not like the popularity of Republican General Taylor. He feared Taylor's popularity would damage his own Democratic Party's prospects. Being vindictive Polk removed most of Taylor's troops and assigned them to General Winfield Scott. Taylor disobeyed orders and went forward with his 5,000 remaining troops. Taylor's troops were outnumbered by more than four to one, however he won an impressive battle against General Santa Anna (General that ordered death to the Alamo defenders in Texas.) Taylor lost 650 men to 3,400 for Santa Anna. Poke's plan backfired with Taylor being a great hero, and later winning the presidency.
March 9-29	Siege of Vera Cruz – General Winfield Scott using cannons and some massive guns borrowed from the navy defeated the Mexican army.
April 17-18	Battle of Cerro Gordo – General Santa Anna was counting on yellow fever to inhibit the Americans. Yellow fever frightened General Scott more than the Mexicans. Yellow fever was a problem, but Scott's forces won a crushing victory.
Sept. 12-15	Battle of Chapultepec – with fierce fighting Scott's army broke through the wall of Mexico City and captured the capitol.
1848	
Feb. 2	War ends with Treaty of Guadalupe Hidalgo. Mexico lost one-third of its original territory since independence. The U.S. gained a great deal of territory, to eventually be the states of California, Nevada, Utah, Arizona

and parts of Colorado, New Mexico and Wyoming.
1846-1847
Of American soldiers who served 13,283 died. OF the casualties 11,562 died mostly of disease. As many as 25,000 Mexicans died. In terms of deaths due to disease, this was the deadliest of all American wars. Seven men died from disease for every man killed from battle.
The main fatal diseases were diarrhea/dysentery, yellow fever, malaria and smallpox. The diarrheas and yellow fever resulted in the highest death rates. Diseases such as influenza, measles, cholera and mumps also took their toll too. Poor sanitation contributed to the spread of disease. Likewise, disease was spread as a result of crowded camps resulted in epidemic proportions of influenza, smallpox and measles.

Fig. 7.1 The Mexican-American War began May 8, 1846. President James K. Polk managed most aspects of the war.

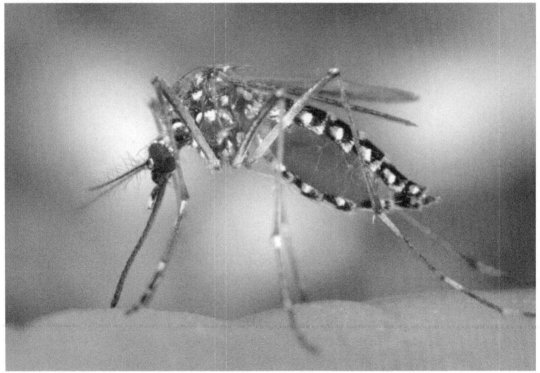

Fig. 7.2 Yellow fever mosquitos transmits the virus to humans.

CHAPTER 8

American Civil War

A. Introduction

The American Civil War (1861-1865) was an armed conflict between 23 northern states and 11 southern states that had seceded from the Union to form the Confederate States of America. Many families were torn by divided loyalties, and close relatives often fought each other.

a) Background – During the 1850s, there was almost continuous quarreling between sections of the country. All the various sectional demands were mixed up with the slavery issue. Antislavery forces demanded that Congress should keep slavery out of the expanding country's new territories. The Whig party broke up over the slavery question. In its place appeared the new Republican party, dedicated to preventing slavery from expanding to the territories. Abraham Lincoln soon joined the new party.

In Kansas, opponents and supporters of slavery poured into the new territory and clashed in armed conflict. The south wanted to force slavery on "bleeding Kansas". Abolitionists were persons who wanted to end slavery. In 1859, a fanatical abolitionist named John brown led a raid on Harpers Ferry, Va. He planned to seize the federal arsenal and start a slave uprising. Government troops under Col. Robert E. Lee captured Brown, and he was later hanged. But Southerners thought that Northern leaders had encouraged Brown's scheme.[1]

Lincoln became the Republican presidential candidate in the election of 1860. Before the election, many Southern leaders had urged secession or withdrawal from the Union, if Lincoln should win. Many Southerners favored secession as part of the doctrine of states' rights. Secessionists held that the national government was a league of sovereign states, and that any state had a legal right to withdraw from the Union. Lincoln won the election, but prior to his inauguration in March 1861, seven southern states led by South Carolina adopted an ordinance of secession. On February 9th the Confederacy selected Jefferson Davis as its president.

b) Causes of the War – There is a lack of agreement on causes of the Civil

War. Some would believe that the slavery issue was the basic cause. However, others would claim that the major issue was States Rights, does a state have the right to withdraw from the Union?

Lincoln in his presidential campaign and in his inaugural address noted "I declare that I have no purposes directly or indirectly, to interfere with the institution of slavery in the states where it exists. His only intention was to prevent slavery from spreading into new states and territories.[2] Lincoln's goal was to save the Union, not to end slavery in the states where it existed.

c) **Beginning and end of the war** – The Civil War started on April 12, 1861, when Southern artillery shelled Fort Sumter in the harbor of Charleston, South Carolina. The garrison was forced to surrender on April 13, 1861. On April 15, Lincoln called for troops to enforce the nation's laws. The South regarded this move as the equivalent of a declaration of war. The brutal war ended four years later on April 9, 1865, when Confederate General Robert E. Lee surrendered to Union General Ulysses S. Grant at Appomattox, Virginia. Besides the horrible carnage of the war, two main results were that states did not have the right of secession from the Union and slavery was ended in the country.

d) **Death from Disease** – Union troops died of diseases with 63% of Union fatalities from disease, 12% due to wounds and 19% of Union deaths were due to the death on the battlefield. Likewise, 2/3 Confederate troops died of infection. It was also found that more men died throughout this four-year period than in any other war experienced in the U.S. Between 620 and 750 thousand soldiers died during the Civil War.[3]

Of those who died, by far the leading cause of death was disease. Unsound hygiene, dietary deficiencies, and battle wounds set the stage for epidemic infection, while inadequate information about disease causation greatly hampered disease prevention, diagnosis, and treatment.

B. Military Activity

It is estimated that hostilities occurred on 8,000 occasions in the Civil War. The military significance of the battles into four classes were as follows: decisive, major, formative and limited. Wikipedia has described 384 battles.[4] Civil War Highlights are noted in Table 8.1. There were 50 major battles and about 100 others that had major significance. The present report will be limited to selected decisive and major battles of significance. The selected battles are as follows:

a) **First Battle of Bull Run (July 21, 1861)** – After the Confederates attacked Fort Sumter, Bull Run near Manassas was the first major battle. General Irwin

McDowell's troops marched from Washington, D.C. toward the Confederate capital of Richmond. Initially, the larger Union forces had an upper hand, causing Confederate troops into retreat. However, reinforcements arrived just in time under the southern commander General Thomas Jackson and checked the Union forces. This event earned the general the popular nickname "Stonewall" Jackson and helped the Confederates under General Pierre Beauregard launch a counter attack and claim victory. Many civilians had followed the Union troops, expecting a quick victory. This was not to be.[5]

b) Battle of Fort Henry (February 6,1862) – When Kentucky's fragile neutrality fell apart in the fall of 1861, Ulysses Grant and his volunteers took the small town of Paducah, Kentucky, at the mouth of the Tennessee River. In February 1862, in a joint operation with the U.S. Navy, Grant's ground forces applied pressure on Fort Henry, and it surrendered. The fall of Fort Henry opened up the Union War effort in Tennessee and Alabama.

c) Battle of Fort Donelson (February 11-16, 1862) - After the fall of Fort Henry, Grant moved his army overland 12 miles east to capture fort Donelson on the Cumberland River. The Confederates struck at Grant's forces to establish an escape route; however, Grant was able to rally the Union troops to prevent the escape. The Confederate forces, under General Simon Bolivar Buckner, finally surrendered Fort Donelson on February 16. Grant's surrender demand to Buckner was popular throughout the Union, "No terms except unconditional and immediate surrender." The general was colloquially known from then on as "Unconditional Surrender" Grant. President Abraham Lincoln promoted Grant to major general of Volunteers.[6] The surrender of Fort Donelson was a tremendous victory for the union war effort; 12,000 Confederate soldiers had been captured in addition to the bountiful arms in inventory of the fort. Battles of Fort Henry and Fort Donelson were the first two major Union victories of the Civil War.[7]

d) Battle of Shiloh (April 6-7, 1862) – Major General Grant moved the Union army deep into Tennessee. On the morning of April 6, 40,000 Confederate soldiers under the command of General Albert Sidney Johnson led a surprise attack. They hoped to defeat Johnson's army before he was reinforced by Major General Carlos Buell's Army of the Ohio. The Confederates were dominant throughout the day driving the Union Army back by over two miles. Reinforcements finally arrived, and Grant was able to defeat the Confederates during the second day of battle.

The battle left behind a bloody legend: 1,723 southern soldiers dead, 1,754 northern soldiers dead and more casualties than in the Revolutionary War, War of 1812, and Mexican War combined. During the engagement,

Confederate General Johnson was killed, and Union General William Sherman was shot twice with two of his horses killed.

Despite the criticism, Grant emerged from Shiloh a hero. Northern newspapers called Grant a great general, for unlike other union military leaders, he stubbornly resisted the Confederates, and he exuded noble qualities; calmness, self-control, and fortitude under fire.[5,7]

e) Battle Monitor and Merrimack (March 9, 1862) – The Confederates had raised a sunken federal ship, the Merrimack and covered it with iron plates. This ship battled the Northern ironclad, the Monitor. Neither ship won the battle, but wooden ships in the future would not be able to compete.

f) Battle of Fort Pulaski (April 10-11, 1862) – In Georgia a Union blockade closes Savannah, Georgia. The fort fell because of a new weapon, the Parrott rifle. This cannon would do more than damage a fort's wall; it would destroy a fort making masonry forts obsolete.

g) Second Battle of Bull Run (August 28-30, 1862) – This battle was fought on the same ground in Virginia as the first Battle of Bull Run. The Union was defeated, with one major reason for the defeat was that General George McClellan would not provide the requested reinforcements to General John Pope. It was later learned from correspondence of McClellan to his wife, that he deliberately withheld troops from Pope, as he did not wish Pope to have success on the battlefield. General Henry Halleck and Lincoln had given direct orders to reinforce Pope's troops, which McClellan ignored. Many believe McClellan's actions were treasonable and that he should have been court-martialed and jailed.[7]

h) Battle of Antietam (September 17, 1862) – In June 1862 General Robert E. Lee had the ambitious plan to invade the border state of Maryland and northern state of Pennsylvania with the goal of severing important railway routes. The battle of Antietam began when General Lee's forces crossed the Potomac River into Maryland. Union General George McClellan attacked Lee along Antietam Creek. The Union won under McClellan, however Lincoln was disgusted with him, as he had refused to pursue Lee after the battle and let him escape. Had McClellan been more daring, Lincoln believed, he could have smashed Lee's army and ended the war. The Battle of Antietam resulted in 23,000 casualties, the bloodiest single day battle of the entire war.[8]

i) Battle of Fredericksburg (December 13, 1862) – The president replaced McClellan with General Ambrose Burnside, who decided to attack Lee at Fredericksburg, Virginia. Burnside's union forces received a crushing blow with more than 12,000 union soldiers killed or wounded.

j) Battle of Chancellorsville (April 30 – May 16, 1863) – General Joseph "Fighting Joe" Hooker replaced Burnside as commander of the Army of the Potomac. By the spring of 1863, the army numbered 120,000, with the Confederates at half that number. With the battle on May 2, Stonewall Jackson attacked Hooker's right, while Lee struck in front. The Confederates won the battle. Hooker retreated having 17,274 casualties to Lee's 12,826. Confederate victory cost the life of Jackson, Lee's ablest general, who was shot accidentally by his own men. Lee had won a famous battle but had lost his right hand" in Stonewall Jackson.[5]

k)   Battle of Gettysburg (July 1-3, 1863) – After his successes at Fredericksburg and Chancellorsville, in July Lee invaded the North again and fought the Union, under General George Meade, at the 3-day battle at Gettysburg, Pennsylvania. For the first three days of July, a northern army of 90,000 men met a Southern army of 75,000 in the greatest battle ever fought in the Western Hemisphere. The Union won, with many considering this the turning point of the Civil War. The battle is remembered for the full assault of close to 15,000 Confederate infantry men against the center of the Union line on Cemetery Ridge. Now famously known as Pickett's Charge, this failed attack by Lee is cited as the primary reason for the Confederate defeat. Lee's army conceded the field on the 4th of July and staggered back to Virginia. Another northern invasion had failed. There were close to 50,000 casualties over three days.

As Lee withdrew on July 4 from Gettysburg, he found his retreat south blocked by the flooded Potomac River. Lincoln ordered General Meade to pursue the enemy, but Meade hesitated, and once the Potomac subsided Lee escaped. An angry Lincoln said, "Our army held the war in the hollow of their hand, and they would not close it." Lincoln was ready to look for a new commander of Union forces.[7]

With the great Union victory at the Battle of Gettysburg in July 1863, the stage was set for Lincoln's address at the Gettysburg battlefield cemetery on November 19, 1863. Defying Lincoln's prediction that "the world will little note, nor long remember what we say here", the Address became the most quoted speech in American history.[9] He defined the war as an effort dedicated to these principles of liberty and equality for all.

l) Campaign of Vicksburg (July 4, 1863) – Union war strategy called for taking control of the Mississippi River by the Union army and navy and cutting the Confederacy in half. This involved a long siege of the fortress city of Vicksburg on the Mississippi River. The Confederates held on for over 40 days and finally surrendered unconditionally on 4th of July. Grant captured

30,000 men, and the North took control of the Mississippi River (Fig.8.1). This was followed 5 days later by the surrender of Port Hudson in Louisiana, splitting the western from the eastern Confederacy. During the Civil War, in general the Union had done poorly in 1861 and in 1862. However, in 1863 historians consider the Battles of Vicksburg and Gettysburg to be the turning points of the war.[7]

m) The Overland Campaign, Battles of the Wilderness, Spotsylvania and Cold Harbor (May 5 – June 3, 1864) – In November 1863, Lincoln made Grant a lieutenant general, and he became the commander of all Union forces giving him command of more than half a million men and the chance to implement his own strategies. He stopped capturing cities and went after the major Confederate forces. This strategy proved bloody but successful.

On May 5th, 1864, Grant attacked the Confederate forces, headed by General Lee himself, at the Battle of the Wilderness. The battle ended in a draw, with great losses on both sides. Grant's next battles were at Spotsylvania and Cold Harbor. Both Confederate and Union soldiers were slaughtered in great numbers. Cold Harbor was an utter defeat for the Union. In a month of fighting, Grant had lost almost 55,000 men. From the Wilderness to Cold Harbor, Grant had hammered Lee for 70 miles. In each engagement his losses had been fairly matched by Lee's, except at Cold Harbor, and the net benefit had been with Grant. Both armies had been shattered, but Lee had fewer men to spare. Lincoln told a crowd "Grant had the grip of a bulldog, when he once gets his teeth in, nothing can shake him off."[10]

n) Siege of Petersburg (June 20, 1864 – April 2, 1865) – Grant realized he could not destroy Lee's army without a siege. His men dug trenches around the city. Lee's weary troops did the same. The deadly siege of Petersburg began on June 20 and dragged on for nine long months.

Union troops tried several times to break through the Confederate line. The most unusual attempt, the Battle of the Crater, took place on July 30. Northern engineers had dug a 511-foot tunnel under the Confederate lines and set off a gigantic powder charge at the end. The explosion blew a huge crater over 170 feet long. Northern soldiers poured forward, but milled about helplessly in the crater, at the mercy of Southern fire. The Confederates beat back the attack, which Grant called a "stupendous failure."[11]

o) Battle of Mobile Bay (August 2-23, 1864) – The blockade of Southern ports grew more and more effective. Union forces worked steadily to seize the main ports still open to blockade runners that slipped through the ring of Northern ships. In August 1864, a naval squadron under Rear Admiral David G. Farragut sailed into the harbor of Mobile, Alabama. Farragut was warned that the harbor bristled with mines, which were called torpedoes in those days. "Damn the torpedoes! Full stream ahead!" Farragut bellowed, and drove on, resulting in a complete blockade of the port.[11]

p) March to the Sea (November 15 – December 21) – On September 2, 1864, 60,000 Union troops under General William Tecumseh Sherman captured Atlanta, Georgia. Sherman had begun a campaign from a victory at the Battle of Chattanooga to capture Atlanta and Savannah, Georgia. The Battle of Atlanta had ended with the city in flames. On their march to Savannah, Union troops destroyed civilian properly and laid waste to everything that might help the South continue fighting.

On December 21, Savannah was captured, ending the March to the Sea. General Sherman offers the city to Lincoln as a Christmas present. Sherman next turned to go through South Carolina. There was more destruction of South Carolina than Georgia as Sherman was vindictive to South Carolina, as this state had started the war.[1]

q) Battle of Cedar Creek (October 19, 1864) – Grant sent General Philip Sheridan into the Shenandoah Valley with orders to make it a "barren waste." Sheridan followed Grant's order "that a crow would have to carry its own rations flying over the valley." On October 19, after three battles Sheridan's army defeated Confederate General Early's forces. Lincoln telegraphed Sheridan: "With great pleasure I tender to you and your brave army the thanks of the nation and my own personal admiration.

Grant wired Lincoln a message from Sheridan who noted how badly the Confederacy was losing men and supplies. Sheridan noted: "If the thing is pressed, I think Lee will surrender." Lincoln wired Grant: "Let The Thing Be Pressed"[7]

r) Battle of Appomattox Court House (April 9, 1965) – Lee was forced to retreat to Appomattox Court House by Union forces and in the end had no choice but to surrender. On April 9, 1865, Grant accepts the surrender of Confederate General Lee. The effect of this was to end the war in Virginia and to trigger a wave of surrenders across remaining Confederate territory.

Grant offered generous terms that did much to ease tensions between the armies and preserve some semblance of Southern pride, which was needed to reunite the warring sides. After cessation of hostilities President Lincoln invited Grant and his wife to see a play at Ford's theater. Grant declined which saved his life, as John Wilkes Booth had planned to kill both Lincoln and Grant.

C. Diseases during Civil War

Civil War stories of heroic battlefield actions and adventures have been recorded in many books and presentations. The undignified death of hundreds of thousands who died horrible, at times painful, deaths due to disease and wound infection contradicts the image of the noble soldier. The total reported sick cases for all disease was over 5.8 million. We must always remember the famous statement of General William T. Sherman, "All War is Hell!"

The Civil War represents a landmark in military and medical history as the last large-scale war fought without knowledge of the germ theory of disease. Unsound hygiene, dietary deficiencies, and battle wounds set the stage for epidemic infection, while inadequate information about disease causation greatly hampered disease prevention, diagnosis, and treatment.

At the time of the Civil War epidemic diseases were still thought to be caused primarily by "maismas," invisible poisons in the air. The poisonous maismas were thought to result primarily from "decompositions" of animal or vegetable matter. Marshes and swamps were an important source, and the resulting toxic air was sometimes described using the Italian term "malaria," or "bad air." Later by the British the term "zymotic diseases" was used on the concept that ferments or "zymes' were pathogenetic agents. For American physicians during the Civil War diseases now called infectious were classified in the official records as "zymotic diseases".[12]

The major cause of death during the Civil War was disease. Disease killed more people than everything else combined including gunshots, artillery, accidents, drowning, starvation, suicide etc. There are various opinions on the total death loss due to the war. Recorded military deaths have been reported as 620,000. However, the number has also been noted to be 660,000 with deaths by others suggested closer to 750,000. There seems to be agreement that about two-thirds of Civil War deaths were from Disease. Up until the Vietnam War, the number killed in the Civil War surpassed all other wars combined. Table 8.2 are deaths in major or U.S. wars.[13]

The biggest thing that all these Civil War diseases had in common was that nobody had any idea how to prevent or cure them, with the exception of malaria.

Most disease information is from Union records. Reliable numbers on the number of Confederates who suffered from disease are less available. Sadly, when Richmond was burned at the end of the War, many medical records were lost. However, some of the records were retrieved.

a) **Civil War Medicine and Camp Conditions** – During the war doctors had yet to develop bacteriology and were generally ignorant of the causes of disease. Generally, Civil War doctors underwent only two years of medical school. Medicine in the United States was woefully behind Europe. Harvard

Medical School did not even own a single stethoscope or microscope until after the war. Most Civil War surgeons had never treated a gunshot wound and many had never performed surgery. Medical boards admitted many "quacks," with little to no qualification. Yet, for the most part, the Civil War doctor (as understaffed, underqualified, and under-supplied as he was) did the best he could, muddling through the so-called "medical Middle Ages." Some 10,000 surgeons served in the Union army and about 4,000 served in the Confederacy. Medicine made significant gains during the war. However, it was the tragedy of the era that medical knowledge had not yet encompassed the use of sterile dressings, antiseptic surgery, and the recognition of the importance of sanitation and hygiene. Obviously, if handwashing by troops and surgeons had been recognized as a singularly critical activity in preventing and controlling disease, the results might well have been different. As a result, thousands died from diseases such as typhoid or dysentery.[14]

At the beginning of the Civil War, medical equipment and knowledge was hardly up to the challenges posed by the wounds, infections and diseases which plagued millions on both sides. Illnesses like dysentery, typhoid fever, pneumonia, mumps, measles and tuberculosis spread among the poorly sanitized camps, felling men already weakened by fierce fighting and meager diets. Additionally, armies initially struggled to efficiently tend to and transport their wounded, inadvertently sacrificing more lives to mere disorganization.

For doctors in the field during the Civil War, germ theory, antiseptic (clean) medical practices, advanced equipment, and organized hospitalization systems were virtually unknown. Medical training was just emerging out of the "heroic era," a time where physicians advocated bloodletting, purging, blistering (or a combination of all three) to rebalance the humors of the body and remedy the sick. Physicians were also often encouraged to treat diseases like syphilis with mercury, a toxic treatment, to say the least. These aggressive "remedies" of the heroic era of medicine were often worse than patients' diseases; those who overcame illness during the war owed their recoveries less to the ingenuity of contemporary medicine than to grit and chance. Luck was a rarity in camps where poor sanitation, bad hygiene and diet bred disease, infection, and death.[15]

Civil War medicine was not yet advanced enough to connect a lack of hygiene with disease. For example, during a Civil War surgery cleanliness was a mere afterthought. Surgeons would often use the same tools continuously on patient after patient never cleaning them. They might wipe off on their apron, but that was about as much cleaning as any piece of equipment received.

There are characteristics of every army that influence public health in wartime: they live in crowded circumstances; environmental conditions in the field that were primitive. Clearly there is evidence that lack of sanitation was widespread and responsible for much of the illness among troops in both armies. Interestingly, it was not because the relationship between sanitation and disease was unknown at the time of the Civil War that lapses of sanitation occurred. Unfortunately, military objectives sometimes override sanitary ones.

Dr. Joseph Woodward, a surgeon in the army, documented breaches of sanitation in camps. He noted that in great armies in time of war personal cleanliness is often nonexistent. The men are unwashed, their clothes filthy, bodies full of vermin, and heaps of garbage lie about. What was especially needed was policing the latrines. The trench is too shallow, not the requisite five feet deep and daily covering with soil being entirely neglected. Large numbers of the men did not use the latrines, but instead use clumps of bushes and every fence border. It was impossible to step outside the encampment without having both eye and nostril continually offended.[16,17]

Contamination of the water was a serious problem. Simple things such as placing a latrine downstream and away from clean water supply were often overlooked. Even more important, men were not using the latrine and the feces deposited haphazardly, with the ground in the vicinity sloping down to the stream, from which all water in the camp is obtained.

Not only did the soldiers have to endure an unhealthy living environment when they went to the field hospital, they were operated on by a surgeon who had blood and pus on his coat from the previous patient. Then while he was operating on his patient, if he dropped his instruments, he would pick it up, rinse it off and continue to work on his patient. Bloody fingers often were used as probes. Bloody knives were used as scalpels.

In addition to the high number of soldiers affected by illness, many were also wounded from bullets. Due to the disproportionate ratio of soldiers to surgeons, the surgeon had to look at a soldier briefly and determine how he was going to be treated. If he was slightly wounded, in the interest of saving as many soldiers as possible, he was overlooked. However, if he was wounded on a limb the surgeon would amputate within ten minutes (Fig.8.2). First the doctor would give the soldier a dose of whiskey and then place chloroform on a cloth over his nose to place him in an unconscious state for the amputation. One witness described surgery as such: "Tables about breast high had been erected upon which the screaming victims were having legs and arms cut off. The surgeons and their assistants, stripped to the waist and bespattered with blood, stood around, some holding the poor fellows while others, armed with long, bloody knives and saws, cut and sawed away with frightful rapidity, throwing the mangled limbs on a pile nearby as soon as removed." If a soldier survived the table, he faced the awful surgical fevers. However, about 75% of amputees did survive, if they did not succumb to fevers or gangrene.[14]

According to the great American poet and Civil War nurse, Walt Whitman, surgeons were butchers because limbs would be amputated to minimize pain and prevent further spread of infections to other soldiers, but these surgeons did little to minimize pain. At times death or infection set in because the two and four wheeled carts used as ambulances were unreliable and overcrowded.

Amputation was by far the most common surgery in the Civil War. During the war it is estimated that about 60,000 surgeries were performed. Of these, nearly 75% were amputations. There were several reasons why amputation was the main procedure. Bullet wounds made by the slow moving Minié ball caused major damage. They often shattered bones beyond repair. Also, if a man was wounded in the head, stomach or chest, he rarely lived long enough to be taken to a field hospital.[18]

In addition to socioeconomic background affecting a soldier's susceptibility of acquiring a disease, living and sanitary condition also affected their chance of survival. Coming into the military with a good nutritional background also increased survival rate. The wounded and sick suffered from the haphazard hospitalization systems that existed at the start of the Civil War. As battles ended, the wounded were rushed down railroad lines to nearby cities and towns, where doctors and nurses coped with the onslaught of dying men in makeshift hospitals. These hospitals saw a great influx of wounded from both sides and the wounded and dying filled the available facilities to the brim.

Bad sanitary practices and infrequent bathing generated offensive, "sickening" odors thought to cause disease. Military sanitation was the worst, as illustrated by one commander who dismissed complaints from inspectors because "an army camp is supposed to smell that way." Physicians gradually impressed line officers with the need to enforce the army's rules about sanitation and the data show that the incidence of enteric diseases, especially acute diarrhea and dysentery, decreased considerably in the later years of the war. Personal cleanliness remained a persistent problem; soldiers rarely bathed. Some soldiers failed to wash their bodies and their clothes since they were used to being taking care of by either their mother or wife. It was said that a Civil War army on the march could be smelled before it could be seen.[12]

Confederate surgeon, J. Julian Chisholm, author of *A Manual of Military Surgery* (1861) wrote, the "fire of an enemy never decimates an opposing army. Disease is the fell destroyer of armies, and stalks at all times through encampments. Where military weapons have destroyed hundreds, insidious diseases, with their long train of symptoms, and quiet, noiseless progress, sweep away thousands. To keep an army in health is, then, even more important than to cure wounds from the battlefields."[19]

b) Diseases for Civil War Recruits

Disease was a greater problem with recruits, then for older troops. Enlistment records show that over 50% of Union soldiers came from rural areas. Among the Confederates, an even higher proportion was from rural areas; the most common occupation on both sides was farmer. There had often been inadequate physical examinations of recruits. Many unqualified recruits entered the military and diseases should have weeded out those excluded by physical exams. There was no knowledge of the causes of disease. Troops from rural areas were crowded together for the first time with large numbers of other individuals and got diseases to which they had no immunity.[12] Not having experienced the common diseases of childhood, the new soldiers fell prey to them as adults.

Many men were not previously exposed to the diseases sometimes called "crowd diseases," such as measles, that mostly occurred in childhood and gave immunity. As a result, measles appeared in epidemic form as soon as recruits gathered to await transportation to training camps and later in their service the disease was much less common. Measles contracted in childhood is mild but is severe for adults and prepares the systems for other attacks. Later research showed adults with measles develop complications including pneumonia, bronchitis, hepatitis, middle ear infection and sinusitis.[17] In the Union army over 67,000 men had measles and more than 4,000 died. During the first year of the war alone, there were 21,676 reported cases of measles and 551 deaths of Union soldiers mainly from respiratory and cerebral brain involvement.

On a personal observation, both measles and chickenpox were treated as part of growing up, with little or no danger of significance. In fact, when a neighborhood child had either measles or chickenpox, we were encouraged to play with that child in order to contract the disease. I was born in the 1940's and only much later did I learn that measles was a problem for adults.

c) Most predominate diseases

1) Diarrhea and Dysentery – The number one disease killer on both sides was diarrhea and dysentery. This has been true in all armies in all wars before and after the Civil War. Dysentery is considered diarrhea with blood in the stool. Diarrheas were a constant feature of army life, and most cases were treated at sick call and did not enter the records. The true incidence of diarrhea was even higher then recorded

Diarrhea and dysentery accounted for around 45,000 deaths in the Union army and around 50,000 deaths in the Confederate army. The reason dysentery and so many other diseases were able to spread so rapidly through both armies was primarily because of lack of sanitation practices and contaminated water. Proper hygiene during this time was nonexistent. There were frequent references to the interplay of flies, fingers, feces and food.

The total recorded Union cases was 1,528,098. Thousands of the afflicted went into battle fatigued with abdominal pain, malaise and dehydration. If wounded, they often died due to their poor constitutional state, but were not counted as a death from disease.[20]

Chronic diarrhea and chronic dysentery were diagnostic entities and a much larger problem. The case fatality rates for the chronic forms were quite high: 16.2% for chronic diarrhea and 12.6% of the cases diagnosed as chronic dysentery. Together they accounted for 23% of all deaths caused by disease in the Union army. The terms usually meant prolonged, severe, daily diarrhea with frequent liquid or unformed stools accompanied by weakness and weight loss, progressing to severe incapacitation.[12]

These diseases include watery stools that can cause shock and death without replacement of fluid and chemicals required for the body to function. Patients recovering from these usually pass bacteria in their stools for 7 to 10 days.

Soldiers had many names for the diarrheal diseases. Among the Southern troops it was simply called the "Confederate disease". In the east, Union soldiers often called diarrhea the "Virginia Quickstep," whereas the western army called it the "Tennessee Trots".

These diseases are spread to healthy individuals from carriers who harbor and excrete the bacteria in their stools. Flies living outdoors play a crucial role in spreading diarrhea/dysentery. They appear about ten days after climate becomes favorable for their breeding; they disappear with the onset of severe frost. Since 1912 house flies were proven to carry bacillary dysentery, contaminating food by vomiting or defecating on it after feeding on dysenteric stools. Hairs on fly legs in contact with infected material are the most common conveyers of the bacteria to food, probably because they provide a much larger surface area to which the bacteria can cling.[17] Of course fecal contaminated water is another source.

Amoebic dysentery (caused by parasite Entamoeba histolytica) was the most lethal of diarrheal infections due to its infestation of not only the intestines, but the lungs, brain, and other important organs. This parasite was commonly transmitted through feces-contaminated food and water, which were bountiful in filthy encampments. Civil War physicians treated diarrhea following the usual practices of the time. They used opiates effectively, often administered as an alcoholic solution (tincture of opium or paregoric). A long list of other medicines was used, including turpentine, but none was as popular as opium and calomel.

2) Typhoid Fever – Typhoid was another killer, the second leading killer after diarrhea/dysentery. This was one of the most feared and often fatal epidemic diseases of the nineteenth century. Typhoid fever is most likely to attack recruits, and as a general rule affects the individual but once during his lifetime." The disease was a result of contaminated water or food. The disease is caused by the bacterium *Salmonella typhi*. Survivors shed the bacterium in their stools that was often passed to others via hands unwashed after a bowel movement. Typhoid killed around 30,000 Confederate and 35,000 Union troops during the war. One third of people who contracted the disease died of it.[3]

3) Pneumonia – Pneumonia was the third leading killer disease of the war, after diarrhea/dysentery and typhoid. Pneumonia was responsible for the deaths of 20,000 Union and 17,000 Confederate troops. 1 in 6 people who got this disease died from it. Pneumonia was more of an opportunistic type of disease. It looked for weak people to inject itself into. If you became wounded on the battlefield or became sick with something else there was a good chance pneumonia was going to find you. Stonewall Jackson died from pneumonia after being shot by his own men during the battle of Chancellorsville.[3]

4) Malaria – Malaria was transmitted by mosquitoes. However, this was not determined until 1897, three decades after the Civil War ended. Malaria is a parasitic infection that is transmitted through the bite of an infected mosquito. Prior to the war medical experts believed it was caused by humidity or a harmful air or odor.

Malaria was the second most common disease diagnosed; only diarrhea and dysentery were more frequent. The Union forces had almost a million recorded cases of the intermittent fevers which were the major symptom of the disease. The overall incidence of malaria during the 4 years of the fighting averaged 1.8 diagnosed attacks per soldier annually (actually, 1794 cases per 1000 per year); although calculated on an annual basis, most of the cases occurred during the four warmest summer months.[12] After outbreaks of malaria forced significant setbacks in many Northern campaigns, Confederate General Robert E. Lee had such confidence that malaria would continue to plague the Union army that, in the summer of 1863, he said "the climate in

June will force the enemy to retire."

General Ulysses S. Grant's forces, which were exposed to the swamps along the Mississippi River during the siege of Vicksburg, had the highest incidence of malaria of any Union army. Fortunately, the Union army had access to the effective drug, Quinine, to treat malaria. Due to the naval blockade, Southern soldiers could not access Quinine and had to resort to weaker native plants and medicinal herbs to combat the illness. One could argue the Confederate Army's struggle with the parasite was a contributing factor to the outcome of the war. One of the reasons the Union siege of Vicksburg was successful was because the Confederates were debilitated by an outbreak of malaria. This seemingly small outbreak across a Confederate encampment changed the course of the war immensely, because it turned the Mississippi River into the North's hands, consequently splitting the Confederacy in half.[21]

5) Tuberculosis (TB) – Tuberculosis killed about 14,000 soldiers during the war. There was no known cure for it. Today it is treatable but never cured. Once you get this disease you get it for life. Tuberculosis for many years was known as consumption. Since it is treatable, most cases are found in developing countries. Pre-enlistment physical examinations were rudimentary or worse at the beginning of the war, and clearly many men with TB were enlisted. As a result, was most frequent during the first 2 years of the war. Many men with obvious TB died or were discharged and examinations became much more thorough, especially after the draft was inaugurated in 1863, and incidence of the TB decreased in subsequent years.

6) Smallpox – During the war there were smallpox cases, with a major epidemic of the disease in the U.S. in 1863 and 1864 causing a marked incidence in both armies. As a highly contagious disease, isolation or quarantine was necessary to control spread of the disease. Where possible separate hospital units were set up for soldiers with smallpox. Vaccination had originally occurred as early as the Revolutionary War.[12]

The worst period of the epidemic was in 1864; the incidence in white troops was 7.4 cases per 1000 troops, whereas among black troops it was 61.1 per 1000 troops. The much higher incidence among the black soldiers suggests that the black troops had not been vaccinated when they were slaves, and the policy of vaccinating newly enlisted troops with no vaccination scars had not been enforced with this group.

The troops feared smallpox but feared vaccination almost as much. Mass vaccinations were performed to stem local outbreaks, but the vaccine materials were often ineffective and could themselves cause serious illness. Fear of vaccination was understandable. An exudate called "lymph" obtained from previously vaccinated individuals without worrying about cleanliness was then inserted into the arms of others by making crude painful gouges with a knife, which was not cleaned. These injections often resulted in severe local infections with some men dying from "blood poisoning".[12]

Some Civil War surgeons on both sides specifically blamed "spurious vaccination," meaning complications arising from contaminated or ineffective vaccine, on "indiscriminate vaccination and revaccination from arm to arm". In many prisons, new captives were constantly added despite containing smallpox outbreaks among previous prisoners. It was claimed to be an inhumane practice of putting prisoners into camps infected by smallpox. It was equivalent to murdering many of them by torture of a contagious disease. There was no evidence that anyone on either side purposely intended harm. President Lincoln had a mild case of smallpox affecting him for about a month. Many people were always waiting to see him, usually asking for favors. The president remarked to a visitor, "There is one good thing about this. I now have something I can give to everybody".[22]

7) Yellow Fever – Like malaria, yellow fever was transmitted by mosquitoes. It was once thought the yellow fever was caused by some form of filth on ships that generated the "bad air" that resulted in devastating epidemics, primarily in port cities. Yellow fever was widespread in lowland areas in the southern states during the mosquito season. New Orleans was one of the city's most severely affected by yellow fever before the war. In 1853 between 8,000 and 9,000 people died of yellow fever, and severe epidemics also occurred in 1854 and 1855; in 1858 another 5,000 people died from the disease. During the Civil War the relationship between mosquitoes and the disease was unknown. In 1881 a Cuban physician, Carlos Finley suggested that the mosquito transmitted the disease and later a U.S. army doctor, Walter Reed, proved the disease was carried by a mosquito.

During the war southern cities felt protected from Union forces as yellow fever would greatly reduce Union troop strength.[23] In September 1862, in the midst of the Civil War, a severe epidemic of yellow fever in Wilmington, Delaware occurred after a blockade running vessel from the Bahamas docked. In the zeal to off-load the ship, quarantine laws were apparently overlooked. The yellow fever spread rapidly. Deaths numbered as high as 18 in a single day, and one time as many as 500 cases were being treated. The epidemic lasted less than three months with about 1,000 people dying.[24]

An epidemic of yellow fever occurred in Union-occupied New Bern, North Carolina, in September, October, and November of 1864. It attacked 571 Union soldiers, causing 278 deaths among the troops stationed there, a typical case-fatality rate for the disease (48.7%).[12]

8) Nutritional Deficient Diets – Unfortunately much of the food of both armies were dehydrated or overcooked and lacked certain nutrients. Many of these diets were lacking vitamin C, vitamin A and certain B-vitamins. Vitamin A deficiency was seen with cases of night blindness, and scurvy with lack of vitamin C.

Scurvy was the vitamin deficiency disease most observed. Prior to the Civil War, scurvy was the most common disease in the United States army. Scurvy was prevalent for both Union and Confederate troops, but records of Union scurvy cases are more complete. Scurvy was diagnosed in 46,931 Union troops. More deaths were recorded from diarrheas than from scurvy, however due to the immune function of vitamin C many believe adequate vitamin C status could have moderated or prevented the effects of other disease conditions including diarrheas.[25]

Death directly attributed to scurvy was 3,000 Union soldiers imprisoned at Andersonville, Georgia. This represented 25% of total deaths of the 12,000 captured soldiers. Due to the relationship of diarrheas and scurvy, 90% of the mortality at Andersonville was either directly or indirectly the result of scurvy.[26] The physicians at Andersonville were aware of the importance of fresh vegetables and fruits in prevention and treatment of scurvy. However, wartime conditions made scurvy preventing foods unavailable.[27] The present author personally believes that many deaths were due to pellagra (niacin deficiency) based on the high corn diets, severe diarrhea and other signs attributable to the disease.

Scurvy resulted because of the wide use of dried vegetables in winter. There were requests for donations of potatoes and onions to be sent to the troops as their anti-scurvy properties were well known. As a result of scurvy, wounds failed to heal and slight abrasions such as rubbing of a shot, a bruise, the scratch of a mosquito bite, the prick of a splinter or vaccination scars, tended not to heal, but to turn into scorbutic ulcers.[28]

9) Venereal Diseases – Syphilis and gonorrhea were serious health problems during the Civil War. There were 102,893 cases of gonorrhea and 79,589 cases of syphilis with only about 130 deaths. Union General Joseph Hooker's 1863 directive to improve soldier morals by allowing prostitutes into his encampment has forever associated his name with prostitutes.[20] These sexually contracted diseases were from attending brothels or from prostitutes. The treatment often was harsh with the toxic mineral mercury and cauterization of the ulcers.[29]

10) Other diseases and factors – In addition to the major diseases there were other disease conditions in the military. In addition to flies and mosquitoes, other parasites and insects were troublesome like fleas, lice and ticks. Childhood diseases such as measles, mumps, chicken pox and scarlet fever could be problems for adults, which was particularly true as previously mentioned for measles. Other diseases could have been debilitating or potentially fatal such as viral hepatitis, typhus, rheumatic fever, influenza, cholera, tetanus and arthritis. In the case of cholera, this was one of the deadliest epidemics of the 19th century, with case fatality rates reaching 70%. However, no epidemics occurred in the U.S. during the Civil War.

Sickness among recruits, in particular colds, measles, mumps, and typhoid fever, affected some early military campaigns. Besides decreasing the number of men available for duty, sick soldiers tied up personnel and other resources for their care, and the resulting deaths demoralized newly mobilized troops. Measles contributed to the failure of General Lee's first field assignment, the recapture of the western counties of Virginia (later West Virginia) in August 1861.[12] Lee, in a letter to his wife on September 1, 1861, wrote: "We have a great deal of sickness among the soldiers, and now those on the sick list would form an army. The measles is still among them, though I hope it is dying out. The constant cold rains, mud, with no shelter but tents, have aggravated it. And these drawbacks, with impassable roads, have paralyzed our efforts.[30]

j) Disease and Death of Civil War Prisoners

Deaths were frequent in both Confederate and Union prisons. Some of the suffering was unavoidable as overcrowding stretched limited medical resources, food supply and complete disregard for sanitation. For prisoners' war mortality rate was 15.5% and for Confederates was 12%.

The causes of death among Union prisoners at Andersonville Prison from March 1-August 31, 1864, are as follows: typhoid/typhus – 199 deaths, malaria– 119 deaths, smallpox/measles/scarlet fever– 80 deaths, diarrhea/dysentery – 4,529 deaths, scurvy- 999 deaths, bronchitis– 90 deaths, inflammation of the lungs– 266 deaths, other disease– 844 deaths, wounds– 586 deaths.

Likewise, the causes of death of Confederate prisoners in Northern prisons as follows: typhoid/typhus– 1,100 deaths, malaria– 1,000 deaths, smallpox/measles/scarlet fever- 3,500 deaths, diarrhea/dysentery- 6,000 deaths, scurvy- 351 deaths, bronchitis- 133 deaths, inflammation of lungs- 5,000 deaths, other- 1,700 deaths. It is clear that disease trumps battlefield casualties at this time period.[3] Bollet reported in Northern prison camps late in the war that pneumonia caused the most deaths among Confederate Prisoners of War.[12]

The Confederate surgeon Joseph Jones inspecting Anderson stockade documented breach of sanitation. He wrote of one stream filled with "the filth and excrement of twenty thousand men, the stench was disgusting and overpowering; and if it was surpassed in unpleasantness by anything, it was only in the disgusting appearance of the filthy, almost stagnant, waters moving slowly between the stumps and roots and fallen trunks of trees and thick branches of reeds, with innumerable long-tailed, large white maggots, and fermenting excrement, and fragments of bread and meat.[24]

Other diseases spread but poor sanitation also developed as soon as men gathered; if they produced immunity, as typhoid fever does, they also were mostly seen among recruits because after short periods of service the men had either died of the disease or developed immunity, even if the episode of the disease had been too mild to be diagnosed.[17]

With the extremely poor sanitation of Civil War encampments, the swarms of flies that plagued all campsites, virtually no opportunity for washing, and many veterans who were chronic typhoid carriers, it is not surprising that recruits quickly became infected.[17]

D. Summary

The American Civil War was an armed conflict between 23 Northern states representing the Union and 11 Southern states that seceded from the Union and formed the Confederate States of America. In 1860 Abraham Lincoln was elected president. Prior to his inauguration in March 1861, seven states led by South Carolina had seceded from the Union and on February 9th the Confederacy selected Jefferson Davis as its president. The principal causes of the war were the issues of slavery and that of States Rights. Does a state have the right to withdraw from the Union? Lincoln declared prior to the election that he would not interfere with the institution of slavery in states where it existed. As president Lincoln stated that individual states had no right to leave the Union and his determined goal was to save the Union.

The Civil War began on April 12,1861 with the Confederate attack on Fort Sumter in South Carolina. The war ended four years later April 9, 1865, when Confederate General Robert E. Lee surrendered to Union General Ulysses S. Grant at Appomattox Court House, Virginia (Fig.8.3). Major and decisive battles included Bull Run, Fort Henry, Fort Donelson, Shiloh, Antietam, Fredericksburg, Chancellorsville, Gettysburg, Vicksburg, Wilderness, Spotsylvania, Cold Harbor, Petersburg, Mobil Bay, Chattanooga, Atlanta Cedar Creek and Appomattox Court House. Historians consider the Battles of Vicksburg and Gettysburg to be turning points of the war. The Civil War was American's bloodiest conflict. The unprecedented violence of battles such as Shiloh, Antietam, and Gettysburg shocked citizens and international observers alike.

There are disputes on number of Civil War deaths, estimates ranging from 620 and 750 thousand soldiers, and perhaps more. There seems no disagreement that two-thirds of the deaths of soldiers were caused by uncontrolled infectious diseases, and epidemics played a major role in halting several major campaigns.

The Civil War was the last large-scale war fought without knowledge of the germ theory of disease. Unsound hygiene, dietary deficiencies and battle wounds resulted in epidemic infections. Lack of information on disease cause hampered disease prevention, diagnosis and treatment. Medicine in the U.S. was woefully behind Europe. Harvard Medical School did not even own a single stethoscope or microscope. Medical knowledge did not include the use of sterile dressings, antiseptic surgery or the importance of sanitation and hygiene.

Some diseases could have been prevented by simple handwashing. Medical equipment and knowledge were not up to the challenges posed by wounds, infections and diseases which affected millions on both sides. Illnesses like dysentery, typhoid fever, pneumonia, mumps, measles and tuberculosis spread among the poorly sanitized camps killing men already weakened by fierce fighting and nutrient inadequate diets. New recruits had to deal with outbreaks of disease on crowded battle fields, trenches and encampments. A recruit from a healthy background who had limited exposure to disease had a lower immunity to disease compared to a man from an unhealthy background. For example, measles contracted as a child would not be dangerous, but contracted by recruits as an adult could have serious consequences.

Medical training was just beginning to leave the concept where physicians advocated bloodletting, purging, blistering (or a combination of all three) to rebalance the humors of the body and remedy the sick. Physicians would treat syphilis with mercury, a very toxic element. The aggressive "remedies" of medicine were often more dangerous than the patients' diseases. During surgery cleanliness was an afterthought. Surgeons would use the same tools continuously on patient after patient, never cleaning them.

Clearly lack of sanitation was widespread and responsible for much of the illness among troops. Often the men were unwashed, their clothes filthy with their bodies full of vermin. One of the most serious problems was the location and policing of the latrines. Poor location and lack of use of the latrines resulted in fecal material in ground water and sources of drinking water. Defecation outside of tents attracted flies which spread diseases to food.

The number one disease killer was diarrhea/dysentery, accounting for around 45,000 deaths in the Union and 50,000 deaths for the Confederacy. The reasons for this was lack of sanitation and contaminated water. The second leading killer of troops was typhoid fever, also caused by contaminated water and food. Pneumonia was the third leading killer. Other leading diseases were malaria, tuberculosis, smallpox, yellow fever, nutritional deficiencies (e.g. scurvy and night blindness) and venereal diseases. Additional serious health problems mainly for young recruits were childhood diseases such as measles, mumps, chicken pox and scarlet fever that were problems for adults. Other dangerous and debilitating diseases included viral hepatitis, typhus, rheumatic fever, influenza, cholera, tetanus and arthritis. In conclusion the Civil War resulted in more deaths than any other war, with diseases by far the greatest cause of death. Deaths for Civil War prisoners were very high due to overcrowding limited medical resources, inadequate and poor-quality nutrition and complete disregard for sanitation. It is good to remember and to repeat the words of Union General William Sherman that "all war is Hell!"

Table 8.1 Civil War Highlights[11]

1960	
Nov. 6	Lincoln elected president.
Dec. 20	South Carolina secedes from the Union.
1861	
Feb. 9	Jefferson Davis president of Confederacy.
Mar. 4	Lincoln inaugurated president.
Apr. 12	Confederate troops attacked Fort Sumter.
Apr. 15	Lincoln issued a call for troops.
Apr. 19	Lincoln proclaimed a blockade of the South.
May 21	Richmond, Va. Was chosen as the Confederate capital.
July 21	First Battle of Bull run (Manassas), Union troops retreated in disorder.
1862	
Feb. 6-16	Grant's Union troops captured Ft. Henry and Ft. Donelsen
Mar. 9	The ironclad ships *Monitor,* and *Merrimack* battled to a draw.
Apr. 6-7	Battle of Shiloh won by Union, heavy losses both sides.
Apr. 10-11	Confederate Ft. Pulaski in Savannah, Ga. destroyed because of new weapon, the Parrott rifle.
Apr. 18-29	A Union fleet under Farragut captured New Orleans.
June 6	Memphis fell to Union armies.
June 25-July 1	Confederate forces under Lee saved Richmond in the Battles of the Seven Days.
Aug. 29-30	Lee and Jackson led Southern troops to victory in the second Battle of Bull Run.
Sept. 17	Confederate forces retreated in defeat after the bloody Battle of Antietam (Sharpsburg).
Oct. 9	Battle of Perryville ended Confederate Bragg's invasion of Kentucky.
Dec. 13	The Union suffered a terrible defeat at Fredericksburg.
Dec. 31-Jan. 2	Battle of Murfreesboro, Union troops under Rosecrans defeat Confederates.
1863	
Jan. 1	Lincoln issued the Emancipation Proclamation.
Mar. 3	The North passed a draft law.
May 1-4	Northern troops under Hooker were defeated in the Battle of Chancellorsville.
July 1-3	The Battle of Gettysburg ended in a Confederate defeat and marked a turning point in the war.
July 4	Vicksburg fell to Northern troops giving the north control of the Mississippi River.

July 8	Northern forces occupied Port Hudson, La.
Sept. 19-20	Southern troops under Bragg won the Battle of Chickamauga.
Nov. 19	Lincoln delivered the Gettysburg Address.
Nov. 23-25	Grant and Sherman led Union armies to victory in the Battle of Chattanooga.
1864	
Mar. 9	Grant became General in Chief of the North.
May 5-6	Union and Confederate troops clashed in the Battle of the Wilderness.
May 8-12	Grant and Lee held their positions in the Battle of Spotsylvania Court House.
June 3	Battle of Cold Harbor, Union suffered heavy losses.
Aug. 5	Farragut won the Battle of Mobile Bay.
Sept. 2	Union troops under Sherman captured Atlanta.
Oct. 19	In Shenandoah Valley Sheridan's army defeated Confederates after three battles.
Nov. 8	Lincoln was re-elected President.
Nov. 15	Sherman began his march to the sea.
Dec. 15-16	The Battle of Nashville destroyed Hood's Confederate Army.
Dec. 21	Sherman's troops occupied Savannah, Ga.
1865	
Apr. 2	Confederate troops gave up Petersburg and Richmond.
Apr. 9	Lee surrendered to Grant at Appomattox.
Apr. 14	Lincoln was assassinated.
Apr. 26	Johnston surrendered to Sherman.
May 4	Confederate forces in Alabama and Mississippi surrendered.
May 26	The last Confederate troops surrendered.

Table 8.2 Estimated deaths in major U.S. wars[13]

Wars	No. of Deaths
King Philip's	6,000
American Revolution	4,435
War of 1812	2,283
Mexican-American	13,283
Spanish American	2,246
Civil War	620,000-750,000
World War I	116,516
World War II	405,399
Korea	33,746
Vietnam	58,152

8.1 Under Ulysses Grant defeat of Confederates at Battle of Vicksburg. This gave the Union control of the Mississippi River.

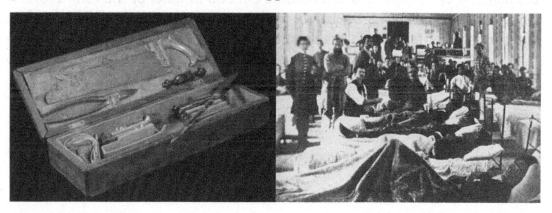

8.2 Amputation Kit. Amputation was by far the most common surgery in the Civil War. It is estimated that about 60,000 surgeries were performed, of these 75% were amputations.

8.3 March 9,1864 Ulysses Grant became General in Chief of the Union forces. On April 14, 1865, President Lincoln was assassinated. This was five days after surrender of Confederate forces to end Civil War.

CHAPTER 9

Spanish-American War

A. Introduction

The Spanish-American War was an armed conflict between Spain and the United States in 1898. Between 1895 and 1898 Cuba and the Philippine Islands revolted against Spain. There was revulsion among Americans against the ruthless tactics employed by Spain to suppress a revolt in its colony Cuba. The Spanish government sent 100,000 soldiers to suppress the uprising. Thousands of Cubans were put into concentration camps, where many died of starvation and disease.

President William McKinley increased pressure on Spain to end the atrocities against the Cuban people. In early February 1898 the Battleship USS Maine was sent to Havana, Cuba to provide a naval presence and to protect American interests and civilians there.[1]

On February 13 a massive explosion sank the vessel, killing 266 sailors (Fig.9.1). Sensationalist newspaper articles and advocates of war accused the Spanish of destroying the ship, and a naval inquiry soon concluded that a mine had caused the disaster. With the rallying cry "Remember the Maine" galvanizing Americans, and threatening Spain with military action. Today still no one knows for sure what sank the USS Maine, was it a Spanish mine or an internal explosion?[2]

There was a great debate on whether to go to war with Spain. President McKinley was against war. Fellow Republican Theodore Roosevelt declared the president had "no more backbone than a chocolate éclair". On April 25 there was a declaration of war with a reluctant McKinley requesting an armed intervention.[3]

The Spanish-American War was fought in two theaters, the Caribbean and the South Pacific. Officially the war lasted less than 4 months, from April to October. Actually, the war involved 118 days of hostilities. The war graphically demonstrated the consequences of inadequate medical resources, particularly in preventive medicine, and on troop health in garrison settings. Poor sanitation and disease killed thousands. Tropical diseases would prove to be the greatest enemy of U.S. troops.

The actual military encounters of the war occurred mainly in Cuba and involved approximately 22,000 U.S. soldiers in combat before the Spanish forces surrendered on August 12, 1898. The victorious U.S. emerged from the war as a world power with far-flung overseas possessions and a new stake in international politics that would soon lead it to play a determining role in the affairs of Europe and the rest of the globe.

B. Military events in Spanish-American War

Battles and Events in the Philippines, Cuba and Puerto Rico are as follows:

1) The Philippines – When it appeared that there would be military action between Spain and the U.S., Assistant Secretary Theodore Roosevelt of the Navy sent a telegraphic order to Commodore George Dewey on February 25th commanding him to concentrate the ships of the Asiatic Station at Hong Kong. In the event of war, he was to take his squadron and destroy the Spanish ships in Philippine waters.

The first battle between American and Spanish troops was at Manila Bay where on May 1, 1898, Commodore George Dewey, commanding the U.S. Navy's Asiatic Squadron aboard USS Olympia acted. In a quick victory Dewey defeated a Spanish squadron of Admiral Patrico Montoyo's force of seven wooden vessels in Manila Bay. Dewey lost no ships, and nine Americans were wounded; Spanish losses were estimated at over 370.[4]

When news of this triumph reached Washington, McKinley authorized a modest army expedition to conduct land operations against Manila, a step in keeping with the desire to maintain constant pressure on Spain in the hope of forcing an early end to the war. The actual occupation of Manila was delayed until August, after the arrival of 11,000 troops from the United States. Commanded by Major General Wesley Merritt, the Americans, with the support of Filipino revolutionaries, forced the Spanish garrison to capitulate on August 14. General Merritt formally accepted the surrender and declared the establishment of a U.S. military government in occupation. At the same time, it was recommended that the U.S. retain control of the Philippines, possibly granting independence in the future.

2. Cuba – At the time of the naval attack in the Philippines, the North Atlantic Squadron under Rear Admiral William Sampson had begun a partial blockade of Cuba while scouting in the Caribbean Sea for a fleet that had left Spain under the admiral. Finally, on May 28, American ships located Cervera's fleet, which had anchored in the landlocked part of the island. While the navy placed a blockade and landing a force outside the harbor, the army hastily prepared to send an expeditionary force to assault Santiago by land.

Major General Shafter's troop transports departed Tampa on June 14, meeting with their navy escorts the following day. The expedition arrived off Santiago on June 20 and began to disembark east of the city at Daiquiri two days later. In addition to providing escort for the convoy, Sampson's ships furnished fifty-two steam launches, sailing launches, whaleboats, lifeboats, and cutters to help the army and its equipment ashore. Shafter expressed deep appreciation for the navy's assistance in this matter, as the boats on the army's transports were too few to disembark the expedition in any reasonable length of time.[4]

Sampson's armored ships had maintained a tight blockade of Santiago de Cuba. On the morning of July 3, Admiral Cervera attempted to break out of the American blockade, thus precipitating the Battle of Santiago de Cuba. He tried to escape westward along the coast. In the ensuing battle, all his ships came under heavy fire from U.S. guns and were beached in a burning or sinking condition.

Theodore Roosevelt (T.R.) Assistant Secretary of the Navy and future president, was important in the Spanish-American War. As Assistant Secretary of the Navy, he called for a buildup in the country's naval strength, particularly the construction of battleships. Roosevelt also began pressing his national security views regarding the Pacific and the Caribbean on McKinley. Roosevelt was particularly adamant that Spain be ejected from Cuba to encourage the latter's independence and to demonstrate the U.S. resolve to reinforce the Monroe Doctrine.[5]

When war was finally declared, T.R. quit his job of Assistant Secretary of the Navy. Now he formed a cavalry regiment called the "Rough Riders". In it were wealthy polo players from the East and hard-riding cowboys from the West. T.R. was asked to command the first regiment, but he deferred to the more experienced Leonard Wood's higher rank, but the men of the First U.S. Volunteer Cavalry – the "Rough Riders" – looked to T.R. as their forceful leader.

The U.S. Army, under General William Shafter, landed on the coast east of Santiago and slowly advanced on the city to force Cervera's fleet out of the harbor. General Shafter launched a full-scale two-pronged assault on Santiago on July 1. He sent nearly half of his men against a small Spanish force strongly defending a stone fort at El Caney. The remainder made a frontal assault on the main Spanish defenses at Kettle Hill and San Juan Hill.

T.R. and the Rough Riders had a short, minor skirmish known as the Battle of Las Guasimas; they fought their way through Spanish resistance and, together with the Regulars, forced the Spaniards to abandon their positions.[6]

Under T.R.'s leadership, the Rough Riders became famous for the charge up Kettle Hill (part of San Juan Heights) on July 1, 1898, while supporting the regulars (Fig.9.2). Roosevelt had the only horse and rode back and forth between rifle pits at the forefront of the advance up Kettle Hill, an advance that he urged despite the absence of any orders from superiors. He was forced to walk up the last part of Kettle Hill, because his horse had been entangled in barbed wire. The victory came at a cost of 200 killed and 1,000 wounded.[7]

Roosevelt commented on his role in the battles: "On the day of the big fight I had to ask my men to do a deed that European military writers consider utterly impossible of performance, that is, to attack over open ground an unshaken infantry armed with the best modern repeating rifles behind a formidable system of entrenchments. The only way to get them to do it in the way it had to be done was to lead them myself. Years later he would say, "San Juan was the greatest day of my life." Roosevelt's victory along with that of the U.S. navy, forced Spain's navy to flee Santiago harbor. In 2001, Roosevelt was posthumously awarded the Medal of Honor for his actions.[5] Another famous American had shown conspicuous bravery, First Lieutenant John Pershing (Blackjack Pershing). Pershing would be the U.S. commander in World War I.

3) Puerto Rico – Major General Nelson Miles began an invasion of Puerto Rico on July 25th with 1,300 infantries which landed on the island's south coast off Port Guancia. The first organized armed opposition occurred in Yauco in what became known as the Battle of Yauco. This encounter was followed by the Battle of Fajardo. The United States seized control of Fajardo on August 1 but were forced to withdraw on August 5 after a group of 200 Puerto Rican-Spanish soldiers led by Pedro del Pino gained control of the city, while most civilian inhabitants fled to a nearby lighthouse. The Americans encountered larger opposition during the Battle of Guayama and as they advanced towards the main island's interior. All military actions in Puerto Rico were suspended on August 13, after Spain relinquished its sovereignty over Puerto Rico.[8]

4) The Peace Treaty – With the Treaty of Paris, signed on December 10, 1898, Spain officially ended its rule over Cuba, and for $20 million it transferred the Philippines, Puerto Rico, and Guam to the United States.

5) Philippine–American War – Armed conflict broke out between U.S. forces and the Filipinos when U.S. troops began to take the place of the Spanish in control of the country after the end of the war, quickly escalating into the Philippine-American War. The U.S. had to put down a long and bloody insurrection that did not end until 1902. The war had stared in February 1899. The brutal war raged in which the United States committed 70,00 troops and for three years lost more men than in the entire conflict with Spain. The war resulted in 4,196 deaths, 1,020 due to combat and 3,176 mostly from disease. There were over 20,000 Filipino combat deaths. As many as

200,000 Filipino civilians died from violence, famine and disease. There were epidemics of cholera and malaria.[8]

C. Diseases during the Spanish-American War

Disease was the main death loss during the Spanish-American War. Of the 1691 combat casualties, 385 were fatal. However, the ravages of yellow fever, typhoid, malaria and dysentery were so severe that, by the beginning of August, less than one-quarter of the army that had gone ashore on June 22, 1898, remained fit for service.[10]

Previously in the Civil War (1861-1865) many soldiers died of disease, often even before reaching the battlefield. Sanitation was abysmal. Epidemics of dysentery, pneumonia ("camp lung"), and typhus swept the camps. And yet, nothing was done after the war to change things. Despite horrific losses, little had been learned in the Civil War that significantly advanced medical theory. Ignorance of the role of microbes in contagion and the infection of wounds proved an insurmountable obstacle to medical progress.

Many men died of typhoid fever (often with pneumonia), yellow fever, dysentery and malaria. Without question, the military and medical leadership were woefully unprepared despite the medical and military knowledge available to them.

A commission concluded that the Army Medical Department was short on personnel and was not organized to meet the demands of a war. In addition, it discovered that the department did not investigate the sanitation at the camps, that it employed too few nurses and did not recognize the value of the female nurses, and it was at the mercy of the quartermaster corps for distribution of medical supplies.

The brief Spanish-American war was fought in the tropics, notably Cuba and the Philippines. Disease came close to defeating the U.S. Army. Typhoid, dysentery and yellow fever plagued American troops who were fighting in the tropics for the first time in U.S. history. In all, while the Spanish only killed 385 American soldiers around 2,061 U.S. soldiers died from disease.

All of the diseases of the Civil War still affected the troops but to a lesser extent due to the shortness of the war. Smallpox was then quite well controlled with vaccination and malaria deaths were reduced due to the medication quinine. The three big killers in the war were typhoid fever, yellow fever and dysentery. Death also resulted from heat exhaustion and food poisoning. Canned meat would sometimes arrive already spoiled. Poor food selection would also result in nutrient deficiencies (e.g., scurvy). Scurvy, a vitamin C deficiency results from lack of fruits and vegetables.[11]

During the Spanish-American War, as in almost all previous wars, many more soldiers died from diseases than from enemy bullets. For every American soldier who died in combat, more than seven died from disease (Table 9.1), despite the advances in scientific medicine and public hygiene that had taken place since the Civil War.[12]

The deadliest diseases during the war were typhoid fever, yellow fever and dysentery:

1) Typhoid Fever – As was true for the Civil War, typhoid was one of the most feared and often fatal epidemic diseases of the 19th century. Typhoid fever has an onset characterized by fever, headache, constipation, chills, confusion, delirium, intestinal perforation and death in severe cases.

Also, troops stationed away from the fighting faced danger. Typhoid fever was the major killer of American soldiers during the Spanish-American War, running rampant through the national encampments. In preparation for hostilities, 108,000 volunteers from various states had been assembled in a handful of national encampments located in Georgia, Florida, Virginia, and Pennsylvania. As a result, the sanitary facilities in the camps rapidly became overwhelmed, and the resultant situation was appalling. Typhoid fever epidemics broke out in all of the encampments. Regiments in these camps suffered 20,738 cases of typhoid fever, which resulted in 1,590 fatalities (Table 9.2). Typhoid fever accounted for 87% of all deaths attributable to disease.[15] Pneumonia often accompanied typhoid and the two diseases together most often had fatal consequences.

By the time of the war in 1898 the causative agent of typhoid fever, *Salmonella typhi* had been identified, the Widal serodiagnostic test was available, the mode of transmission via infected feces was established, and effective preventive measures were known. Yet typhoid, a preventable disease, became the major killer of the war. The failure to protect the soldiers' health became a national scandal. Having knowledge of prevention of the disease was not enough, medical officers had little power to enforce sanitary regulation, and line officers with scant training in the value of camp hygiene proved largely uncooperative. Nursing care was another bone of contention, as officers released only their least competent soldiers for nursing duty. The hostility between line officers and medial officers resulted in tragic consequences for health of American soldiers.[14]

English physician William Budd, as early as 1839, believed the causative agent of typhoid spread through contaminated water supplies. However, the majority of army surgeons were opposed to the contagion theory. Budd's theory did not explain how typhoid could be spread by healthy carriers, flies, contaminated milk, and infected food. Also, most army doctors still believed that fevers could originate spontaneously.[15] Contamination of water resulted in spread of the disease. Simple procedures such as placing a latrine downstream to ensure a clean water supply was often overlooked. As important, men often did not use the latrine and defecated near the water supply.

To prevent and control typhoid, Budd recommended thorough disinfection of all privies, drains, intestinal discharges at the moment of passage, body and bed linens before laundering, and the hands of anyone having contact with typhoid patients.

Sanitation procedures had enormous implications for the military, since one could expect the severest outbreaks of typhoid fever under camp conditions where common latrines served as receptacles for the daily excreta of an many as 60,000 men, such as inhabited Camp Thomas during the Spanish-American War. Army sewage studies later determines 60,000 men discharge an average of 9.4 tons of feces a day.

In 1893 George Sternberg, a leading bacteriologist, became surgeon general. Sternberg realized that disease would be the leading cause of death of American soldiers in the impending conflict with Spain. He also understood that high morbidity and mortality rates from disease were not inevitable and could be checked by existing preventive measures.

On April 25, 1898, Sternberg issued Circular No. I, which outlined the rules of personal hygiene and camp sanitation. This included detailed instructions for strict sanitary police with the provisos that sinks (pit latrines) should be dug before a camp is occupied, that all fecal matter in camp sinks should be covered with fresh earth or quicklime daily, that every man who fails to use the sinks should be punished and that all discharges from fever patients should be disinfected immediately with solutions of carbolic acid or chlorinated lime. Had these recommendations been carried out, there would have been little sickness. Unfortunately, they were largely ignored, and typhoid fever rapidly overran the camps.[16]

On the eve of the Spanish-American War, it was not difficult to differentiate between typhoid fever and malaria. Yet, American medial officers continually misdiagnosed typhoid fever as malaria during the Spanish-American War. Misdiagnosed cases had much to do with the spread of typhoid fever in the camps in 1898. Surgeon General Sternberg concluded that "failure to make an early diagnosis, mistaking typhoid fever for malarial fever, led very largely to the camp infection.[16]

Who was responsible for this widespread error in diagnosis? Most placed the responsibility for the prevailing ignorance with the medical schools. "The fault lies in reality with the system of teaching which permitted these young men to go out into practice without a thorough knowledge of typhoid fever."

Also, the training in American medical schools ranged widely, and training in laboratory skills was still the exception. Only a small percentage of medial officers had the advantage of top quality clinical and laboratory experience.

Volunteer recruits were the greatest offenders of hygiene and sanitation. Regular Army veterans knew how to care for themselves and paid closer attention to sanitation. They were more conscientious than the green recruits in using company pit latrines and were not guilty of defecating promiscuously about the surrounding countryside. Illustrating the problem at Camp Thomas, the board found the pit latrines full to the top with fecal matter; soled paper was scattered about the sinks, and the woods behind the regimental camp was strewn with fecal matter.... fecal matter was deposited around trees, and flies swarmed over these deposits not more than 150 feet from company mess tents; the odor in the woods just outside of the regimental lines was an intolerable stench.[12]

Human contact, direct and indirect, was determined to be the predominant means of spreading the infection in the military camps. (Table 9.3) The disease bacterium shed in infected patient stools was often passed to others via hands unwashed after bowel movement. Nurses could be in contact with the feces containing the organism and carelessly pass on the contamination to others. An individual may become the bearer and distributor of the infecting agent of typhoid fever without developing the disease themselves.

In addition to realization that typhoid was primarily due to contaminated water, Walter Reed and his associates established the importance of human contact and flies in the epidemiology of typhoid fever, developed the concept of healthy typhoid carriers as agents of infection. Later the outstanding example of a typhoid carrier was "typhoid Mary", a lady with no effects of the disease who spread the disease widely.[17]

Next to personal contact, flies were shown to be the most active agents in the spread of typhoid in the national encampments in 1898. Numerous accounts mentioned that clouds of flies swarmed around the sinks (pit latrines), and often alighted on the excrement before it is covered up with soil or quicklime. One report noted that after latrines were sprinkled with quicklime, flies with whitened feet were observed walking on food in the mess tents. The aerial route from the sink to the kitchen, became "a literal highway of disease." Flies were such a nuisance that men "ate with one hand and fought flies with the other."[18] Typhoid died out in the fall, coincident with the seasonal disappearance of flies.

2) Yellow Fever – At one time it was believed that yellow fever was caused by filth on ships that generated the "bad air" that resulted in devastating epidemics. The disease was widespread in lowland swampy areas in the southern states during the mosquito season. New Orleans was often affected by yellow fever. In 1853 between 8,000 and 9,000 died of the disease. In New Orleans there were further epidemics in 1854 and 1855, 5,000 dying from the 1855 epidemic. From 1817-1905 yellow fever epidemics took more than 41,000 lives in New Orleans. Many had died from the disease during the Civil War (1861-1865).[19]

Yellow fever had first appeared in the late 17th century. The deadly virus continued to strike cities, mostly eastern seaports and Gulf Coast cities, for the next two hundred years, killing hundreds, sometimes thousands in a single summer.

The disease of yellow fever starts like a common flu with headache, fever, muscle pain, nausea and vomiting. But roughly 15 percent of patients progress to a severe form of the disease: high fever, jaundice, internal bleeding, seizures, shock, organ failure and death. Up to half of those who develop severe disease will die.[20,21]

Yellow fever was first reported in Cuba in 1649, when one-third of Havana residents died from the disease. From 1856 to 1879, the disease struck the city nearly every month. Spanish troops occupying Cuba were particularly susceptible, with 16,000 troops dying from the fever between 1895 and 1898. At the onset of war with the United States, illness had decimated the Spanish fighting force, with 55,000 troops out of an army of 230,000 healthy enough to fight. U.S. officials were aware of the dangers from the disease.[19]

Army Major Walter Reed, a physician who would later head the U.S. Army Yellow Fever Board in Cuba, offered advice to a friend who expected to be deployed there. Surmising incorrectly that the germ for yellow fever was inhaled, Reed wrote that a "plug of cotton in the nostrils would be advisable." Even knowing that yellow fever would strike in the summer rainy season, U.S. troops invaded Cuba June 22nd.

In July, after the Battle of Santiago Lieutenant Colonel Theodore Roosevelt of the Rough Riders unit foresaw the dangerous conditions of yellow fever in a letter to Secretary of War Russell Alger: "If we are kept here, it will in all human possibility mean an appalling disaster, for the surgeons here estimate that over half the army, if kept here during the sickly season, will die." But the troops were ordered to hold their ground in Santiago until Spanish forces surrendered. They did on July 17, but the damage had already been done.[13]

Fewer than 400 American soldiers were killed in combat during the war. But more than 2,000 contracted yellow fever during the campaign. Of the 5,000 that died of disease many of the deaths were due to yellow fever according to records of the U.S. army Yellow Fever commission. Disease, said General William Shafter, was a "thousand times harder to stand up against than the missiles of the enemy." On July 6 in the town of Siboney, the first case of yellow fever among U.S. troops occurred. For the next several weeks, more troops were struck by malaria and dysentery. Yellow fever began to spread, which officers and doctors incorrectly blamed on infected buildings in Siboney. In response, General Nelson Miles ordered Siboney evacuated and burned on July 11. An infantry unit of black soldiers, incorrectly thought to be immune from yellow fever, were brought in to tend to the afflicted. More than a third of their regiment died from yellow fever or malaria.

Approximately 50,000 U.S. troops were stationed in Cuba at the conclusion of the war. U.S. officials focused on preventing future outbreaks of yellow fever and other diseases, which were all caused, according to Major William Crawford Gorgas, the chief sanitary officer in Havana, "by filth, dirt, and general unsanitary conditions." Cleanup measures helped control diseases spread by unsanitary conditions such as typhoid and dysentery. But by July 1899, yellow fever returned to Cuba, though to a lesser degree than the previous year.[19]

Yellow fever posed a major threat to continued military operations in the Americas; hence, on May 23, 1890, Sternberg appointed the Yellow Fever Board (led by Walter Reed) to investigate this disease, its etiology, and possible means of prevention. Carlos Finlay, a Cuban physician, believed that the disease was mosquito borne, though his inoculation experiments had been inconclusive. Experiments by the board were begun by raising mosquitoes individually from eggs, letting them feed on patients with the disease, and then allowing them to bite members of the team. In the end this board would prove, to the surprise and disbelief of many, that a common domestic mosquito spread the disease.[14]

Major William Gorgas, as the chief sanitary officer of Havana, took immediate action by carrying out a mosquito eradication program and within a year for the first time in history, the city was free of yellow fever, as the mosquito eradication program in Cuba was successful. Dr. Gorgas convinced President Theodore Roosevelt to grant funding on an eradication effort in Panama. Prior to 1906 roughly 85% of canal workers had been hospitalized with either malaria or yellow fever. Workers were so terrified of yellow fever that they fled the construction site in droves at the first hint of the disease. Tens of thousands of workers had died.[21]

The Panama Program fumigated private homes with insecticides and sprayed areas of standing water with oil to interrupt mosquito breeding. Finally, on November 11, 1906, the last victim of yellow fever on the Panama Canal died. The yellow fever epidemic was over. In the 1940s, the yellow fever vaccine was developed.

3) Diarrhea and Dysentery – Many deaths were attributed to diarrhea and dysentery. Dysentery is considered diarrhea with blood in the stool. Diarrheas were a problem in all armies in all wars fought before the 20th century. The diarrheas and so many other diseases were able to spread rapidly primarily because of lack of sanitation practices and contaminated water. The same lack of sanitation conditions that favored typhoid fever favored dysentery and diarrhea. There was lack of hygiene with frequent references to the interplay of feces, flies, fingers and food. Food and water had been contaminated with feces. Hands were not washed frequently, and flies would move from feces to food.[20]

Incidence of diarrheas and dysenteries among United States troops was slightly lower than among troops during the Revolutionary War and Civil War. The number of cases were 426 per 1,000 troops, with number of deaths of 1,595. This was a rate of 3.3 troops per 1,000. Diarrheas occurred in severe epidemic form in U.S. troops in the Philippines shortly after the American occupation in 1899-1900.

These diseases are characterized by watery stools that may cause shock and death, without replacement of fluid and chemicals required for the body to function. Patients recovering from these usually pass bacteria in the stools for 7 to 10 days. These diseases are spread to healthy individuals from carriers who harbor and excrete the bacteria in their stools. Flies living outdoors could now spread the diarrhea/dysentery to others. Hairs on fly legs in contact with infected material were the most common conveyers of the bacteria to food.

There was a relationship of the diarrheas to typhoid fever (often with pneumonia) and yellow fever. Individuals with sever diarrheas are in a weakened condition and are less able to fight off diseases. A person contacting either typhoid or yellow fever would likely lack sufficient immunity to fight these diseases. Both dysentery and typhoid are deadly in their own right, but when a person has both at the same time it is almost impossible to recover.[22]

4) Malaria – The symptoms of malaria are headache, fever, chills, sweating, cough and vomiting. Fevers were prevalent in the military camps during the Spanish War, which were diagnosed by the majority of medical officers as malaria or a combination of malaria and typhoid. It was shown that the army surgeons were no better in detecting typhoid fever than their civilian counterparts. In fact, only 1% of the cases examined proved to be malaria; the rest were typhoid. Medical officers went into the southern camps expecting to encounter nothing but malaria, but they were wrong.[12] Malaria was not a great problem during the war, with the effective treatment of quinine.

D. Summary

The Spanish-American War lasted less than four months in 1898. Between 1895 and 1898 Cuba and the Philippine Islands were in revolt against Spain. There were ruthless tactics by Spain to preserve their colonies. The U.S. Battleship USS Maine exploded in Havana, Cuba killing 266 sailors. Spain was believed to be responsible, and this was one of the main reasons war was declared on Spain on April 25, 1898.

In the first battle on May 1st, Commodore George Dewey destroyed the entire Spanish fleet (10 ships) in Manila Bay. In Cuba a naval blockade was in effect. In the Battle of Santiago de Cuba. Spanish Admiral Cervera tried to break out of the blockade resulting in all of the Spanish ships destroyed. On July 1 U.S. forces defeated the Spanish at Kettle Hill and San Juan Hill. At this time under the leadership of future president Theodore Roosevelt's "Rough Riders" made the famous charge up Kettle Hill for victory. On August 12th the Spanish-American War officially ended. On August 14, a Spanish garrison in Manila was defeated and the U.S. military government in occupation was established.

For the war, a commission concluded that the Army Medical Department was short on personnel, unorganized and ill-equipped to meet the demands of war. Disease came close to defeating the U.S. army due to typhoid fever (often with pneumonia), yellow fever, diarrhea/dysentery and malaria. Lack of sanitation in training camps in southeast U.S. resulted in 20,700 typhoid outbreaks, with more than 1,500 deaths. Also, because of inept sanitation practices, water and food were contaminated with feces resulting in many deaths. Lack of hygiene resulted in interplay of feces, flies, fingers and food. Yellow fever epidemics had been common in S.E. U.S. and were devastating in Cuba causing many deaths. Over the years yellow fever had, likewise, been devastating to Spanish troops, from 1895-1898 16,000 troops died from the disease. In early August 1898 the ravages of yellow fever, typhoid, diarrhea/dysentery and malaria resulted in only one-quarter of the army fit for service. The result of the war for the U.S. was that 385 soldiers died from battle, while around 2,061 died from disease. Towards the end of the war and later the role of sanitation became clearer and mosquitoes were found responsible for yellow fever.

The victorious U.S. emerged from the war as a world power with far-flung overseas possessions and became more involved in international politics.

Table 9.1 Total United States Army Deaths from All Causes
in the Continental United States, Cuba, Puerto Rico, and the
Philippine Islands during the Spanish-American War
(1 May to 30 September 1898)[12]

Cause of Death	Officers	Enlisted Men	Total
Killed in Action	23	257	280
Died of Wounds	4	61	65
Died of Disease	80	2,485	2,565
Total	107	2,803	2,910

Table 9.2 Morbidity and Mortality from Typhoid Fever among United States
Army Recruits in the National Encampments from April to December 1898[12]

Army Camp	Location	Typhoid Fever		Deaths from all diseases
		Cases	Deaths	
Thomas	Chickamauga, GA	10,339	761	866
Tampa	Tampa, FL	1,498	99	112
Alger	Falls Church, VA	2,226	212	259
Meade	Middleton, PA	2,690	150	168
Cuba Libre	Jacksonville, FL	3,985	368	427
Total		20,738	1,590	1,832

Note: Ninety-two regiments (107,973 officers and men) were studied.

Table 9.3 The Epidemiology of Typhoid Fever Occurring among United States
Army Recruits during the Spanish-American War[12]

Mode of transmission	Percentage of cases
Contact	62.8
Flies	15.0
Waterborne and airborne	22.2
Total	100.0

Table 9.4 Highlights of Spanish-American War[2,5,8]

1864	Yellow fever was first reported and one-third of Havana, Cuba died.
1895-1898	Deaths from yellow fever for 16,000 Spanish troops in Cuba.
1895-1898	Attempted revolution of Cuba and the Philippines against Spain.
Feb. 15,1898	Explosion of U.S. the Battleship USS Maine in Havana, Cuba, killing 266 sailors.
April 25, 1898	U.S. declaration of war with Spain.
April 25, 1898	Theodore Roosevelt resigned as Assistant Secretary of the Navy and formed a cavalry regiment called "Rough Riders".
April 25, 1898	George Sternberg issued instructions and rules of personal hygiene and camp sanitation. These rules were largely ignored.
April – Aug., 1898	Disease came close to defeating the U.S. Army particularly due to typhoid, yellow fever and dysentery.
April-Aug. 1898	A commission concluded that the Army Medical Department was short on personnel and was not organized to meet the demands of a war.
May 1, 1898	Naval battle in Philippines where Commodore George Dewey destroyed entire Spanish fleet.
May 1, 1898	Beginning of a Naval blockade of Cuba by Rear Admiral William Sampson.
July 1, 1898	U.S. General Shafter launched a full-scale assault on Fort El Caney and the main Spanish defenses at Kettle Hill and San Juan Hill.
July 1, 1898	Under the leadership of future President Theodore Roosevelt and his "Rough Riders", they made the famous charge up Kettle Hill for victory.
July 6, 1898	The first case of yellow fever among troops, later more than 2,000 contracted the disease.
July-Nov. 1898	Lack of sanitary conditions in training camps in southeastern U.S. resulted in 2,070 typhoid outbreaks, with more than 1,500 deaths.
July 17, 1898	Many U.S. troops died from yellow fever during and after Battle of Santiago.
July 17, 1898	Spanish forces surrendered in Cuba.
July 25, 1898	An invasion of Puerto Rico resulted in the Battles of Yauco, Fajardo and Guayama.
Early Aug., 1898	Ravages of yellow fever, typhoid, dysentery and malaria resulted in only one-quarter of the army fit for service.
Aug. 1898	Walter Reed and associates established the importance of human contact and flies in spreading typhoid fever.
Aug. 14, 1898	With support of Filipino revolutionaries, Major General Wesley Merritt and U.S. forces forced the Spanish garrison in Manila to surrender.

Aug. 12, 1898	The Spanish-American war officially ended.
Aug. 18, 1898	The U.S. Army typhoid Board, led by Major Walter Reed was established.
April-Aug., 1898	The Spanish killed 385 soldiers while around 2,061 died from disease.
Dec. 10, 1898	With the Treaty of Paris, Spain officially ended its rule over Cuba, and transferred the Philippines, Puerto Rico and Guam to the United States.
Feb. 1899	The Philippine – American war began and lasted until 1902.
May 23, 1890	Yellow fever continued to be a major threat to military operations. Walter Reed was appointed to investigate and found that the disease was spread by mosquitos. With this information mosquito eradication programs were put in place which ended epidemics of the disease and allowed building of the Panama Canal.

9.1 The explosion of the Maine helped bring on the Spanish-American War.

9.2 The Rough Riders Regiment won national fame for its charge up Kettle Hill in Cuba in 1898. Lt. Col. Theodore Roosevelt, on horseback, led the assault.

CHAPTER 10

World War I

A. Introduction

World War I began June 28, 1914, when Archduke Franz Ferdinand, heir to the throne of Austria-Hungary, and his wife Sophie were assassinated in the Austrian Provence of Bosnia. The assassin was a young Bosnian who lived in Serbia. On the day that the Archduke was killed Austria-Hungary declared war on Serbia. By October 30, the Central Powers – Austria-Hungary, Germany and the Ottoman Empire (Turkey) – were at war with the allies – France, Great Britain, Russia, Belgium, Italy and Serbia. Other countries joined in the fighting including New Zealand, Australia, Canada, India and Belgium, with the United States on April 6, 1917. In total the Central Powers fought more than 20 allied nations. The war ended when the Central Powers signed armistices between September 29 and November 11, 1918. Armed conflict lasted about four years.[1] The war has been erroneously referred to as "a war to end all wars."

There were several basic causes of World War I. These causes included the growth of nationalism, the system of military alliances that created a balance of power, the competition for colonies and other territory, and the use of secret diplomacy.

The total number of military and civilian causalities in World War I, was around 40 million. There were 20 million deaths and 21 million wounded. The total number of deaths includes 9.7 million military personnel and about 10 million civilians. The Allies lost about 5.7 million soldiers while the Central Powers lost about 4 million. Most of the casualties were due to war related famine and disease.

B. Military events in World War I

Major battles of World War I in Chronological order are:

1) Battle of Tannenberg (August 26-31, 1914) – This battle was fought between Russia and Germany. By end of the month, the Germans had taken 92,000 prisoners and destroyed half of the Russian 2nd army. In total, the Russians lost about 250,000 men as well as military equipment. The only positive from the Battle of Tannenberg was diverting the Germans from attacking France. That allowed the French to counterattack at the First Battle of Marne.[2]

2) First Battle of Marne (September 6-9, 1914) – German armies had a plan to encircle the French army from the north and capture Paris. This did not work out as the French Army drove Paris taxis and buses to attack German troops through a gap opened by France's Sixth Army and the British Expeditionary Force. Shocked by this military tactic, the German armies lost communication with one another and after several days of bitter fighting were retreating in what is now known as the "race to the sea." This battle marked the end of German incursion into France and beginning of the trench warfare so widely associated with World War One.[3]

3) Battle of Gallipoli (April 25, 1915 – January 9, 1916) – This battle was an attempt for allied forces to knock out those of the Turkish Ottoman Empire. The Battle has become known as one of the Allied Powers most unsuccessful attempts to gain the upper hand in World War I. The battle began with the British and French initiating a naval attack on Turkey's Dardanelles Straits. The plan aimed to force the Ottoman Empire to surrender. The plan failed miserably in part due to the outdated allies' fleet, and many ships that were sunk by Ottoman cannons and mines. Allied plans were based on the mistaken belief that the Ottomans could be easily overcome. The Battle of Gallipoli saw 58,000 Allied soldiers' casualties.[4]

4) Battle of Jutland (May 31, 1916) – This was the biggest naval battle of the war between Britain and Germany. The battle occurred in the North Sea and was a bloody battle that involved 250 ships and about 100,000 troops. Although the German forces eventually retreated on the 1st of June, they claimed victory due to having taken down 14 British ships and 6,784 British soldiers, compared to Germany's 11 ships and 3,058 fatalities. The British, however, claimed victory, because they were able to maintain their blockade against the Germans. Regardless, after the Battle of Jutland, German forces were never able to reclaim their previous level of power or control.[3]

5) Battle of Somme (July 1 – November 16, 1916) – This campaign or battle lasted until November. It started as an allied offensive against German forces on the Western Front and is now known as one of the bloodiest battles of the war. Over 1.5 million troops killed by its end in November.[5]

6) Battle of Verdun (Feb. 18 – Dec. 16, 1916) – This was the longest and most savage battle of the war. Nealy three-quarters of the French army fought in this battle. In the initial days the Germans breached the French front lines.

Later in the year the French attacked and retook territory they had lost in February. The Germans had lost over 430,000 men killed or wounded and the French approximately 550,000.[4]

7) The United States actively enters the War (June 26, 1917) – The war in Europe began in August 1914, but U.S. President Wilson announced U.S. neutrality. On May 7, 1915, a German submarine sank the British passenger ship *Lusitania*, killing more than 1,100 people, including 128 U.S. citizens. The U.S. public reacted angrily and demanded action. For the first time, public opinion shifted toward the Allied side. Former President Theodore Roosevelt publicly advocated a massive rearmament to get the United States ready for war.[5]

In January 1917, Germany announced a policy of unrestricted submarine warfare: Germany threatened to torpedo and sink any ship, including U.S. ships that traded with the Allied Powers. In the next three months, German submarines (U. Boats) sank three U.S. ships, killing 36 sailors. German leaders hoped to defeat the Allied Powers before the U.S. could fully mobilize.[6]

On April 2, 1917, war was declared on Germany. In Wilson's speech he noted, "the world must be safe for democracy." Further agitating the U.S. was the Zimmerman telegram sent to the German ambassador in Mexico. Mexico was asked to join in war against the U.S. If the Mexican government agreed, Germany promised a return of the territory lost to the United States in the Mexican-American War. There was an overwhelming popular response to the war with partisan clamor almost silenced.[7]

American entry into World War I resulted in American troops on the Western Front under General John Pershing being engaged in 13 campaigns during the period 1917-1918 (Fig.10.1). Major battles began November 20, 1917, and ended November 11, 1918.

8) Third Battle of Ypres (July 31 – Nov. 10, 1917) – This was also referred to as the Battle of Passchendaele. In this battle there were many casualties and widespread mud. Many men and horses drowned in the mud. The battle of Ypres was fought along the British lines. British and Canadian forces claimed victory. The battle had 325,000 British and allied casualties and 260,000 German casualties.

9) Battle of Cambrai (Nov. 20 – Dec. 4, 1917) – This was in northern France between the British and Germans. This was the first time that battle tanks were used on a massive scale in battle. This was combined with air power and heavy artillery. The Battle of Cambrai opened the way for use of sophisticated arms tactics and armored warfare in years that followed. Both the German and British each had casualties of about 45,000.

10) Second Battle of Marne (July 15 – Aug. 6, 1918) – The first Sunday in June 1918 was the most dismal day in the whole war for the Germans.[7] German outpost moving on Paris had reached the Marne and halted for their support to come up. Partly by aid of American units, the German advance was halted at this point. On July 14th while the Germans were preparing to renew their attack, the offensive was suddenly snatched from them by French General Ferdinand Foch, the supreme commander on the Western Front. The combined French, British and American forces pushed them back and from then until November 11th they could never recover the initiative. The second Battle of the Marne would be considered the turning point of the war. The Franco-American troops, with an estimated 300 tanks had forced the Germans to retreat.

11) St. Mihiel and Meus –Argonne (Sept. 12 – Nov. 11, 1918) - The battles took heavy casualties and played its part in foiling the German lunge toward victory on the Western Front. By August, Pershing had enough troops to take over a sector, and he carried out independent offensives in September at St. Mihiel and in the Meuse-Argonne.

This offensive stuck at the German's main supply line and involved the largest number of American troops, and casualties (117,000) in any engagement the army ever fought – larger than the Battle of the Bulge in World War II. The final offensive was at Meuse-Argonne. The battle took the allied armies to the German frontier. After a decisive allied victory, Germans accepted defeat and signed for peace. An American hero was at Meuse-Argonne, Sgt Alvin York, who single-handedly killed 15 Germans and captured 132.

12) End of War (Nov. 11, 1918) – The war ended with armistices signed from late September to early November in 1918. The Kaiser abdicated on November 9 and fled to exile in the Netherlands. For the war 126,000 U.S. men died in combat of wounds and disease, making this the third deadliest war in all of American history, despite its being the second shortest.[5]

C. Diseases during World War I

It is well known that in nearly all past wars, preventable disease had killed more men than had perished from wounds. This was true for the following: French and Indian War, American Revolution, War of 1812, Mexican-American War, Civil War and Spanish-American War.

Infectious diseases will always be with us. In previous centuries, they were the major causes of death, both during wars, and during peace. It was not until the late 19th century that the germ theory of disease became firmly established. Virus disease was not recognized until into the 20th century. With recognition of micro-organisms came great advances in public health to control the spread of diseases. Early attempts at immunization against common diseases, particularly smallpox, were successful even without knowing the bacterial or viral basis for diseases. The late 19th century saw the development of more and better vaccines, notably against typhoid fever and tetanus. Other diseases, such as malaria and yellow fever, could be controlled by identifying the insect vectors and either eliminating or controlling them. Prophylaxis against malaria was available and routinely used. In many ways, the years before World War I marked the beginning of the conquest of infectious diseases, but only the beginning. In 1917, antibiotics were still 20 years in the future. Most of today's vaccines had not yet been developed. Many among the general public knew nothing of prevention from such diseases as tuberculosis and bacterial pneumonia which were common by today's standards. Overall, disease had caused more deaths in the American Army than did enemy action.[4]

After dramatic medical advances in the prewar years, the government went into the war with unprecedented confidence in its ability to keep soldiers healthy. First, a generation of scientific medical discoveries promised to control many infectious diseases and gave medical officers an inflated sense of their ability to prevent or cure disease, encouraging overly optimistic public expectations of the army's good health during World War I.

For World War I far fewer British troops had died of disease (113,000) than from shells and bullets; 418,000 were killed in action and 167,000 died from wounds. The statistics for the German Army showed a similar ratio with 1,531,048 killed in battle, and 155,013 died of disease. In contrast, in the Crimean War (1854-1856, 730,000 British, French and Russian combatants) 34,000 were killed in action, 26,000 died from wounds and 130,000 died from diseases, with diagnoses of cholera and typhus fever being recorded as particularly important causes. The ratio of deaths from disease and those from combat was much the same in the British Army in its first big 20th century war – the South African War (1899-1902). The average annual strength of the army during the war was 210,000 of whom 5,774 were killed in action, 2,018 died of wounds and 13,250 died of disease, of which 8,227 were killed by typhoid fever.[8]

Had it not been for the Spanish flu, more U.S. troops would have died from military action versus disease. The national government raised and commanded an army of young men in part by assuring them and their families that they would be well cared for and would fight in glory against the enemy. But most American soldiers who lost their lives died in bed – killed not in combat by the powerful German army, but by a less glorious, unseen enemy. According to the War Department's official figures, the 57,460 soldiers who died of disease outnumbered the 50,280 who died in combat. Thus, while the U.S. Army helped win the war and enjoyed the glory of victory, the medical officers stood impotent before a killer flu.[9]

Diseases during World War I were as follows:

1) Influenza and Pneumonia – Public confidence in the health and welfare of the nation's soldiers was vital to the government's ability to conduct the war. However, this confidence was lost when the devastating disease influenza resulted in many deaths (Fig.10.2). People also called it the Spanish Flu, or La Ga Grippe and it was a huge epidemic toward the end of the war in 1918, spreading throughout the world.

The sum of American sailors and soldiers who died of the flu and pneumonia in 1918 is over 43,000. The Army Medical Corps almost attained its goal of making this the first war in which the United States lost fewer soldiers to disease than in combat.[10] The influenza epidemic exploded the optimistic health expectations and delivered an experience in failure to army physicians who could do nothing to prevent the flu or to treat the deadly pneumonia that often ensued. To some it seemed a frightful throwback to the nineteenth-century plagues of cholera, typhoid, and yellow fever that devastated cities and armies. The flu epidemic thus damaged the army Medical Department's hopes and promises of defeating the infectious diseases that traditionally followed armies.[11] For every American soldier who died in battle or as result of wounds or gas in World War I, 1.02 died of disease.

Victims of influenza would often develop a deadly type of pneumonia and would suffer from headaches, aching muscles, a persistent dry cough, fever, weakness, a sore throat, and blood poisoning. Once someone was infected, they would usually die within three days in excruciating pain and with swelling of the body. Since there was no cure, gauze masks were distributed among populations to prevent transmission of the disease.[12]

The influenza epidemic of 1918 killed more people in one year than World War I killed in four years. The flu went on to kill almost three times more people than the 17 million soldiers and civilians killed during World War I. This pandemic ranks among the Justinian Plague of the sixth century A.D., which ravaged the ancient world; the Black Death of the fourteenth century, which killed as much as one-third of the population of Europe; and the epidemics that devastated the Indian populations in the Americas during the period of European conquest, killing almost 90% of native Americans in the Americas.

As one of the deadliest pandemics in human history, the 1918 influenza sickened at least one-quarter of the world's population, killing from 2 to 3 percent of those stricken, usually from the complications of pneumonia. An army epidemiologist wrote, "if the epidemic continues its mathematical rate of acceleration, civilization would easily have disappeared from the face of the earth within a matter of a few weeks."

Influenza flooded hospitals with patients, closed schools and churches, killed millions of people throughout the world, and sent millions more to bed, pale and helpless for weeks. In the United States, an estimated 25 million people became ill and 675,000 died. The disease changed life expectancy statistics in the U.S., with both men and women losing 12 years in 1918.

Worldwide mortality estimates range widely from just over 20 million to 50 million. While University of Chicago bacteriologist Edwin Jordan's 1927 estimate of 21 million provided the baseline for decades, more recently scholars have determined that as many as 17 million people died in India alone, increasing the estimate for the global mortality to 40 or 50 million.[14] Some newer estimates suggest that there were over 50 million deaths.

As in previous wars, the training camps in the United States were breeding grounds for disease. In addition to training camps navy personnel on crowded ships were particularly vulnerable. The major childhood diseases, measles, mumps, and chicken pox could sweep through a camp. More serious diseases such as meningitis and pneumonia were a constant threat. Recruits were screened for infectious diseases at entry, which helped somewhat. Colds and influenza were a constant problem, with pneumonia carrying a real risk of death. Simple seasonal influenza was constant but was rarely fatal. All that changed in 1918 when a nightly virulent influenza became a worldwide pandemic. According to the Centers for Disease Control and Prevention, the influenza pandemic made its U.S. appearance in military personnel, infiltrating military training camps across the nation.[15]

One could follow the course of influenza at Camp Jackson, South Carolina. On September 19, 1918, soldiers feeling achy and feverish were hospitalized. Influenza had reached the camp only the day before. It swept the camp quickly, sending 1,000 men to the hospital the first week, and ultimately sickened more than 10,000 of the 38,000 men in the camp. Influenza cases peaked after four weeks, followed by pneumonia cases a week later. Despite efforts, more than 400 people died, including five nurses caring for the soldiers.[16]

Flu was highly contagious and struck quickly with little warning. After the war the Medical Department concluded that literally every soldier was exposed to influenza, "no other disease spreads so fast." The suddenness of the onset was so acute that patients could, as a rule tell the hour they were taken sick. The virulent strand of influenza was so virulent that it caused many serious complications, especially acute infections for the lungs (pneumonia).[11]

Generally, a flu would usually kill the very weak in a population, the youngest and very oldest people. However, the 1918 flu was deadliest for young adults ages twenty to forty, killing not only the weak, but also the strongest people in the population. During the peace negotiations in Paris, the flu incapacitated many of the principals, including President Woodrow Wilson, who was ill for several days.[17]

The origin of the flu has long been a mystery, and the responsible virus was not discovered and identified until 1997. The best understanding is that a strain of influenza first appeared in March 1918 in the United States in Kansas, sickening students at a school in Haskell and soldiers in Camp Funston near Fort Riley, and in Georgia, among soldiers at Camp Oglethorpe. The virus then traveled to Europe, probably with men on the troop ships, to the wretched conditions of trench warfare where it would thrive. That spring the flu struck thousands of soldiers but killed very few.

After a summer lull, however, the flu became increasingly virulent and exploded in a worldwide pandemic in late August 1918. It swept the United States, attacking military training camps, cities, towns, and rural communities. In Europe influenza attacked Allied and German armies with equal virulence, filling field hospitals and transport trains with weak, feverish men all along the Western Front. In October 1918, at the height of military offensives in the St. Mihiel and Meuse-Argonne sectors, more American soldiers died in army camp beds than in the battlefields of France. By the War Department's own account, flu sickened 26 percent of the army – more than one million men – and accounted for 82 percent of total deaths from disease.[9]

The flu virus had appeared in three waves, the first in March 1918 in the U.S., affecting many, but killing few. The second wave of the flu was in late August 1918 and was deadly, virulent, and exploded in a worldwide pandemic. The second wave subsided only to reappear in January and February 1919. The third wave was less powerful than the second, but it was still deadly and spanned the globe.

While physicians had recently gained control over a number of deadly infectious diseases, medical officers were helpless with regard to respiratory diseases, and knew it. Treatment of the flu was a professional disaster for physicians, especially army medical offices, and an experience in failure for the national government. Medical professionals did their best to save those stricken by flu and pneumonia, but without the virology and antibiotics that scientists would develop later in the century, they lacked the tools to control the epidemic.[14]

The war created the influenza epidemic by producing an ecological environment in the trenches in which the flu virus could thrive and mutate to unprecedented virulence. The influenza virus exploited conditions in military camps, battlefields, and trenches to transform from a common winter ailment dangerous only to the infirm, into a lethal disease that could sicken at least a quarter of all people it came in contact with and could kill even the very strongest.

The resulting epidemic in turn impacted the war by striking down millions of soldiers of all armies and spreading disease and death to countries throughout the world. The United States was not a major military player until late 1917, not experiencing the first three years of the war. The American's brief military participation colored much of the American combat experience. Both were concentrated in September, October, and November 1918. Once it arrived in its deadly form in early September, the flu dramatically affected American war activities. Influenza hospitalized 25 to 40 percent of the men in U.S. Army training camps and killed almost thirty thousand of them before they could even go to France. Men carried the flu virus on board the troop ships, and many soon fell ill, toxifying the ships as they crossed the Atlantic.

Another problem made worse by the flu was that of evacuating the disabled from battle to hospital. At best, evacuation in wartime is difficult, and the fighting in the Meuse-Argonne sector produced 93,160 wounded in the American First Army between September 26 and the end of the war. The casualties had to be moved to the rear along broken, muddy roads and through traffic jams that stretched the full lengths of those roads. On top of these casualties came a completely unexpected avalanche of 68,760 medical cases, the bulk of them flu or secondary complications of that disease like pneumonia and bronchitis.

The average flu case was even more trouble than the average case of battle injury. A skyrocketing pneumonia rate convinced the United States Medical Corps that flu could not be treated cavalierly. The flu cases couldn't be sent to wait at the end of the line, nor shuffled from one hospital to the next in search of one with empty beds. To do so would be almost tantamount to murder, for the patients would be very likely to get pneumonia, and the death rate among pneumonia cases in the first half of October was 35 to 45 percent. Medical officers came out with strong recommendations of "Do not transfer patients with pneumonia or respiratory tract infections; absolute rest is as vital to them while they are meeting and overcoming the infection as operation is for penetrating wounds of the abdomen."[18]

The influenza pandemic killed more Americans in Europe during the second phase of the Meuse-Argonne offensive. The records understate the deadliest of the pandemic because they attribute to it only those deaths primarily due to flu or pneumonia. For the sake of giving Spanish influenza full credit as a destroyer of soldiers, let us consider the pandemic as a secondary cause of deaths, i.e., let us consider how many deaths primarily ascribed to wounds or gas should be secondarily blamed on the pandemic. How many wounded died in their holes, lying in rain and waiting for shelter or banging around in ambulances on congested roads, all because the whole evacuation and hospital system was clogged with an unanticipated number of flu victims?[18]

The flu epidemic during the climax of the American military campaign, compromising performance in its largest campaign of the war, the Meuse-Argonne Offensive. During that operation, influenza clogged transportation lines along the battlefront, choked hospitals, killed thousands of soldiers, and rendered many more "noneffective" – unable to conduct their training or fighting missions. Army epidemiologist Haven Emerson later observed that when the influenza epidemic struck in September it coincided "with the period of maximum American Expeditionary Forces participation in combat" and was so powerful that it overwhelmed all other diseases. "In the mass of acutely sick men, "99 of every 100 were suffering from influenza and/ or pneumonia." The War Department later calculated that the army lost a staggering 8,743,102 days to influenza among enlisted men in 1918. The flu thereby depleted and demoralized troops, and distracted military and political leaders from fighting the war to combating disease.[14]

The allied armies provided plenty of examples of how the pandemic hobbled an army's ability to fight. As the 26th Division prepared to take its place in the front line in the Argonne halfway through October, flu swept through its ranks. On October 14 the disease forced Brigadier General Shelton to give up command of the division's 51st Infantry Brigade. The disease struck Captain Nathaniel Simpkins, one of the Division Commander's most valued aides, on the twelfth, and he died ten days later. Every battalion and company lost officers and men hitherto considered indispensable.

While medical officers were responsible for enforcing War Department regulations and policing soldiers' health and behavior, they also often lobbied their superiors for more resources and authority in order to improve health conditions for the soldiers. Politically, while medical officers reported and were subordinate to the army General Command and General Staff, they did not always agree with army policies. Although medical officers did more than other officers to prevent war conditions from fostering disease, they were the ones who were put on the defensive by virulent epidemics and by soldiers' families, elected officials, and military leaders who held them accountable for the sickness and death resulting from those outbreaks. Medical officers thus often found themselves caught between their oath to the army and the nation and the Hippocratic oath.

One of the major impacts of the outbreak was on the result of the war. Though the flu hit both sides, the Germans and Austrians were affected so badly that the outbreak derailed their offensives. German General Erich Ludendorff in his memoir, My War Memories, 1914-18, wrote that the flu was one of the reasons for Germany's defeat. Germany launched its Spring Offensive on the western front in March 1918. By June and July, the disease had weakened the German units. "Our Army had suffered. Influenza was rampant...It often left a greater weakness in its wake than the doctors realized," he wrote. The Armistice was signed on November 11, 1918, that ended the War. But the flu would continue to ravage parts of the world for many more months.[18]

The statistics on what was happening to the German armed forces were harder to come by. However, the German army was badly bloodied and was yielding ground everywhere. On October 17 Ludendorff acknowledged that influenza was again raging in the German front lines. He attributed its especially lethal nature to the absolute weariness of his army: "A tired man succumbs to contagion more easily than a vigorous man." Oddly, for a few days the pandemic helped shore up the hopes of Ludendorff, Hindenburg, and even their monarch that there was still some possibility of survival for their armies. The Kaiser returned again and again to the idea that flu would somehow cripple the Allied armies while leaving his own relatively unaffected. But presently the reality of thousands of sick German soldiers on the Western Front and long lines of hearses filing out of Berlin to the cemeteries swept away this illusion.

Influenzas gummed up the German supply lines and made it harder to advance and harder to retreat. It made running impossible, walking difficult, and simply lying in the mud and breathing burdensome. From the point of view of the generals, it had a worse effect on the fighting qualities of an army than death itself. The dead were dead, and that was that: they were no longer assets, but neither were they debits. But flu took good men and made them into delirious staggering debits whose care required the diversion of healthy men from important tasks. Few things could be more troublesome to a front-line squad than a trench mate with a temperature of 104° F.

2) Trench Diseases – Two major trench diseases were trench fever (Fig.10.3) and trench foot. Trench conditions were awful. Poorly nourished, living in trench conditions, soldiers of all armies were susceptible to all of the epidemic diseases, and others besides. Most American troops spent relatively little time in the trenches and were spared the worst of trench diseases.

Trench fever was also known as quintan fever and was caused by a bacterium called Bartonella quintana found in body lice. Body lice would breed and grow in the soldiers' clothing by clinging on to the seams of the cloth. Trench fever transmission was through body louse, not by bite, but by inoculation of louse feces during scratching. Headaches, severe shin pain with tenderness, rash and continued attacks of a fever that came and went for weeks were its hallmarks. Incapacitation often lasted 60 – 70 days and was ubiquitous because lousiness was almost universal in the trenches.

Soldiers could contract the disease more than once and the number of infections rose to nearly one million at its peak. The disease was also linked to poverty, overcrowding, displacement of resources and homelessness, and could affect the civilian population as well. Fires were forbidden in the trenches. As a result, troops huddled for warmth, facilitating the transfer of body lice. If a soldier was diagnosed with the disease, it meant he would be off duty for a minimum of three months and his country would lose a valuable resource. On the other hand, its low mortality rate also made it a savior for many men who would have otherwise lost their lives on the battlefield.[8]

Trench foot was an infection which made soldiers' feet turn red or blue in color. It was a major problem during the initial stages of the war and was caused by the wet, cold, and unsanitary environment. Men would stand in waterlogged trenches for long periods of time without being able to move their legs or remove their socks. If the condition worsened it would make the legs numb and lead to gangrene and sometimes amputation. The number of cases of trench foot rose to over 75,000 in the British Army and around 2,000 in the US Army. Toward the end of the war the problem was reduced by providing dry socks, with an improved quality of boots.[12]

3) Childhood diseases – The major childhood diseases, measles, mumps, and chicken pox, could sweep through a camp. More serious diseases such as meningitis and pneumonia were a constant treat. Recruits were screened for infectious diseases at entry, which helped somewhat. Colds, and influenza were a constant problem. Disease affecting the lungs (cold and flu) if they were in combination with pneumonia would be serious. As was true with the Spanish Flu, when combined with pneumonia death was a real risk because of no antibiotics. In terms of days lost, the most important disease was mumps. There were 82,000 cases recorded in U.S. troops with only 43 deaths, but with 1 million days lost to illness. There were 8,200 cases of measles, with 86 deaths. Diphtheria struck 4,700 soldiers with 82 deaths. Meningococcal meningitis is particularly deadly. The disease can spread in populations of young people living in crowded conditions. The U.S. soldiers recorded 1,965 cases with 911 deaths.[19]

4) Malaria – Often soldiers and civilians were affected by malaria resulting from mosquitoes during the First World War, and many people died of the disease. Several sources indicate that British, French and Austria-Hungarian troops together had over 20 million cases and the number of deaths per month averaged 80,000. For the U.S. entering the war later, soldiers had less exposure to infected mosquitoes. For U.S. troops malaria, while not often fatal, was seen in 850 cases with four deaths.[12]

5) Typhoid fever – For U.S. troops typhoid claimed 1,200 cases with 155 deaths. This was a great improvement over the previous Spanish-American War with casualties' of 142/1000 soldiers, for World War I it was less than 1 per 1000 troops. Death rate was low due to a typhoid vaccine and greatly improved sanitation (e.g., clean water).

6) Smallpox – Smallpox was a reduced problem due to a near-universal vaccination. However, there were 30 cases reported with 5 deaths.

7) Diarrhea/dysentery – This was the scourge of U.S. armies in the past, but now was less of a problem as was typhoid fever due to greatly improved sanitary measures such as clean water. Nevertheless, there were 6,200 cases with 31 deaths.

8) Tuberculosis (TB) – TB was a major disease during the war but was reduced in troops due to screening for the disease. Overall, it was estimated that 10,000 soldiers served with TB. It was caused by slow breeding bacterium called *Mycobacterium tuberculosis*. There were two stages to tuberculosis: the primary and the secondary stage. The symptoms of the secondary stage included a cough, bloody sputum, weight loss, and a high temperature. Figures from the army medical department showed that 4,200 cases were recorded in the U.S. troops with 433 deaths.[12]

9) Tetanus – There was a great success in preventing and treating tetanus. U.S. troops had 500,000 wounds and injuries, with only 23 cases and no deaths. The spores of clostridium tetani are found widely in soil and can survive for a long time. Entering the body through a wound, the spores become live bacteria, and release the toxins which produce the clinical symptoms. Tetanus antiserums were used as well as surgical cleaning of wounds, greatly reducing the incidence of tetanus.[20]

10) Typhus – World War I started between Austria – Hungary and Serbia. By 1915 an enormous typhus epidemic started and killed at least 150,000 in

Serbia, causing military activity on both sides to be suspended for 6 months. During the war, typhus caused three million deaths in Russia and more in Poland and Romania. Delousing stations were established for troops on the Western Front, but the disease ravaged the armies of the Eastern Front. Fatalities were generally between 10 and 40 percent of those infected, and the disease was a major cause of death for those nursing the sick. Between 1918 and 1922 typhus caused at least 3 million deaths out of 20-30 million cases.

The disease is associated with rats and lice. A strange phenomenon of the war was the total absence of typhus from the Western Front. This is unexplained because soldiers in the trenches on this front were as universally lousy as soldiers have always been, so typhus was not a problem for U.S. troops.[8]

11) Venereal diseases – Sexually transmitted diseases, primarily syphilis and gonorrhea, were a chronic problem for all armies. The number of these infections grew massively during the war and eventually spread to the unaffected populous. At that time, the cure for venereal disease was very expensive, time-consuming and largely ineffective. In syphilis, the treatment involved mercury compounds, toxic in themselves. As these diseases led to the weakening of the fighting force, many countries introduced strict medical policies and performed medical examinations on soldiers and prostitutes to curb the disease.

The conclusion for diseases in the war was the devastation and lack of control for influenza. However, the first World War saw the rise of many well-established and new diseases, and the treatment of these diseases provided an opportunity for the medical community to research and find new cures. The research carried out during World War I into many disorders enabled us to better prepare for future global epidemics and wartime disease.

D. Summary

Highlights of World War I are noted in Table 10.1. World War I, beginning June 28, 1914, was between the Central Powers of Germany, Austria-Hungary and Ottoman Empire against the allies. There were more than 20 allied nations, with major fighting by France, Great Britain, Russia, Belgium, Italy and the United States. The U.S. did not enter the war until June 26, 1917. A major reason for the U.S. entrance into the war was due to loss of American lives resulting from German submarine warfare. It was suggested that "this was a war to end all wars." President Wilson noted concerning the war that, "the world must be safe for democracy."

The war ended after about four years, in November 1918, with the defeat of the Central Powers. The total military and civilian deaths from the war was around 40 million. For the U.S. 126,000 men died in combat of wound and disease, making this the third deadliest war in American history, despite its being the second shortest. Official War Department figures were 57,460 military personnel died of disease while 50,280 died in combat. For each American in the military who died from battle, 1.02 died of disease.

In previous wars disease had killed many more troops than had died from combat. There was great hope of better control of disease as the germ theory had been established, immunization against common diseases (e.g., smallpox), vaccines (e.g., typhoid fever, tetanus), and improved sanitation. Likewise, there was now better control of insect vectors (e.g., malaria, and yellow fever). The hope of less disease for World War I was dashed by the horrible and devastating Spanish Flu of 1918.

The Spanish flu killed many of the troops. Army physicians could do nothing to prevent the flu or the deadly pneumonia that often ensued. Once infected, patients would usually die within three days. The sum of American sailors and soldiers who died of the flu and pneumonia in 1918 was over 43,000.

Other diseases during the war included malaria, typhoid fever, smallpox, diarrhea/dysentery, tuberculosis, tetanus, typhus and venereal disease. Relatively new diseases were trench diseases, trench fever and trench foot. These diseases resulted from the conditions of trench warfare and were related to wet conditions and transfer of body lice. Childhood diseases including mumps, measles, chicken pox and meningitis were also problems.

Table 10.1
Highlights of World War I[1,2,5]

1914	
June 28	Archduke Franz Ferdinand assassinated.
July 28-Aug 4	War is declared between Central Powers (Germany, Austria-Hungary and Turkey) and allies.
August	There were 20 allied nations, with major flighting from France, Great Britain, Russia, Serbia and Belgium. Other allied nations joined the fighting including New Zealand, Canada and India.
Aug. 26-31	The Germans crushed the Russian second army at Tannenberg.
Sept. 6-9	The allies stopped the Germans in the First Battle of the Marne.
September	After the First Battle of Marne was the beginning of trench warfare, resulting in lice induced diseases trench fever and trench foot.
1915	
Early 1915	An enormous typhus epidemic killed at least 150,000 in Serbia, suspending military action for 6 months.
Feb. 18	Germany started to blockade Great Britain.
Apr. 25-Jan. 9	The British and French tried unsuccessfully to eliminate war activities for the Turkish Ottoman Empire at the Battle of Gallipoli.
May 7	A German submarine sank the liner Lusitania.
1916	
Feb. 21	The Germans opened the Battle of Verdun.
May 31-June 1	The British fleet fought the German fleet in the Battle of Jutland.
July 1-Nov. 18	Allies advanced in the Battles of the Somme, one of the bloodiest battles of the war.
1917	
Feb. 1	Germany began unrestricted submarine warfare, resulting in three U.S. ships sunk.
Apr. 2	The U.S. declared war on Germany. President Wilson noted, "the world must be safe for democracy".
June 26	American troops began landing in France.
July 31-Nov. 10	Germany stopped the allies in the third Battle of Ypres.
October	The Kaiser believed the flu would cripple the allied armies more than the Central Powers. However, the flu was equally destructive to both armies.
Dec. 15	Russia signed an armistice with Germany.
1918	
Jan 8	President Wilson announced his fourteen points (including League of Nations) as a basis for peace.
March	A deadly strain of influenza first appeared in Kansas and Georgia, USA.

Mar. 21-May 27	Germany launched offensives at Somme, Ypres and Aisne.
July 15-Aug. 6	In the Second Battle of Marne the Germans moved on Paris, but were defeated by French, British and American forces. This would be considered the turning point of the war.
August	A second wave of flu became increasingly virulent and exploded into a worldwide pandemic. The influenza attacked allied and German armies with equal virulence. The third wave was in Jan.-Feb. 1919.
Sept. 12-Nov. 11	The Germans at the Battle at St. Mihiel and Meuse-Argonne failed in their campaign on the Western Front. General Pershing and American troops struck at the German's main supply line. For the U.S. this was the largest number of American troops and casualties (117,000) in any engagement the army ever fought.
Sept. 26	The allies began their final offensive on the Western Front.
October	In military offensives in the Mihiel and Menuse-Argonne sectors of France more U.S. soldiers died of the flu than on battlefields.
Sept. 29-Nov. 11	Defeated Central Powers signed armistices ending the war.
1914-1918	The number of military and civilian casualties in World War I was around 40 million. For the war 126,000 U.S. men died of wounds and disease. Most deaths were from disease. The Spanish flu devastated both armies.

Fig. 10.1 World War I resulted in American Troops on the Western Front under General Perishing during 1917-1918.

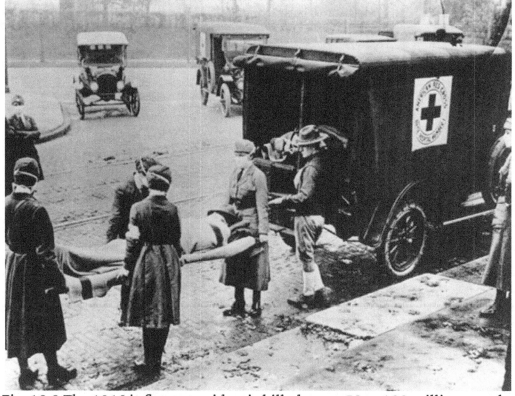

Fig. 10.2 The 1918 influenza epidemic killed some 50 to 100 million people around the world and was most serious disease during World War I.

Fig 10.3 Soldiers undergo delousing on the Serbian front of World War I, an effort to reduce diseases like trench fever.

CHAPTER 11

World War II

A. Introduction

World War II killed more persons, cost more money, damaged more property, affected more people, and probably caused more far-reaching changes than any other war in history. The number of people killed, wounded, or missing between September 1939, and September 1945, can never be calculated. More than 10 million Allied servicemen and nearly 6 million military men from the Axis countries died in the war. An estimated 45-50 million people were killed. This included 6 million Jews murdered in Nazi concentration camps as part of Hitler's diabolical "Final Solution", now known as the Holocaust. World War II cost more than $1,150,000.[1]

The causes of the great war included: (1) The problems left unsolved by World War I, (2) the rise of dictatorships, and (3) the desire of Germany, Italy, and Japan for more territory. Many believe that the roots of World War II related to the Treaty of Versailes which ended World War I. With adherence to the treaty, Germany suffered from widespread unemployment, severe currency inflation and shortages of food and raw materials. Political unrest brought the Nazis into power under Adolf Hilter. The dictatorships came into power with Hitler in Germany, Benito Mussolini in Italy, Communists under Lenin and Stalin in Russia, Francisco Franco in Spain and Emperor Hirohito of Japan.

The war pitted the Allied Powers led by Britain, the United States, Russia, Australia and France, against the Axis powers of Hitler-led Nazi Germany, Fascist Italy, and Imperial Japan. Battles were fought in almost every part of the world. More than 50 countries took part in the war, and the whole world felt its effects. Tanks were in heavy use by both sides (Fig.11.1).

B. Military Events in World War II

The following includes chronological listings of major events and battles of World War II:

a) Early Military Activities
Germany in 1938 annexed Austria and was moving against

Czechoslovakia. World War II began in September 1939 with Germany's invasion of Poland. At this time Britain and France declared war upon Germany. During this time Italy joined Germany for the war.

On September 1, 1939, Germany attacked Poland. Within a three-month period, Germany had defeated six countries – Denmark, Norway, Belgium, Luxembourg, The Netherlands, and France. They failed to knock out Great Britain by bombing and submarine blockades. In March 1941 the U.S. started a "lend-lease" program that furnished arms and aid to nations at war (e.g., Great Britain and Russia). Some historians would suggest that World War II did not begin with the invasion of Poland, but rather it started when the Japanese invaded Manchuria on September 18, 1931. Likewise, war began with Axis Power Italy, Benito Mussolini sending troops to invade Ethiopia in 1935.

b) Military Battles in Europe

1) Battle of the Atlantic (September 1939 – May 1943) – This battle began at the start of the war. Submarine warfare was destroying merchant ships. The merchant ships took to sailing in large convoys, protected by screens of destroyers and corvettes armed with depth charges and sonar. Nevertheless, daring U-Boat commanders carried out many torpedo attacks. In the end, the Battle of the Atlantic was eventually won by technology. This included radar to detect U-Boats from the surface, radio interception, and code-breaking all played a part. At wars end 3,000 merchant ships had been sunk, as well as almost 800 U-Boats.[2]

2) Battle of Britain (July to October 1940) – After the fall of France, Hitler expected the British to seek a peace settlement with Germany, but Britain continued to fight. The German invasion would only succeed with air superiority. For four months the German Luftwaffe carried out air attacks on British airfields, radar stations, aircraft factories, and British cities. The Royal Air Force was able to defeat the airpower of Germany, forcing Hitler's invasion plans to be put on hold.[3]

3) Battle of Moscow (October 1941 – January 1942) – More than a million German troops were employed to attack Moscow. For almost five weeks, the Germans drove the Red Army back, and captured thousands of prisoners. As the Germans advanced, the Russians burned or destroyed food supplies and everything else they could not move. Due to freezing weather and inability to get supplies, the Soviet defense held off the Germans. The Germans were pushed back by more than 100 miles by January. Russian casualties were heavy (approx. 4 million) but the German momentum was broken.[2]

4) Battle of Stalingrad (July 1942 – February 1943) – German artillery and airpower virtually demolished the city but failed to dislodge the defenders. Russia's defenses were based on thousands of strong points in apartments, office buildings and factories, all with orders forbidding retreat. The German army suffered many losses, after which it began its full retreat and the war turned in favor of the allies.

Some historians consider this battle the turning point of the war.[2] The battle was devastating with nearly two million military and civilian casualties. More Russian soldiers died at Stalingrad than the entire war dead of the U.S.A and Great Britain combined.

5) Battle of Normandy (D-Day) (June to August 1944) – The allies under General Dwight Eisenhower launched the largest amphibious invasion of Normandy in history to free German-occupied Western Europe (Fig.11.2). The allies had 5,000 large ships, 4,000 smaller landing craft, and more than 11,000 aircraft.

About 160,000 troops crossed the English Channel on the same day and over two million Allied troops had reached France by the end of August. The allies suffered high casualties on the beaches of Normandy. On August 25th Paris was liberated. By August 30 the German forces had retreated across the Seine.[3]

6) Battle of the Bulge (December 1944 – January 1945) – Following the D-Day invasion of June 1944, the Allies broke out of Normandy and advanced rapidly across France and Belgium. Hitler aimed to halt them by a surprise Blitzkrieg. Before the Allies could cross the Rhine, they had to face a last-stand German onslaught in the Ardennes Forest. At one point U.S. troops were surrounded and U.S. Gen. Anthony McAuliffe was asked to surrender. His interesting one-word reply was "nuts". American forces held on stubbornly despite heavy casualties – more than 19,000 died. The Germans had limited supplies and could only fight for a few days before fuel and ammunition ran out, so the offensive ended. After the battle Germany lacked resources for another offensive and the end was inevitable.[1]

7) Battle of Berlin (April – May 1945) – A final engagement was the Battle of Berlin between the Russians and Germans. It was a massive and extreme bloody action as three quarters of a million German troops, under the personal command of Hitler, fought a desperate final defense against the encroaching Red Army. The Russians had assembled more than 4 million men. Artillery demolished defensive strongpoints in a city already devastated by heavy bombing. Casualties were heavy, including thousands of civilians. From all directions, allied armies closed in on the Germans. On the 30th of April Hitler killed himself rather than surrender, effectively ending the war in Europe.[2]

C. Military Activity and Battles with Japan

1) Pearl Harbor and the U.S. going to War (December 7, 1941) – During the early part of the war in Europe, the U.S. was neutral with a policy of isolationism. However, President Roosevelt (FDR) had signed a "lend-lease" bill in March 1941 to enable the nation to furnish arms and aid to nations at war with Germany and Italy. This change in U.S. foreign policy stimulated German submarine warfare in the Atlantic.[4]

While confronting the European crisis, FDR had to deal with Japan's occupation of parts of China and French Indochina. Due to the occupations, FDR prohibited shipments of scrap iron and oil to them and froze their credit in the United States.[5] Denying Japan's access to oil and scrap iron was in the Japanese viewpoint an act of war by the United States.

On December 7, 1941, the Japanese bombed Pearl Harbor in Hawaii and America was drawn into the war (Fig.11.3). Roosevelt noted in a speech "the date would live in infamy." Four days later Germany and Italy's declarations of war against the United States brought the nation irrevocably into the war with Germany, Italy, and Japan.[6]

The devastating attack on the U.S. naval base was a complete surprise. On November 26 a Japanese fleet including six aircraft carriers, two battleships, three cruisers, and eleven destroyers sailed 275 miles north of Hawaii. About 360 planes were launched from this point for the final assault. A total of 2,403 Americans died in the attack and 1,178 others were wounded. The Japanese believed that once the U.S. fleet was out of their way, the road to conquering all of Southeast Asia and the Indonesian archipelago would open up for the Japanese.

Should FDR be condemned, at least in part, for the Pearl Harbor disaster? He certainly could be criticized for insisting on moving the Pacific Fleet to Pearl Harbor, resulting in many ships being lined up like sitting ducks. Roosevelt made Admiral H. Kimmel, Commander-in-Chief of the U.S. Fleet. Kimmel's predecessor, Admiral James Richardson, had protested FDR's decision to move the Pacific Fleet from San Diego and Long Beach to Pearl Harbor. Richardson warned him to his face, at the White House, that putting these ships in the middle of the Pacific would make them more vulnerable to attack. Stung by Richardson's opposition, FDR removed him.[7]

Far worse, did FDR deliberately encourage an assault that would move reluctant Americans who believed in isolationism to demand involvement in war. FDR had once noted that "the Japanese are notorious for attacking without warning," and the question was "how to maneuver them into firing the first shot without too much danger to ourselves.

FDR acted quickly to make sure that serious blame was not placed on himself, but rather the commanders in Honolulu with "dereliction of duty." The president appointed a commission to investigate Pearl Harbor. Supposedly FDR's panel was independent, but it was not and was chosen so there was no possibility to implicate him in the disaster.[7]

The chairman of the Senate Foreign Relations Committee, Tom Connaly frankly told FDR that he "could not understand why we were taken off our guard" at Pearl Harbor. Connaly kept asking, "Mr. President how could this thing happen?"

There was valuable intelligence that offered clues that Japan was shortly planning a spectacular surprise attack against U.S. forces in Hawaii. The chief officers Kimmel and Walter Short were not adequately informed by Washington of the imminence of war.[4]

Admiral Kimmel, who had been charged with "dereliction of duty", claimed that FDR, Marshall, and their Washington Circle had "deliberately betrayed the men in Hawaii and made me the scapegoat." They wanted to get the United States into war. FDR was the architect of the whole business. "It's obvious he wanted the Japanese to attack. May God forgive you for what you have done to me, for I never will."

Kimmel continued, "You betrayed the officers and the men of the Fleet by not giving them a fighting chance for their lives" and you betrayed me by not giving me information you knew I was entitled to." The conclusion of the Pearl Harbor disaster was that FDR was elegant in his speeches, but definitely shared in the disaster and did not come out smelling like a rose.[7]

2) Battle of Midway (June 1942) – Midway was a catastrophic defeat from which the Imperial Japanese Navy never fully recovered. Much of the credit goes to the codebreakers who revealed the Japanese's plan to ambush U.S. forces in time for the Allies to plan a counter-ambush. At the end of the two-day battle, Japan had lost four aircraft carriers and a major part of its air armada. These aircraft carriers were part of the force that attacked Pearl Harbor. The Battle of Midway proved to be one of the most decisive victories in history. It ended Japanese threats to Hawaii and to the United States.[1]

3) Battle of Guadalcanal (August 1942 – February 1943) – On Guadalcanal, the allies had success against Japanese forces in a series of battles, helping turn the tide further in the Pacific. In mid-1943, allied naval forces began an aggressive counterattack against Japan, involving a series of amphibious assaults on key Japanese-held islands in the Pacific. This "island-hopping" strategy proved successful, and allied forces moved closer to their ultimate goal of invading the Japanese mainland.[8]

4) Atomic bomb and Japan's surrender (August – September 1945) – Heavy casualties sustained in the campaigns at Iwo Jima and Okinawa, and fears of the even costlier land invasion of Japan led President Truman to authorize the use of a new and devastating weapon. The atomic bomb was unleashed on the Japanese cities of Hiroshima and Nagasaki in early August. On September 2, U.S. General Douglas MacArthur accepted Japan's formal surrender aboard the USS Missouri in Tokyo Bay.[8] Highlights for military events are noted in Table 11.1

C. Diseases during World War II

Disease, the partner of war, has often caused more deaths in past conflicts between nations than the arms of opposing forces. Conditions favorable to the communication of disease exist wherever large numbers of persons are gathered; these conditions are intensified when movements of armies and civilian populations are carried out under the stress of War. Soldiers engaged in combat may suffer a lack of food or receive food not properly prepared; the men may sleep in cold and rain and may undergo fatiguing marches which greatly lessen their powers of resistance. Civilians may be congregated for munitions work in areas where housing accommodations are poor, and sanitation facilities are limited. The use of disease as a weapon of war may add to suffering caused by the normal upward trend of disease rates.[9]

As the Second World War raged in Europe, the U.S. military recognized that infectious disease was as formidable an enemy as any other they would meet on the battlefield. So they forged a new partnership with industry and academia to develop vaccines for the troops. Vaccines were attractive to the military for the simple reason that they reduced the overall number of sick days for troops more effectively than most therapeutic measures.

This partnership generated unprecedented levels of innovation that lasted long after the war was over. As industry and academia began to work with the government in new ways to develop vaccines, they discovered that many of the key barriers to progress were not scientific but organizational.[10]

Wartime vaccine programs expanded the scope of the military's work in vaccines well beyond its traditional focus on dysentery, typhus and syphilis. These new research initiatives targeted influenza, bacterial meningitis, bacterial pneumonia, measles, mumps, neurotropic diseases, tropical diseases and acute respiratory diseases. These diseases not only posed risks to military readiness, but also to civilian populations. The first approved vaccine was for the flu. There was a great fear that a flu would return to equal the verosity of the flu of 1918-1919, which killed over 50 million worldwide. Fortunately, a severe devastating flu did not develop during World War II years.

Wartime programs, like the flu commission, developed or improved a total of 10 vaccines for diseases of military significance, some in time to meet the objectives of particular operations. For instance, botulinum toxoid was mass-produced prior to D-Day in response to (faulty) intelligence that Germany had loaded V-1 bombs with the toxin that causes botulism. Japanese encephalitis vaccine was developed in anticipation of an Allied land invasion of Japan. Some of these vaccines were crude by today's standards. In fact, some might not receive broad FDA approval today, but they were effective and timely.[10]

For the war, there was a wide range of preventative measures including immunizations against yellow fever, cholera, plague, influenza, typhus, typhoid fever, smallpox and tetanus. Vaccination was meant to curb or eliminate these diseases during the war. Also, the troops had access to antibiotics including sulfonamides and penicillin to treat both disease and wound infections. Penicillin was tested during World War II, further reducing infection and gangrene deaths. Soldiers also benefited from the availability of blood transfusions, better burn management, synthetic antimalarials and DDT. Modern medical practices and rapid evacuation of wounded also increased battlefield survivor rates. Soldiers who would have died in prior wars now survived.[11] Despite medical advances, for every two men lost to battle in the Southwest Pacific, five men were lost to disease.

Improved sanitation reduced disease casualties. There was better handling of human waste which reduced fecal contamination of food and water. Better sanitation reduced, diarrhea/dysentery, typhoid fever and other diseases.

The improved medical treatment and preventative measures resulted in a 4% died-of-wounds rate for British and American troops, (this rate was later reduced to 2.5% in Vietnam) and death rates from disease markedly fell below the killed-in-action rate of previous wars.[11]

The wartime prevalence of the five quarantinable diseases – smallpox, cholera, plague, epidemic typhus and yellow fever – was insignificant when one realizes the large numbers of men and women operating in areas in which an appreciable hazard of acquiring these diseases existed. The preventative methods protected millions of GIs from the worst of terrible, debilitating, and potentially fatal diseases. Although death from disease was greatly reduced from all previous wars involving the U.S., there still were major disease problems.

Major diseases during World War II include:

a) Malaria – The Japanese and their Axis allies were not the U.S. military's only enemies. Malaria was a threat as significant as Imperial Japan, and one that would stalk U.S. soldiers, sailors, and marines across the islands of the Pacific, around the Mediterranean, and onto the Asian mainland. Malaria also threatened recruits in training camps across the southern and western U.S.

The global threat was made clear shortly after Pearl Harbor. In the days and weeks that followed, U.S. and allied troops and installations were hit hard in the Philippine Islands. The Japanese overran Bataan on April 9, 1942, while the island fortress of Corregidor surrendered on May 9th. When the fortress capitulated, 85 percent of the garrison was suffering from malaria.[12] Over the next four years, malaria proved to be the number one medical problem of World War II, often accounting for more U.S. casualties than the Japanese.

United States victory in the Pacific was tied to the fate of a number of research and development programs. Most famous of these were the Manhattan Project, which produced the atomic bombs, and the Radiation Laboratory, which helped develop radar. Less famous was the antimalarial program, which would safeguard the health and lives of millions of GIs sent to malarious locations around the globe. In 1939, U.S. public health officials and malariologists began to act in response to a looming world war.

The National Research Council (NRC) – a nongovernmental body established by Congress to advise the federal government on technical and scientific matters – put together a Committee on Chemotherapy, focused first and foremost on drugs for malaria. Also, scientists and policy makers at the Rockefeller Foundation expanded their antimalarial programs and discussed how best to proceed in a time of national emergency. For all these concerned experts, priority would shift from issues of combating malaria in peaceful civilian populations to dealing with the disease in conditions of combat and disruption. Joined by their counterparts from the U.S. Army and Navy, they convened a series of conferences and began soliciting and exchanging research on combating malaria. The wartime malaria work was arguably the largest biomedical research program up to this time and a model – both practical and rhetorical – for postwar biomedical research. All this was a sudden response to a disease that had been around for thousands of years.

After Pearl Harbor, the antimalarial program became critical to the war effort. Java (Indonesia) fell to the Japanese in March 1942, cutting off the United States from the source of 90 percent of the world's supply of quinine. With the United States preparing to send millions of troops into malarious areas of the world, the need to replace quinine became acute.

Malaria has had an enormous impact on human populations. Because of the complexity of the disease – malaria is caused by several mosquito-borne protozoans – and its widespread incidence, it had been the subject of research programs on more than one occasion. For the United States, malaria's peak year was 1933, with 125,000 cases reported resulting in 5,000 deaths. The disease was essentially eliminated in the United States by the 1950s, but it drew considerable attention during World War II. While the United States has been malaria-free, it is instructive to recall that throughout much of modern history, including much of the twentieth century, malaria was an endemic disease in large parts of the continental United States, and a persistent problem for military and colonial personnel in many parts of the world.

With regard to the number of people killed, malaria remains one of the deadliest diseases in the world. It has been so for millennia. For every person killed by malaria, there are hundreds who are made sick by the malaria parasites. Exact numbers are hard to know because malaria's scourge is worst in some of the poorest places on earth. The WHO believes that malaria kills one to two million people each year, most of them children under the age of six in Sub-Saharan Africa. Out of the hundreds of millions who are infected, the disease causes serious illness in 10 to 20 million people. It is one of the most frequent causes of sickness and death in the world today, a role it has apparently enjoyed throughout most of human history.[13]

Malaria is caused by a single celled protozoan parasite that is larger and a more complex organism than bacteria. Taxonomically, the parasite belongs to the genus *Plasmodium*. Over 100 species of *Plasmodium* infect birds, reptiles, and mammals. For the human disease complex, there are four recognized species of *Plasmodium: falciparum, vivax, malariae,* and *ovale.* In the case of the *falciparum* malaria, the deadliest kind, its DNA sequence – its genetic fingerprint – is available on the Internet. During the last 175 years, many of malaria's secrets emerged from diverse research projects in many countries. By World War II, most of malaria's basic biology was known. In the confines of military medicine during World War II, it was *P. vivax* and *P. falciparum* that figured most prominently. All four species share characteristic febrile episodes – with chills, rigors, and sweating – as well as a range of other possible symptoms overlapping with those of other illnesses: nausea, headaches, body aches, and general weakness.

All these species of malaria transmit the blood-born microscopic malaria from host to host. The bite of an infected female mosquito is a requisite for nourishing mosquito eggs, the *Plasmodium* enter the bloodstream, via the mosquito's saliva, in a form known as sporozoites.

The control of malaria also has a long history. Eliminating the wetlands associated with fever is an ancient approach. In the seventeenth century, cinchona bark entered the European pharmacopeia. The bark's active principal, quinine, was isolated at the beginning of the nineteenth century. Later, once the parasites and the vector mosquitoes were known, other modes of attack on malaria opened up. Killing or inhibiting the parasites and the mosquitoes at any stage of their complex life cycles were potential avenues for limiting disease. Most famous on the environmental side is the use of DDT (dichloro-diphenyl-trichloroethane) to kill mosquitoes with regard to biomedical history of malaria control, drug development takes center stage.

Quinine is an old antimalarial that predates modern understanding of malaria's etiology. Quinine was valuable because of its capacity to control certain fevers. The close of the war saw the advent of a new wonder drug against malaria, chloroquine. Though still in use today chloroquine's efficacy has been severely limited by the rise of drug-resistant strains of malaria.

Overall, the program was a great success. World War II was the first major U.S. conflict in which fewer U.S. soldiers died of diseases than of contact injuries. While malaria in the developed world was all but vanished in the second half of the 20th century, it continued to kill millions in the developing world. Even today, malaria kills millions every year.

b) Typhus – Typhus was a devastating disease for humans and was responsible for hundreds of thousands of deaths during WWII.[14] There were many deaths in German concentration camps. The causative organism is *Rickettsia prowazekii* transmitted by the human body louse. There was another type of typhus referred to as "scrub typhus" that was spread by a chigger or mite. Typhus fever is caused by the bacteria *Salmonella typhi*. Vaccines and antibacterial treatments were available and generally successful at curing affected individuals.

Prior to major war efforts in 1939, Italy had invaded Ethiopia in 1935 – 1936. They found a high incidence of typhus among Ethiopians. To prevent typhus the Italians had instituted rigid methods of cleanliness, including delousing stations, at the beginning of the war. They were able to report no cases of typhus in their army of 500,000.

In Europe the Germans were reported to be taking measures against the spread of typhus fever found among Polish prisoners of war as early as October 1939. Typhus had reached epidemic proportions in many places in eastern Europe. The Germans closed some areas to travel and took stringent measures to prevent a typhus epidemic in Germany proper.

During World War II, typhus struck the German Army during Operation Barbarossa, the invasion of Russia, in 1941. In 1942 and 1943 typhus hit French North Africa, Egypt and Iran particularly hard.[15]

c) Hepatitis – A World War II hepatitis outbreak was the biggest in history. The hepatitis B virus was responsible for an outbreak of jaundice that struck 50,000 soldiers after they received yellow fever vaccines during the war. Nearly all U.S. and other allied troops had been vaccinated against yellow fever. The outbreak was blamed on yellow fever vaccine that was made with human blood serum. Researchers estimated that 427,000 doses were drawn from the contaminated lots of vaccine. Perhaps 330,000 men were infected with or exposed to the hepatitis B virus over a six-month period in 1941 and 1942, and about 1 in 7 of them became sick.[16]

d) Influenza – The prospect of an influenza epidemic as severe as the First World War was announced in October 1941. Doctors from the St. Louis Health Division noted that influenza had reached epidemic proportions in 25 to 30 percent in communities in December 1940. Nevertheless, the winter of 1941-42 had seen no epidemic of influenza; reports to the United States Health Service for the week ended January 10, 1942, showed only 3,800 cases throughout the nation as compared with 77,820 cases for the corresponding week of 1941. For the military influenza did not have a significant effect on troop strength compared to the devastating pandemic of 1918-1919 during World War I.[10]

e) Tuberculosis – War and armed conflict have a long and well-established impact on morbidity and mortality from tuberculosis (TB). Increases in TB infection, disease, and death are seen in times of war, forced population displacement, and natural disasters. These crises result in conditions that promote the transmission and reactivation of TB, including population crowding and immunosuppression from famine and other infectious conditions.

During World War I TB was reported in 4,200 troops with 433 deaths. However, the incidence of TB and death during World War II as one tenth those seen in World War I. This dramatic decline is attributable not only to the declining incidence of TB in the general U.S. population, but also to the improved screening methods of identifying TB cases and excluding them from entry into service.[17]

f) Typhoid fever – For previous wars typhoid fever resulted in 2,000 deaths during the Spanish American War but only 155 during World War I. For World War II the death rate was very low due to a typhoid vaccine, proper sanitation and isolation.[9]

g) Venereal diseases – Venereal diseases were a leading health problem in the Army and Navy, although the present degree of infection among service men is said to be only about 25 percent of that shown by statistics for the period of the First World War. Surgeon General McIntire of the Navy told a regional conference on social hygiene at New York that the venereal morbidity rate in the Navy and Marine Corps had been 7 percent lower in 1941 than in 1940. He said social diseases could be as deadly as enemy fire in crippling fighting men and called for a public program to reduce infection by curbing prostitution.[9]

Control measures generally had so far prevented communicable diseases (except venereal diseases) from gaining foothold in the armed forces of the United States. Assistant Surgeon, General Vonderlehr said at Cincinnati, February 4, that a rise in syphilis rates was to be expected as a result of war conditions and that venereal diseases ranked second only to battle casualties in rendering manpower ineffective.[18]

h) **Diarrhea/dysentery** – These diseases result from poor sanitation, typically the result of unsanitary water that contains micro-organisms, which damage the intestine. These diseases are spread to healthy individuals from carriers who harbor and excrete the bacteria in their stools. There had been lack of sanitation which had allowed feces to contaminate water and food. Flies had spread feces to food.

Diarrhea/dysentery had been great problems of past wars but starting with World War I the diseases were greatly reduced by good hygiene and sanitization. These diseases were further reduced but not eliminated during World War II.

The average strength of the Army for the years 1942-45 was approximately 6,076,135 men. Within this population and time, 523,331cases of diarrhea and dysentery were reported, a crude rate of 21 per annum per 1,000 average strength. In late 1942 and in 1943, increasing numbers of troops entered North Africa and the Mediterranean, the Middle East, and the China-Burma-India theaters, all north of the Equator. Rates for the total Army rose to 25 per 1,000 and for troops overseas to 66 per 1,000, the 1943 annual rate for all overseas troops being the highest of the war. Rates for the total Army were better in 1944 and 1945, 22 and 22, respectively. Rates overseas fell from 66 in 1943, to 38 in 1944, and to 33 in 1945. Total deaths ascribed to diarrheal disorders were 64 for World War II.[19]

i) **Vitamin deficiencies** – Poor diets for the troops or the general population resulted in vitamin deficiencies.[20] Without a variety of foods, soldiers became malnourished. Some of the vitamin deficiencies diseases reported were beriberi (vitamin B, or thiamin), scurvy (vitamin C) and pellagra (niacin).

Beriberi resulted for troops isolated on the Bataan Peninsula, those on Guadalcanal, and American prisoners of war held by the Japanese subsisted on diets largely of rice. The prisoners were provided a very white "polished rice". A less processed rice would have provided adequate thiamin to prevent beriberi.[20]

In relation to vitamin C, each Italian soldier received a lemon a day so that there were few cases of scurvy. Based on poor diets in Ethiopians, however, scurvy was a problem. The Ethiopian Red Cross reported some 30,000 cases of scurvy along the Somaliland front.[9]

j) Jungle Rot – "Jungle rot" was a term used to describe conditions that resulted from an inability to stay dry. "New Guinea Crud" or "the Creeping Cruds" were terms used by soldiers to describe all kinds of tropical skin disease. These could be similar to aggravated athletes' foot-a fungus infection on the trunk, thighs, face, and scalp. Rashes, impetigo, and scabies also did occur. Treatments for soldiers were to clean the area, paint it with silver nitrate, dress it, and avoid sweating.[21]

k) Other diseases and conditions – Other diseases or conditions affected the military but were much less than the widespread diseases of pandemics. These would include pneumonia, rheumatic fever, scabies, meningitis, dengue fever, trench diseases (trench fever and trench foot), leishmaniasis, childhood diseases, mustard gas poisoning and conditions resulting from extreme cold (e.g., Battle of the Bulge) and heat.

Battlefield fatigue and post-traumatic stress disorder (PTSD) were common for World War II soldiers. Long days, weeks, and months in combat, separation from family, the loss of friends and companions, diseases, heat, rain, lack of food and clean water – all contributed to everyday problems of soldiers.

August 14, 1945, victory over Japan (V-J) Day, marked the end of the war, but not the end of the suffering. Those brave men and women, who endured so much on the battlefields, came home with a variety of post-disease and post-war effects. Suffering from disease and wound complication, service-related hearing loss and/or blindness, skin scarring disorders, and PTSD were common, but not always acknowledged. Long-term effects included skin cancer, parasites, alcoholism, adjustment disorders, and suicide.[21]

D. Diseases of German prison camps and during the Holocaust – In the German prisons and Nazi concentration camps, of the many things that were horrible was disease. Some of the diseases present included malaria, typhus, typhoid, scabies, dysentery, and tuberculosis. The massive amount of disease was due to poor conditions in the camps. As there were no working sewer systems, excrement was everywhere. The people in the camps were not able to clean themselves readily as there were few showers available, and they did not have a change of clothes. Also, disease ran rampant because there were few, if any cures for them, and they had very few doctors in the camps. The doctors that were in the camps were most likely prisoners, and they had no medicine or instruments.

Typhus epidemics killed thousands of prisoners held in appalling conditions in German concentration and death camps such as Auschwitz, Theresienstadt, and Bergen-Belsen during World War II. Of the epidemics, typhus claimed the greatest number of lives. Many prisoners also suffered from tuberculosis, malaria, meningitis, dysentery and typhoid fever. The winter, and also late fall and early spring, saw numerous cases of colds, pneumonia, and frostbite which developed not infrequently into gangrene. The dreadful sanitation conditions caused skin diseases, and above all scabies. Almost all prisoners suffered from boils, rashes, and abscesses that resulted mostly from vitamin deficiency and infections. In camp conditions, all these illnesses were highly acute. A characteristic camp illness was starvation sickness. It was usually accompanied by diarrhea (often bloody), swollen legs, impaired vision and hearing, memory loss, nervous breakdown and, above all, exhaustion to the point of collapse. The majority of prisoners suffered from several medical conditions simultaneously.[22]

Thousands of prisoners as well as Jews and others in concentration camps died of starvation, disease, exhaustion, exposure and brutal treatment. Contagious diseases spread rapidly in such cramped, unsanitary housing. The Holocaust victims were murdered or died of starvation, disease, and persecution. Six million Jews were murdered by the Nazi regime and its allies.[23]

E. Japanese Prisoners of War (POW) – They suffered from brutal mistreatment and disease. The 140,000 allied POW captured by the Japanese during World War II endured horrific cruelties and a comparatively high percentage did not survive. While the death rate of POWs in German camps was about 4 percent, it is generally agreed that the allied POW death rate in Japanese camps was estimated at between 27 to 38%. The relatively high death toll in Japanese camps is partly due to brutal mistreatment and executions (Fig.11.4). Many of the Japanese captors were cruel toward the POWs because they were viewed as contemptible for the very act of surrendering. The guards were conditioned to consider that inhumane treatment was no less than what the POWs deserved; real warriors die.[24] In addition, as the tide of war turned against Japan and its extended supply lines became more vulnerable, the flow of food and medicine declined to camps scattered across Southeast Asia. Moreover, friendly fire caused about one in four POW deaths as the U.S. attacked Japanese convoys, sinking many ships transporting POWs back to Japan because they were unmarked.

Most POWs worked as slave laborers to keep Japan's heavy industry going. They were put to work in mines, fields, shipyards and factories on a diet of about 600 calories a day. Some of the worst conditions and hardship of POWs were those that were sent to build the Burma-Thailand railway. Prisoners of war and Asian laborers worked side by side to build the 260-mile railroad by hand. They were expected to work from dawn to dusk, ten days on and one day off, moving earth, building bridges, blasting through mountains and laying track. Around 61,000 prisoners were put to work on the railroad. Of those 13,000 died. At this location prisoners suffered from malnutrition, ulcers and cholera.

The high death toll was also due to the POWs' susceptibility to tropical diseases due to malnutrition and immune systems adapted to temperate climates. The average prisoner received less than a cup of filthy rice a day. The amount was so meagre that gross malnutrition led to loss of vision or unrelenting nerve pain. Diseases were abundant. Malaria and dysentery were almost universal. Dysentery reduced men to living skeletons. Tropical ulcers were particularly gruesome.

From a Japanese prison camp in Thailand, most ulcers were caused by bamboo scratches incurred when working naked in the jungle…Leg ulcers of over a foot in length and maybe six inches in breadth, with bone exposed and rotting for several inches, were not an uncommon sight.

Diseases besides malaria, dysentery and ulcers, included cholera, typhoid, diphtheria, dengue, typhus, smallpox, blackwater fever (complication of malaria) and tuberculosis. Cholera came in terrifying epidemics, particularly when the monsoon season hit more remote jungle camps, the mortality rate was high. The nematode worm *strongyloides stercoalis* was endemic to tropical areas. *Strongylides* dinfections (with various other intestinal parasites) where diagnosed at some of the larger camps (with microscopical facilities) on the Thai-Burma Railway, with no treatment available.[25]

With the predominantly rice diets, there were vitamin deficiencies. This included thiamin (vitamin B_1) deficiency as beriberi, night blindness due to vitamin A deficiency and pellagra due to niacin deficiency. Likewise, there would have been riboflavin deficiencies. An obvious symptom of riboflavin deficiency was scrotal dermatitis.[20]

When the war was looking like the allies would be invading Japan, prisoners were moved further away from the coast. The official policy of Japan when an invasion began was to behead, bury alive or shoot all prisoners. Instead of invasion Japan was asked to surrender or the U.S. would employ a devastating weapon. Japan refused and the atomic bomb was unleashed on the cities of Hiroshima and Nagasaki. Japan surrendered and war prisoners were eventually released.

The horrors of cannibalism for captive Americans at Chi Chi Jima were learned after the war. The Japanese admitted that eight captured American fliers were executed for the purpose of getting more meat to eat. The meat was cooked and consumed, none of the Japanese liked the taste as they knew it was human flesh.[26]

Highlights of Medical procedures and Diseases in World War II is noted in Table 11.2.

D. Summary

World War II began in September 1939 and was over in September 1945. The main allied powers were led by Britain, the United States, Russia, Australia and France against the axis powers of Nazi Germany, Fascist Italy and Imperial Japan. Actually, more than 50 countries took part in the war. The war killed more people, damaged more property and affected more people than any other war in history. An estimated 45-50 million people were killed. The main causes of the war involved unsolved problems from World War I, the rise of dictatorships and desire for more territory by Germany, Italy and Japan.

Military activities leading up to the war included in 1931 Japan invading Manchuria, and Germany in 1938 annexing Austria and moving against Czechoslovakia. Also Italy invaded Ethiopia in 1935. In September German troops invaded Poland resulting in Britain and France declaring war on Germany. During the early part of the war in Europe, the U.S. was neutral with a policy of isolationism. German submarine warfare was pushing the U.S. towards war, but the final push for war came on December 7, 1941, when the Japanese bombed Pearl Harbor. On December 11, the U.S. declared war on Japan, Germany and Italy.

The far-reaching conflict, World War II, saw an unprecedented number of engagements as axis and allies sought to achieve victory. By the time the U.S. entered the war only Britain and Russia of the major allies remained undefeated.

Important early battles in Europe were the Battle of the Atlantic, Battle of Britain and Battle of Moscow. An important battle for Russia was defeating the Germans in the Battle of Stalingrad (February 1943). This battle was devastating with nearly two million military and civilian casualties. More Russian soldiers died at Stalingrad than the entire war dead of the U.S. and Britain combined.

The allies, under General Dwight Eisenhower, in the Battle of Normandy (June 1944) launched the largest amphibious invasion of Normandy to free German-occupied western Europe. This was followed by the Battle of the Bulge (December 1944) which forced the Germans to retreat. In the final engagement, the Battle of Berlin (May 1945), Russian troops defeated the Germans. Hitler had killed himself, effectively ending the war in Europe.

The Pearl Harbor surprise attack (December 7, 1941) brought the U.S. into

World War II. The Japanese fleet included six aircraft carriers, two battleships, three cruisers, eleven destroyers and about 360 planes. They destroyed many ships, planes and caused 2,403 American deaths. The Japanese believed that by destroying much of the U.S. fleets, they could conquer all of southeast Asia. For the war with Japan, a major battle was the Battle of Midway (June 1942). This provided one of the most decisive victories with the defeat of the Imperial Japanese Navy, this ended threats to Hawaii and the United States.

In the Battle of Guadalcanal (August 1942 – February 1943) the allies had success against Japanese forces in a series of battles, helping turn the tide further in the Pacific. There were heavy casualties in the final two Japanese Battles of Iwo Jima and Okinawa. There was a fear of even a costlier land invasion of Japan, therefore President Truman authorized the atomic bombing of the cities of Hiroshima and Nagasaki. Japan surrendered on September 2, 1945, thus ending World War II.

Diseases during wars had always caused more deaths than the arms of opposing forces. The disease rate was less for World War I than previous wars. Disease rate was further reduced for World War II. As the war was raging in Europe the U.S. military forged a new partnership with industry and academia to develop vaccines for the troops. Wartime programs developed or improved 10 vaccines. As a result, for the U.S. wartime prevalence of the quarantinable diseases of smallpox, cholera, plague, typhus and yellow fever were insignificant when considering many individuals coming together. Nevertheless, disease was an important factor during the war.

Improved sanitation reduced disease casualties. Better handling of human waste reduced fecal contamination of food and water. Improved sanitation reduced diarrhea/dysentery, typhoid fever and other diseases. Also, the troops had access to antibiotics including sulfonamides and penicillin for treating diseases and wounds. Likewise, also reducing death rates were blood transfusion, better burn management and rapid evacuation of wounded.

Although death from disease was greatly reduced from all previous major wars involving the U.S., there still remained disease problems. Death rates from disease were less for the war in Europe versus the more tropical regions in battles with Japanese. Despite medical advances, for every two men lost to battle in the Southwest Pacific, five men were lost to disease.

Malaria was the number one medical problem of the war, often surpassing casualties resulting from the Japanese. It is one of the deadliest diseases of the world. For every person killed by malaria, there are hundreds who are made sick by the malaria parasites. An antimalarial program safeguarded the health and lives of millions of GIs sent to malarious locations around the globe. Malaria was best treated with quinine. This became a problem as Java, Indonesia fell to the Japanese in early 1942, cutting the U.S. off from the greatest source of quinine. The U.S. was able to develop a new wonder drug against malaria named chloroquine. Mosquitoes are responsible for transferring the disease to humans. On the environmental side the use of the insecticide DDT for killing mosquitoes was important in controlling the disease in some areas.

The diseases of typhus and typhoid fever were not serious problems for U.S. troops due to vaccines and proper sanitation and isolation. Rates of tuberculosis were low due to improved screening methods prior to troop enlistments. Due to better sanitation deaths from diarrhea/dysentery were greatly reduced from previous wars. Like other wars venereal diseases were a problem and was believed to be ranked second to battle casualties in rendering manpower ineffective. With poor diets vitamin deficiencies resulted in beriberi, scurvy and pellagra. Other disease conditions included pneumonia, rheumatic fever, scabies, meningitis, dengue fever, trench disease, childhood diseases, mustard gas poisoning and conditions of extreme cold or heat.

In the German prisons and Nazi concentration camps, of the many things horrible was disease. Typhus epidemics killed thousands in German concentration and death camps. Many prisoners also suffered from tuberculosis, malaria, meningitis, dysentery and typhoid fever. In winter there were colds, pneumonia and frostbite which often developed into gangrene. Dreadful sanitation conditions caused scabes and other skin diseases. A characteristic camp illness was starvation sickness, accompanied by diarrhea, swollen legs, impaired vision and hearing and memory loss. Thousands of prisoners as well as Jews and others died in concentration camps of starvation, disease and exhaustion. Six million Jews were murdered by the Nazi regime.

Japanese prisoners of war (POW) suffered from brutal mistreatment and disease. The death rate of POWs in German camps was about 4% compared to an estimated death rate in Japanese camps between 27% to 38%. There was brutal mistreatment and many executions. The high death toll was also due to the POWs susceptibility to tropical diseases, because of malnutrition and immune systems adapted to temperate climates. Malaria and dysentery were almost universal. Dysentery reduced men to living skeletons. Other diseases were ulcers, cholera, typhoid, diphtheria, dengue, typhus, smallpox, black water fever, parasites and tuberculosis. Cholera came in the monsoon season, with mortality rates high. After the war the horrors of cannibalism were learned for some captive Americans.

Table 11.1 Highlights of World War II[1]

1931	
Sept. 18	Japan invaded Manchuria in North China.
1935	
Invasion of Ethiopia by Italians.	
1938	
March	Germany annexed Austria and Czechoslovakia.
1939	
Sept. 1	German troops invaded Poland.
Sept. 3	Britain and France declared war on Germany.
1940	
Apr. 9	Germany attacked Denmark and Norway.
May-June	Germany in control of Denmark, Norway, Belgium, Luxembourg, Holland and France.
Sept. 22	Japan pushed into French Indochina.
1941	
Apr. 6	Germany invaded Greece and Yugoslavia.
June 22	Axis forces invaded Russia.
Dec. 7	Japanese attacked Pearl Harbor.
Dec. 8-11	The U.S. declares war on Japan, Germany and Italy.
1942	
Jan. 2	Manila fell to invading Japanese forces.
Feb. 27	Allies lost the Battle of Java Sea.
Apr. 18	U.S. carrier-based aircraft bombed Tokyo.
Apr. 19	Japanese overran Batan.
May 4-8	The allies won the Battle of Coral Sea.
June 4-6	The Battle of Midway ended Japan's expansion eastward.
July 2	The British halted the Germans at El. Alamein.
Aug. 7	U.S. marines landed on Guadalcanal.
Nov. 7-8	Allied forces landed in North Africa.

Nov. 19	The Russians counterattacked at Stalingrad.
1943	
March 2-5	Allies defeated a Japanese naval force in Battle of Bismark Sea.
May 12	Organized axis resistance in Africa ended.
July 10 – Sept. 3	Allied forces invaded Sicily and Italy.
Nov. 6	The Russians recaptured Kiev.
Nov. 20	U.S. marines invaded Tarawa and Makin.
1944	
Jan 27	Russians broke the siege of Leningrad.
Apr. 22	Allied forces landed at Hollandia.
June 6	The allies landed in Normandy, France.
June 19-20	U.S. forces won the Battle of the Philippine Sea.
June 21	U.S. troops landed on Guam Island.
July 25	U.S. forces broke out of Normandy.
Aug. 15	Allied troops landed in southern France.
Dec. 16	Germans began the Battle of the Bulge.
Dec. 27	The allies halted the German offensive.
1945	
Jan. 9	Allied troops invaded Luzon, Philippines.
Feb. 19	U.S. marines stormed Iwo Jima Island.
Apr. 11	U.S. troops landed on Okinawa Island.
Apr. 22	The Russians reached the suburbs of Berlin.
Apr. 25	U.S. and Russian forces met at Torgau.
May 2	German troops in Italy surrendered.
May 7	Germany surrendered to the allies.
Aug. 6	U.S. dropped an atomic bomb on Hiroshima.
Aug. 9	U.S. dropped an atomic bomb on Nagasaki.
Sept. 8	Japan signed the terms of surrender.

Table 11.2
Medical Procedures and Diseases in World War II

1935-1945
Wartime programs developed or improved 10 vaccines for diseases of military significance.
Military used antibiotics including sulfonamides and penicillin to treat disease and wound infections.
To prevent and treat malaria synthetic antimalarials were developed.
To control malaria the insecticide DDT was used to kill mosquitoes.
Rapid evacuation of wounded troops increased battlefield survivor rates.
Improved sanitation reduced disease casualties.
During the invasion of Ethiopia in 1935 by Italians, 25,000 cases of typhoid fever for Ethiopians was discovered.
In 1939 typhus reached epidemic proportions among Polish prisoners of war.
Wartime prevalence of quarantinable diseases – smallpox, cholera, plague, typhus and yellow fever – were insignificant when considering large number of individuals together, compared to previous wars.
From receiving yellow fever vaccine, 330,000 allied troops were exposed to hepatitis B virus
In March 1942 Java fell to Japan, eliminating quanine for treatment of malaria.
In April 1942 when Japanese overran Bataan 85 percent of garrison had malaria.
Despite medical advances, for every two men lost to battle in the southwest Pacific, five men were lost to disease.
Malaria was the number one medical problem of World War II, often resulting in more causalities than from the Japanese.
Cases of diarrhea and dysentery were 21 per annum per 1,000 troops, very low compared to previous war. Lower incidence was mainly due to improved sanitation.
Jungle Rot described all kinds of tropical skin diseases.
Rates of tuberculosis were one tenth of the incidence of World War I. Most of this was due to improved screening methods to deny entry into service.
Venereal diseases were 25% less than in World War I.
Vitamin deficiencies were found mostly in concentration camps and prisons, the most common diseases were beriberi (Thiamin), scurvy (vitamin C), pellagra (niacin) and scrotal dermatitis (riboflavin).
In German prison camps and during Holocaust, there were high levels of disease including malaria, typhus, typhoid, scabies, dysentery, tuberculosis and starvation.
Typhus epidemics killed thousands of prisoners at German concentration and death camps at Auschwitz, Theresienstadt and Bergen-Belsen .
During the Holocaust in Germany many died from being murdered or died from starvation, disease and persecution. This included six million Jews and many others during the Nazi regime.

There was a high death toll for Japanese prisoners of war from tropical diseases due to malnutrition and immune systems adapted to temperate climates.

In Japanese prisons malaria and dysentery were almost universal, with tropical ulcers particularly gruesome. Other diseases included cholera, typhoid, diphtheria, dengue, typhus, smallpox, and tuberculosis and the nematode worm strongyloides.

The horrors of cannibalism for captive Americans at Chi Chi Jima were learned after the war.

Fig. 11.1 Tanks were in heavy use during World War II by both sides.

Fig. 11.2 President Roosevelt promoted Dwight D. Eisenhower Commander of allied Forces in Europe for World War II.

Fig. 11.3 On December 7, 1941, the Japanese bombed Pearl Harbor, Hawaii, resulting in a declaration of war.

Fig. 11.4 Japanese prisoners of war suffered from brutal mistreatment, execution and death.

CHAPTER 12

Korean War

A. Introduction

The Korean War began June 25, 1950, when North Korea crossed the border into South Korea and ended with a Korean armistice July 27, 1953. The war was between North Korea (with support of China and the Soviet Union) and South Korea (with the support of the United Nations, principally from the U.S.)

a) Background – Japan had conquered Korea during World War II. With the surrender of Japan, at the end of World War II, Korea was divided at the 38th parallel into two zones of separation. The Soviet Union administered North Korea making it Communist, while the U.S. administered South Korea making it a Capitalist state with a form of democracy.

After the Communist North Korea attacked South Korea, President Truman promptly urged the United Nations to intervene. The United Nations Security Council denounced Communist North Korea's invasion and authorized the formation of the United Nations Command and the dispatch of forces to Korea to repel it. These UN decisions were taken without participation of the Soviet Union and the People's Republic of China, both of which supported North Korea. Sixteen UN countries sent troops to help the South Koreans, and 41 countries sent military equipment or food and other supplies. The United States sent more than 90 percent of the troops, military equipment, and supplies. Truman had sent in U.S. troops without Congressional authorization. He had referred to the war as a "police action" and some legislators referred to the action as "Mr. Truman's War".[1]

b) Effect of the war – The Korean War was one of the bloodiest wars in history. About a million South Korean civilians were killed and several million were made homeless. About 580,000 UN and South Korean troops and about 1,600,000 Communist troops were killed or wounded or were reported missing. Almost 40,000 Americans died in action, and more than 100,00 were wounded. Truman kept the war a limited one, rather than risk a major conflict with China and perhaps Russia.[2]

The war in the air resulted in massive U.S. bombing in North Korea. Jet fighters confronted each other in air-to-air combat for the first time in history, and Soviet pilots covertly flew in defense of their communist allies. The war incurred the destruction of virtually all of Korea's major cities, thousands of massacres by both sides, including the mass killing of tens of thousands of suspected Communists by the South Korean government, and the torture and starvation of prisoners of war by the North Korean command. North Korea became among the most heavily bombed countries in history.

B. Military activity

Directly after the end of World War II, the Cold War began which was a battle between the ideas of Communism and Democracy. The Korean War was the first test of the Cold War between the Communists, led by Russia and China and mostly democracies with the U.S. contributing the most. For North and South Korea, the conflict was a Civil War, a struggle with no possible compromise between two competing visions for Korea's future. For the war that erupted in 1950, there were six months of combat raging up and down the Korean peninsula before settling into years of trench warfare. The major battles and actions are as follows:

1) First Battle of Seoul – The first Battle of Seoul was part of an invasion of South Korea by North Korea at the start of the Korean War. On June 25, 1950, supported by the Soviet Union and China, the North Korean troops using the blitzkrieg-style invasion crossed the 38th parallel. Northern forces overwhelm the ill-equipped defenders and captured Seoul in three days. The United Nations condemns the attack and creates a "police" force to help defend South Korea.[3]

2) Air Battles of South Korea – The Air Battle of South Korea was an air campaign in the Korean War occurring roughly from June 25 to July 20, 1950, over South Korea between the air forces of North Korea and the United Nations, including the countries of South Korea, the United States and the United Kingdom. This ended in victory for the UN Air Force, which destroyed the North Korean People's Air Force.[4]

3) Battle of Pusan – On July 5, 1950, the first U.S. Marines, leading the UN force, join battle shortly after landing on the Korean Peninsula (Fig.12.1). U.S. troops suffer heavy casualties, and the four American divisions are driven back into a perimeter around the southern port city of Pusan.[4]

4) Battle of Inchon – On September 15, 1950, U.S. Gen. Douglas MacArthur, Commander of UN forces makes a bold military move and lands an amphibious invasion force of 80,000 Marines at the port of Inchon. This cut off North Korean troops, allowing UN forces to break out of the Pusan parameter. The battle also ended a series of victories by the Communist troops and severed the supply line of the Communist army. On Sept. 26, 1950, Seoul was retaken after house-to-house fighting (Fig.12.2). MacArthur orders troops to continue chasing the retreating North Korean army across the 38th Parallel.[5]

5) China enters the war – On Nov. 25, 1950, China, issuing warnings against the UN that it should cease aggressions against North Korea, sets a trap to crush MacArthur's army. Chinese forces, numbering 300,000 invaded North Korea and pushed UN troops southward in a disorganized, hasty retreat.[1]

6) Battle of Chosin Reservoir – U.S. Marine troops with their backs to the Sea of Japan fought in a brutally cold winter from Nov. 7 to Dec. 9, 1950. Encircled at the Chosin Reservoir, U.S. Marines retreated to the ports of Hungnam and Wonsan. This was known as the Battle of "Frozen Chosin", there were over 5,000 frostbite casualties.[3]

7) Fourth Battle of Seoul – The South Korean capital of Seoul changes hands for the last time as UN troops recapture the battered city on March 18, 1951. MacArthur's army advances slightly north of the 38th Parallel.[3]

8) Operation Courageous – The operation took place between March 23rd and 28th, 1951, to trap a larger number of Communist army troops between the Han and Imjin Rivers. The Communist troops were forced to withdraw from the operation zone allowing the U.S. troops to pursue them.

9) Leadership change for UN – On April 11, because of their disagreement in how to militarily handle the Korean War, President Truman recalls MacArthur as commander of the UN forces, and U.S. Gen. Matthew Ridgeway is given command. MacArthur wanted to win the war even if it meant using the atomic bomb. Truman wanted a negotiated end to the war.[2]

10) Battle of Heartbreak Ridge – This was fought for one month between September and October of 1951 in the hills of North Korea. The American Army began their final assault on the Chinese Army on October 11, 1951, and by October 15, 3,700 Americans and 25,000 Chinese were either killed or wounded with the American army capturing the terrain.[5]

11) Battle of Hill Eerie – The battle was fought between the UN troops and the Communist Forces in 1952 at the Hill Eerie. The outpost was taken several times by both sides. In May, the Philippine Battalion Combat team engaged the Chinese Army at Karhwagol resulting in a high number of Chinese casualties capturing the Hill Eerie. In June 1952, the Chinese launched another attack to capture the hill but were resisted by the Filipino Army bringing an end to the Battle of Hill Eerie.[5]

12) Battle of Old Baldy – There were a series of five battles for control of Hill 266 occurring over a period of several months from 1952 into 1953. The UN troops managed to capture the outposts in a series of battles with the last battle fought on March 23, 1953. The Battle of Old Baldy proved costly to both sides with the UN troops losing 357 men while Chinses casualties were more than 1,000.[5]

13) Peace Talks – There had been peace talks held in July 1951, November 1951, October 1952, and March 1953. These talks were deadlocked with no progress made. It was not until July 27, 1953, that then UN, North Korea and China signed an armistice agreement, continuing the division of Korea. The agreement calls for a 2.5-mile-wide buffer zone across the middle of the Korean Peninsula that closely follows the 38th Parallel. At this date no treaty had been signed between North and South Korea, so technically the two countries are still at war.[1]

C. Diseases during Korean War

a) Medicine and disease prevention – Infectious disease was the primary cause of death in the early wars in the U.S., as was true for the rest of the world. Disease was particularly prevalent in the 19th century wars of the Mexican-American War and the Civil War. Death from diseases was better controlled in World War I as there was a better understanding of the importance of sanitation and of disease control. However, the deadly uncontrollable influenza of 1918-1919 greatly increased death rate for World War I and worldwide. It was responsible for 50 million deaths.

Death from disease was greatly reduced in World War II due to further improvement in sanitation and the use of several vaccines for disease prevention. Also, for World War II the wonder drugs of penicillin and sulfa drugs were available for disease cure and prevention. Also, the use of the insecticide DDT was available to prevent diseases spread by mosquitoes.

For the more recent wars and preparation for future wars, vaccines that prevent disease are essential. Presently vaccination for U.S. troops is quite complicated. The first cluster of vaccines would protect against influenza, meningococcal, measles, mumps, German measles and chicken pox. The second cluster would protect against pathogens posing a threat later in military service (e.g., hepatitis A, hepatitis B, polo virus and tetanus-diphtheria-whooping cough).

For the Korean War vaccines protected against many of the dreaded diseases of the past and were administered to the U.S. troops.[6] However, this was not true for the general Korean population. Here there were acute or chronic infectious diseases such as malaria, typhus, smallpox, typhoid, diphtheria, dysentery and tuberculosis. During the 1950s was a time when war victims, including war orphans, witnessed a high volume of acute infectious diseases such as typhoid fever.

Vaccines for the military included smallpox, typhus, typhoid, tetanus, yellow fever, Hepatitis A, meningococcal, cholera and diphtheria. A rabies vaccine was provided to selected troops who had mission's endemic for rabies. The typhus vaccine prevented louse-borne typhus, but not murine or scrub typhus. A vaccine for Japanese encephalitis was developed during the war.

Tuberculosis (TB), a serious disease incidence for the general Korean population, was not a major disease incidence for U.S. troops. Recruits of the U.S. armed forces had been screened for the disease prior to induction. This included detecting the disease through x-ray and other procedures. Tuberculosis had also been declining in the U.S. at the time of the Korean War.

For the Korean population, the high rate of TB was primarily a legacy of the Korean War. Even when the fighting stopped the poverty, cramped living spaces and limited medical treatment during and after the war created ideal conditions for the TB bacteria to spread.[7]

With World War II there was introduction of penicillin and sulfa drugs, this was continued and improved in the Korean War, reducing infections from wounds as well as diseases such as pneumonia.

b) Diseases and other Health Concerns – In addition to infectious diseases, there were other health concerns with injuries that included radiation, asbestos exposure to airborne toxins, noise, and chemical exposure. Also, exposure to the herbicide agent orange and mustard gas were health problems for United Nation troops.

Predominate diseases and injury during the war are as follows:

1. Malaria – In 1933 there were almost 130,000 malaria patients in Korea and 1,800 patients among them died of malaria. The Japanese Government General took measures to control malaria especially during the 1930s and the number of patients decreased. However, as Japan engaged in World War II, the general hygienic state of the society worsened, and the number of malarial patients increased. The worsened situation remained the same after liberation in 1945 and during the Korean War (1950-1953).[8] Malaria has in times past and in previous wars earned for itself a reputation for producing high ineffectiveness in the troops. Much had been accomplished by the time of the Korean War by the antimalaria drugs and conventional eradication of mosquitos by use of DDT.

During Korean War, U.S. troops were exposed to malaria and received weekly chloroquine chemoprophylaxis. This regimen generally succeeded in preventing malarial attacks while U.S. troops were in the war. Despite the use of the antimalaria drug, during the Korean War, thousands of cases of malaria were diagnosed.[9]

2. Korean Hemorrhagic Fever – In the Spring of 1951, the United Nations was faced with an acute and severe infectious disease that had never been seen before. The disease is an acute viral disease characterized by sudden onset with fever of 3 to 6 days child's, prostration, anorexia, vomiting, widespread capillary damage, hemorrhagic phenomena and renal insufficiency. The widespread abnormalities of blood vessels, chiefly arterioles and capillaries have been considered as a main and initial defect which led to impairment of function in a number of organs. Since every patient developed some degree of kidney failure, fluid restriction was required.

Approximately 70% of cases showed a mild course and 30% have several complications, such as shock, bleeding, renal failure, electrolyte imbalance, pulmonary edema and secondary bacterial infections. Korean hemorrhagic fever is fatal in 5 to 15 percent of cases.[10]

During the Korean conflict, at least 3,000 United Nations troops were affected, including 2,115 cases for U.S. forces. The infection is caused by a hantan virus and is carried by rodents including the striped field mouse (Apodemus agrarius). Hemorrhagic fever was second only to malaria in importance for the Korean War.

3. Diarrhea/dysentery – Diarrheal diseases have influenced the outcome of military/naval campaigns from time immemorial. This problem was particularly widespread in the American Revolutionary, the Mexican-American and Civil War. It was likewise a problem in the Korean War but to a much lesser extent. Starting in World War I diarrheal diseases were greatly reduced by knowledge of the bacterial cause of diarrhea and improved sanitation to reduce incidence of the diseases. Nevertheless, during the Korean War, the American forces lost 79,970 man-days from these diseases. Of a sample of 98 soldiers, 54 developed diarrheas (from a multiplicity of pathogens) within six weeks of arrival in South Korea.[11]

4. Japanese encephalitis – Epidemic encephalitis, a neurotropic virus, had been recognized as a clinical entity in Japan at least since 1924. For the Korean population in general there were 5,548 cases in 1949. There were 402 cases occurring in American troops in Korea during the war years of 1950-1953.[12] Severe neurological manifestations may rapidly progress to death. The disease is probably transmitted by biting Culex mosquitoes that feed on infected birds, pigs and other mammals. During the war a vaccine became available. Americans had a complete susceptibility to the virus which did not exist in the Western Hemisphere.

5. Polio (Paralytic poliomyelitis) – This was the second most important neurotropic virus disease among troops in Korea with 120 cases occurring over the period 1950-1953. Polio was mostly a childhood disease, with the condition more serious in adults. It was not until 1955 that the U.S. government licensed Jonas Salk's polio virus vaccine and one year later there was an oral Sabin's attenuated vaccine.[12]

6. Venereal Diseases – As expected during wars, venereal diseases of syphilis and gonorrhea were serious health problems during the Korean War. Throughout the war the incidence of venereal disease was estimated at 184/1000 soldiers. For some units the incidence reached 500 cases per 1000 soldiers. During and following the Korean War, the U.S. military used regulated prostitution services in South Korean military camp towns. This was in spite of hiring prostitutes being incompatible with military core values. The number of prostitutes for the U.S. army was probably close to the number of U.S. soldiers.[13]

7. Cold injuries – There were injuries due to the extremely low temperatures in Korea. There were health problems due to cold climates like skin cancer in frostbite scars or pain, tingling, or numbness the fingers and toes.

The victims of frostbite, a trivial sounding but terrible affliction is where the flesh freezes solid, then dies and decays. Gangrene is the final stage of frostbite. The fleshy part of the hand or foot often returns to normal, but the frostbitten fingers and toes become withered and black.

The troops were often immobilized, pinned down by enemy fire. There were no replacements. The wounded lay too long on the frozen ground. It was the military situation rather than the harsh climate that produced most of the 5,300 frostbite casualties listed for the U.S. Army and Marines. Cold weather accounted for 16% of army non-battle injuries, and U.S. casualties of cold injury required evacuation from Korea during the winter of 1950-1951.

Korean War troops that served in the Chosin Reservoir Campaign were particularly affected by the subzero temperatures from October through December 1950. They could have been exposed to temperatures which were 50 degrees F below 0 at times, and the wind chill factor reached 100 degrees F below.[14]

C) Diseases of Prisoners of War (POWs)

a) North Korean and Chinese POWs – The POWs (North Korean and People's Republic of China) during the Korean War resulted in 7,614 deaths. Most POWs died as a result of infectious and parasitic diseases. Deaths from infectious disease was 5,013 (65.8%) out of 7,614 deaths followed by external causes including injury, 817 (10.7%). Few POWs died of malaria, typhus, diphtheria, or other parasitic disease, while many such deaths were reported among the general Korean population. This difference could be the result of a better supply of food and water in the camps, more aggressive public health measures amongst a confined population, and better access to medical treatment at the POW camps, compared with the general population.

For the POWs, the 5,013 deaths included sepsis, diarrhea/dysenteries, hepatitis, influenza, parasitic diseases, paratyphoid fever, pneumococcal meningitis, polio, relapsing fever, syphilis, tuberculosis, tetanus and typhoid fever.[15]

The. Vast majority of deaths were from two diseases, diarrhea/dysenteries (45.9%) and tuberculosis (48.0%). As in all wars diarrhea/dysenteries has been a problem. The disease was likewise a problem for United Nation forces. However, tuberculosis was not a serious problem for U.S. troops as recruits had been rejected as a result of screening for the disease.

b) American and UN Prisoners of War – In the beginning of the war the North Koreans generally did not keep prisoners. Americans were usually executed, sometimes after torture or mutilation. Photographs portray American corpses with their hands tied behind their backs and shot in the head. "American soldiers were found who had been burned and castrated before they were shot; others had their tongues torn out. Some were bound with barbed wire, even around the head and mouth."

After the Chinese joined the war, captured Americans were sent to Chinese-run prisoner of war camps in North Korea, usually after forced marches. Prisoners who were unable to continue the marches because of exhaustion were killed by the Communist guards. A total of 6,656 Army troops were taken prisoner. The official death toll in captivity was 38%. That number, however, probably does not include the men who perished before reaching the camps: "The suffering was intense as the weather was extremely cold, and many prisoners froze their feet. The average food ration consisted of one rice ball a day and little or no water. Many died from malnutrition, dysentery, beriberi and pneumonia.[16,17]

Table 12.1 illustrates Korean War highlights.

D. Summary

Japan had annexed Korea in World War II. At the end of the war, Korea was divided at the 38th parallel into two zones. The Soviet Union administered North Korea, making it Communist while South Korea became a Democracy administrated by the U.S. After World War II the Cold War was infect battling between ideas of Communism and Democracy. Highlights of the war are noted (Table 12.1)

The Korean Civil War began in June 1950 when Communist North Korea crossed the border into South Korea. The United Nations and President Truman called for action to protect South Korea. To support South Korea, 16 UN countries sent troops and 41 countries sent supplies. The U.S. sent more than 90 percent of the troops, military equipment, and supplies. North Korea was supported by China and Russia.

For six months combat raged up and down the Korean peninsula before settling into years of trench warfare. South Korea and its allies were ill prepared for the war and were dominated by early victories of North Korea. This changed with the Battle of Inchon in September 1950 when U.S. General Douglas MacArthur, commander of U.N. forces, made a bold military move with an amphibious invasion force of 80,000 marines that cut off North Korea troops. On November 25, 1950, China joined north Korea with 300,000 troops. On July 27, 1953, the war ended with no winner and the two countries still were separated at the 38th Parallel.

In early U.S. wars most, military personal died of infectious diseases. Starting with World War I death from military action was about equal with diseases. For World War II and the Korean War, disease effect was less due to greater knowledge of disease control, improved sanitation hygiene and the use of several vaccines for disease prevention. Also, use of wonder drugs such as sulfa drugs, penicillin and other antibiotics for treatment of wounds and for disease prevention and cure. For example, pneumonia was now more easily treated. The use of insecticides such as DDT was employed to prevent diseases spread by mosquitoes. Due to vaccines disease such as smallpox, typhus, typhoid fever, tetanus, yellow fever, hepatitis A, cholera and diphtheria were now under control.

For the Korean population there was a high incidence of TB. However, rates of TB have been declining in the U.S. and recruits for the military had been screened for the disease prior to induction.

The major disease problems during the Korean War were malaria, Korean hemorrhagic fever, diarrhea/dysentery, Japanese encephalitis and venereal disease. There were thousands of cases of malaria, but the attacks were controlled by antimalaria drugs and eradication of mosquitos by use of DDT. A new disease for UN and U.S. troops was Korean hemorrhagic fever, with the disease fatal in 5 to 15 percent of cases. Better knowledge of bacterial cause of disease and improved sanitation greatly reduced diarrheal diseases compared to early U.S. wars. Japanese encephalitis was transmitted by mosquitoes with 402 cases occurring in American troops during the war years. Venereal diseases were and have always been a problem during wars. Cold injuries were a serious problem with 5,300 frostbite casualties.

Americans and UN prisoners of war were often shot after torture or mutilation (including tongue removal and castration). Others died from long marches, and many died from malnutrition, dysentery, beriberi and pneumonia.

Table 12.1
Korean War Highlights[2,18]

1950	
June 25	North Korean Communist troops invaded South Korea. The UN demanded that North Korea halt the action.
June 27	President Truman ordered U.S. air and naval forces to help defend South Korea.
June 27	The UN asked member nations to aid South Korea. 16 UN countries sent troops to help South Korea and 41 countries sent food and equipment. The U.S, sent more than 90 percent of troops, military equipment and supplies.
June 30	President Truman ordered U.S. ground troops to South Korea.
July 5	In Battle of Pusan U.S. troops suffer heavy casualties.
July 20	In air battles the UN air force destroyed North Korea's air force.
Sept. 8	Allied troops stopped the deepest Communist advance, at the Pusan Perimeter in south-eastern South Korea.
Sept. 15	Commander of UN forces Gen. Douglas MacArthur made a bold move and sent an amphibious invasion force of 80,000 marines landing behind the enemy lines at Inchon.
Sept. 26	General MacArthur's forces announced the capture of Seoul, the South Korean capital.
Oct. 19	The Allies captured Pyongyang, the capital of North Korea.
Nov. 25	China enters the war to aid North Korea with 300,000 troops. The allies retreat with the attack by Chinese.
1951	
Jan. 4	The Communists occupied Seoul.
March 14	The Allies reoccupied Seoul after ending their retreat.
April 11	Truman removed MacArthur and replaced him with General Ridgway.
July 10	Truce talks began but fighting continued.
Oct. 15	Battle of Heartbreak Ridge is won by U.S. troops with 3,700 Americans and 25,000 Chinese Army either killed or wounded.
1952	
April 28	Communist negotiators rejected a proposal for voluntary repatriation of prisoners.
May-June	Battle of Hill Erie, UN troops won the battle. Filipino troops, in particular, resisted Chinese troops.
Oct. 8	The truce talks were broken off.
1953	
March 23	UN troops were successful in the Battle of Old Baldy, with UN troops losing 357 men while the Chinese casualties were more than 1,000.
March 28	The Communists accepted a UN proposal to exchange sick and wounded prisoners.

April 26	The Truce talks were resumed.
July 27	A truce agreement was signed, and the fighting ended.
Throughout total war	
Greatest disease and injury problems were malaria, Korean hemorrhagic fever, diarrheal/dysentery, Japanese encephalitis and venereal diseases. There were 5,300 frostbite casualties.	
About 580,000 UN and South Korean troops and about 1,600,000 Communist troops were killed or wounded. Almost 40,000 Americans died in action, and more than 100,000 were wounded.	

Fig. 12.1 The Battle for the Hills of Central Korea lasted from January 1951 to July 1953. This photograph shows United Nations troops preparing to attack on an enemy hill.

Fig. 12.2 U.S. First Battalion troops move through a roadblock in Seoul as fighting raged in the Republic of Korea capital, September 1950. The battle of the city followed the capture of Inchon, the port of Seoul, on Sept. 14 and 15.

CHAPTER 13

Vietnam War

A. Introduction

The Vietnam War began in 1957 when Communist guerrillas, called Viet Cong, began to attack villages in South Vietnam. The Viet Cong were supported by North Vietnam and consisted of persons from both the South and the North. The fighting gradually developed into a major war that endangered world peace. Communist countries supported North Vietnam, and non-Communist nations supported South Vietnam. The U.S. was South Vietnam's main ally. Their other allies were Australia, New Zealand, South Korea, Thailand, the Philippines and other anti-communist allies. The war ended April 30, 1973, with the fall of Saigon.[1]

a) Background – Vietnam had been a colony of France. Ho Chi Minh, a Vietnamese Communist, gained control of North Vietnam. In May 1954 the Indochina War ended with the defeat of French forces at Dien Bien Phu. Vietnam was then divided into two parts, North Vietnam and South Vietnam. The Viet Cong and North Vietnam began their war to unite South Vietnam with North Vietnam.

President Eisenhower worked to protect South Vietnam by helping the South Vietnamese both militarily and economically. Before Eisenhower left office, the United States had military advisors in South Vietnam to train soldiers. By the time President Kennedy was assassinated (November 22, 1963) he had increased the number of U.S, military that trained and fought with the South Vietnamese troops, from 700 to 16,000. In August 1964 there was the Gulf of Tonkin incidence where a U.S. destroyer was alleged to have clashed with North Vietnam fast attack craft. In response, the U.S. Congress passed the Gulf of Tonkin resolution and gave President Lyndon Johnson broad authority to increase American military presence in Vietnam. Johnson increased troop strength and before the war's end there were 540,000 U.S. troops employed in the conflict.[2]

b) Effect of the war – The Vietnam War was the longest in U.S. history lasting 19 years until the Afghanistan War (2002-2014). U.S. and South

Vietnam forces relied on air superiority and overwhelming firepower forces, artillery and airstrikes. The U.S. also conducted a large-scale strategic bombing campaign against North Vietnam and Laos. In all the major battles the U.S. and allies won. However, beginning in the late 1960's, American involvement in Vietnam became increasingly unpopular in the U.S. There were many antiwar protests against the war.

For the U.S. the causalities of the war were listed as 58,220. One out of every 10 Americans who served in Vietnam was a casualty. Casualties for South Vietnam are estimated at 110,000. Other South Vietnam's allies' deaths were 400 for Australia, and New Zealand 88 and South Korea, 4,400, Vietnam's communist government claimed 1.1 million combatants died between 1954 and 1975.[3]

B. Military activity

At the heart of the war was the desire of North Vietnam, which had defeated the French colonial administration of Vietnam in 1954, to unify the entire country under a single Communist regime modeled after those of the Soviet Union and China. This was a civil war with the South Vietnamese aligned with the west. The war was also part of a larger regional conflict and a manifestation of the Cold War between the United States and the Soviet Union and their respective allies.[3]

Important battles and events in the Vietnam War are as follows:[2-6]

a) **Battle of Van Tuong (Aug. 18, 1965)** – Also called Operation Starlite, this was the first purely American assault on the Vietcong. A Vietcong defector claimed that North Vietnam was planning to attack the American Chu Lai Air Base from Ban Tuong, so it was decided to launch a preemptive strike. This was a resounding victory. Ground forces artillery from Chu Lai, ships and air support combined killed nearly 700 Vietcong soldiers. U.S. forces sustained 45 dead and more than 200 wounded.

b) **Battle of la Drang (Oct.-Nov. 1965)** – This was the first major battle between U.S. forces and North Vietnam. For 35 days U.S. forces pursued and fought the North Vietnam until the enemy, suffering heavy casualties returned to bases in Cambodia (Fig.13.1). Later a North Vietnam regiment ambushed an American battalion with heavy U.S. casualties.

c) **Battle of Khe Sanh (January 21 – April 9, 1968)** – The Battle of Khe Sanh took place in South Vietnam in the province of Quang Tri. The engagement began when the North Vietnamese bombarded the U.S. marine garrison leading to an extensive battle, which lasted 77 days. Despite heavy casualties, both sides claimed victory. Regardless, 205 Marines died at Khe

Sanh, physically counting around 1,600 dead North Vietnamese Army soldiers and estimating North Vietnamese losses between 10-15,000.

d) Battle of Hué (January 331 – February 28, 1968) – The Battle of Hué was one of the bloodiest battles fought during the Vietnam War (Fig.13.2). The Viet Cong and North Vietnamese were driven out in intense fighting with all allies. The North Vietnamese would lose 5,000 in Hué proper and up to 3,000 more in the surrounding area. The city was left in ruins, with around 50% of its buildings destroyed and the ancient citadel ruined. Thousands of citizens were left homeless. Moreover, in addition to the multitudes of civilians killed and wounded in the fighting, thousands of civilians were systematically executed during the brief Communist occupation of the city.

e) Tet Offensive (January 30 – March 28, 1968) – The Tet Offensive began, encompassing a combined assault of Vietcong and North Vietnamese armies. Attacks were carried out in more than 100 cities and outposts across South Vietnam, including Hué and Saigon, and the U.S. Embassy was invaded. The initial attacks stunned the U.S. and the South Vietnamese armies causing them to lose control of several cities. However, they quickly regrouped and launched an offensive that inflicted a heavy casualty on the North Vietnamese. Although Tet Offensive was indeed a massive military defeat for North Vietnam, it had a profound effect on the U.S. Government and its citizens because they had been made to believe that the North Vietnam had been weakened and was unable to launch such an aggressive military operation. This was a marked turning point in the war and the beginning of a gradual U.S. withdrawal from the region. There were still more battles during the Johnson administration. However, in March Johnson signaled his desire to end the war by halting the bombing in Vietnam north of the 20th parallel.

f) Vietnamization – Richard Nixon entered the White House in January in 1969. During his presidential campaign he had pledged to reduce the number of U.S. soldiers fighting in Vietnam. Nixon had entered office with the promise of bringing "peace with honor". The plan to end the war included gradual withdrawals of the U.S. troops from Vietnam as part of the so-called "Vietnamization" program from June 1969. It called upon South Vietnam to do more of the fighting.

Nixon secretly escalated the war into Cambodia and Laos in 1970 and 1971, respectively, to destroy North Vietnamese supply through the Ho Chi Minh Trail to South Vietnam. Fallout from these incursions caused massive protests, which even escalated to violence at Kent State University on May 4, 1970.

g) Battle of Hamburger Hill (May 10-20, 1969) – The North Vietnam army was entrenched on Hamburger Hill in South Vietnam. Despite heavy losses a joint U.S.-South Vietnam force captured the hill. Instead of securing it, however, they were ordered to withdraw, causing outrage and further eroding support for the war. This led to diminishing popularity of the conflict since many felt that the battle was pointless, and many doubted whether the U.S. should be involved in Vietnam further.

h) Easter Offensive (March 30-Oct. 22, 1972) – North Vietnam launched a major offensive in South Vietnam. The Easter Offensive was a victory for South Vietnam and U.S. with heavy North Vietnam casualties from the U.S. destructive air power.

i) Operation Linebackers (Dec. 18-29, 1972) – The U.S. air force and navy campaigns were carried out when secret peace talks collapsed in 1972. Nixon decided to bomb North Vietnam and force them to the bargaining table. The attacks led to more severe damage to the North Vietnam infrastructure. Millions of gallons of petroleum products were also destroyed in the process. The air assaults were roughly 36,000 tons of bombs on North Vietnam cities. The increased air strikes proved to be the most severe in history to that point, but they worked. In January 1973, a cease-fire agreement was signed between the United States, South Vietnam, and North Vietnam, ending U.S. involvement in Vietnam.

j) Fall of Saigon (April 30, 1975) – In January 1973, South Vietnam, the United States, and the Communists signed a cease-fire agreement. Later in the year, the United States removed its last combat troops from Vietnam. But the Communists soon launched another offensive against South Vietnam and Saigon fell to the Communists. Now the Communist were in control of all of Indochina, Vietnam, Cambodia and Laos.

Although America's war in Vietnam failed to salvage the Republic of South Vietnam, it bought time in which neighboring countries improved their economies and defensive capabilities, and it may have discouraged greater communist activism in places like the Philippines.

C. Diseases during Vietnam War

a) Diseases that were now better controlled – U.S. troops must be prepared to be deployed anywhere in the world, often on very short notice, whether it is for actual combat, for a training exercise, or to serve as peacekeepers. Given the political instabilities in many parts of the world, U.S. war fighters must be ready to be deployed into environments where the risk of exposure to infectious diseases may be significant. In the most recent deployments, military preventive medicine measures such as the provision of safe water and food and the use of vaccines, chemoprophylaxis, and vector control measures – along with favorable combat conditions – have kept the number of casualties from infectious diseases low. Therefore, decision makers often must rely on estimates of the potential of newly emerging infectious diseases, the extent of emerging microbial resistance to chemoprophylactic agents, and the regionally important illnesses for which epidemiologic information may be incomplete and for which proven vaccines or medical countermeasures do not exist.[7,8]

Until World War II deaths due to infectious disease outnumbered those due to direct combat injuries. Even more so infectious diseases were less for the Korean and Vietnam Wars. Infectious disease that had been the primary cause of death in the early American wars were now more under control. For the Vietnam War no longer were there massive deaths from smallpox, typhus, typhoid fever, yellow fever, cholera and diphtheria. Vaccines were given just prior to induction to the military or received during childhood. Illustrating the importance of vaccines, cholera was epidemic in Vietnam but not a single case of cholera was seen in U.S. troops. Smallpox, one of the deadliest diseases was being eliminated worldwide. Polio, normally a childhood disease, was now no longer a problem since effective vaccines were developed in the 1950s.[8]

There were still a wide variety of infectious diseases that affected American war fighters in Vietnam. Although the use of vaccines against plague and cholera significantly minimized the incidence of those diseases among U.S. troops in Vietnam, disease for which vaccines were not available – for example, leptospirosis, melioidosis, and shigellosis – were prevalent. Even in recent years, U.S. troops have been deployed to geographic regions where there exist endemic infectious disease agents against which the U.S. military did not have immediately available either suitable, safe, and effective vaccines or appropriate chemoprophylactic agents. Infectious diseases continue to contribute substantially to morbidity during deployments. The Vietnam War experience resulted in focused attention on malaria, viral hepatitis, dengue, scrub typhus, murine typhus, leptospirosis and bacterial diarrheas.

Vaccination programs of U.S. troops today are quite extensive. The first cluster of vaccines would protect against influenza, mumps, German measles, and chicken pox. The second cluster of vaccines would protect against pathogens posing a threat later in military service, that included hepatitis A, hepatitis B, polio virus, and tetanus – diphtheria – whooping cough.[8]

Fatal casualties of the Vietnam War have listed 58,220 records. A total of

41,872 were killed in action or died of wounds. Only 938 of the 58,220 died of an infectious disease or some other illness. Although serious this is a small percentage indicating that many infectious disease threats of the past are no longer as dangerous as they were in previous wars.[9]

b) Diseases in the Vietnam population – The most common diseases were malaria, tuberculosis, hepatitis B, trachoma, intestinal infections, dengue fever, leprosy, diphtheria, cholera, tetanus, whooping cough, measles, poliomyelitis, chicken pox, typhoid fever, acute encephalitis, acute meningitis, and sexually transmitted disease.[10] The prevalence of epidemics of bacterial, viral, and parasitic diseases was attributed to the unsanitary environment. There was an outbreak of Bubonic plague, spread by fleas during the Vietnam War. Trachoma, the world's leading cause of preventable blindness, has been dramatically reduced in recent years.[11]

c) Diseases and other Health concerns for the military – In addition to infectious diseases, there were other health concerns some of which show their affects after the war is over such as use of the defoliant Agent Orange and Post-Traumatic Stress Disorder. Some of the infectious diseases were food or waterborne including diarrhea/dysentery, hepatitis A and typhoid fever. These diseases involved fecal contamination; better sanitation reduced these conditions. Vector borne diseases included dengue fever, malaria and Japanese encephalitis. These diseases would be controlled by reducing the impact of mosquitos. (e.g., draining swamps and mosquito netting).[12]

The main troubling disease conditions were as follows:

1) Malaria – Tropical diseases were frequent in Vietnam with malaria the most important. Over 40,000 cases of malaria were reported in Army troops alone between 1965 and 1970 with 78 deaths. However, this was less than had been seen in earlier wars because of the effectiveness of weekly chloroquin-premaquin prophylaxis against vivax malaria. There are four kinds of malaria that affect humans, each characterized by a different species of the Plasmodium parasite.[13]

When a person is bitten by a mosquito bearing Plasmodium, the parasite is injected into the bloodstream, where it lives out its life cycle in red blood cells and concentrates in the vital organs, principally the liver. Plasmodium falciparum is the predominant type of malaria worldwide and likely accounted for 90 percent of malaria illnesses reported in Vietnam. It is also the most feared, because it can affect the brain. Mosquitos spread malaria from one infected person to another.[14]

With the disease there is fever, chills, sweats, anemia, severe flu like symptoms such as shivering, joint pain and headaches. If not properly treated it can lead to organ failure and death. Control or prevention of malaria is to control mosquitos by draining swamps and standing war, use of antimalaria drugs, using mosquito netting and widespread use of the insecticide DDT.

2) Diarrhea/dysentery - These diseases have always been of major military importance because of their severe debilitating effects and the speed with which epidemics may occur. It includes specific infectious diseases such as shigellosis. Shigellosis was recognized as the most common specific bacterial cause of acute diarrheas.[15]

Peak incidence months for diarrheas were April, May and June. Sanitation measures involving "food, feces, flies and fingers" are most important. Carriers are common and complicate control measures. Ampicillin was the antibiotic drug of choice.

During the Vietnam War, hospital admissions for diarrheal diseases outnumbered those for malaria by nearly 4 to 1. Diarrhea ranks #1 of the infectious disease threats for the military based on its impact on readiness.

3) Tuberculosis (TB) – This is the most fatal infectious disease and the seventh leading cause of death in Vietnam. During the Korean War TB was a major health risk as it is today. In a 2013 report Vietnam ranked 12th in the world for most TB patients with nearly 200,000 new cases and 30,000 deaths recorded each year. A current challenge is TB patients who are resistant to TB medicines. It was estimated that up to 20 percent of TB patients in Vietnam cannot be treated due to their resistance to drugs.[11]

Contrary to the Vietnam population, TB was not a serious disease incidence for U.S. troops during the Vietnam War. In the more recent wars military recruits have been screened for TB prior to induction through X-ray and other procedures. There were also vaccines and medications for those detected during the war.[10] Likewise the incidence of TB in the U.S. has been steadily declining with relatively few cases encountered.

4) Dengue Fever – The disease often occurred in U.S. troops in Vietnam. Attack rates were high and periods of convalescence up to 3 ½ weeks beyond the acute illness. During May 1965-April 1966, the average monthly incidence of the dengue virus in U.S. personnel in Vietnam was 3.5 cases per 1,000 troops. It was under reported due to lack of laboratory capabilities. Dengue can lead to a more severe illness, dengue hemorrhagic fever.

Dengue fever is a viral disease transmitted by the Aedes mosquito. Sometimes this is called "breakbone fever" because of the intense pain it produces, the disease is characterized by fever, frontal headaches, aching bones and joints, nausea and vomiting.[10]

A study of fevers of unknown origin among 87 soldiers deployed to the rural Mekong River Delta in 1967 found that 3% of cases were caused by dengue. In 1967, the monthly incidence of dengue was 57-87 cases per 1,000 troops.

5) Parasites – A U.N. World Health Organization study in 2007 found that 55 million of Vietnam's 83 million people had intestinal worms.[10] Parasites were also a problem for U.S. troops during the Vietnam War. They were much more numerous and diverse in tropical Vietnam than would have been experienced in the U.S.

Returned U.S. veterans have died of bile duct cancer which is also called cholangiocarcinoma. This cancer was caused by consuming raw or undercooked fish which contained parasitic liver fluke worms. These worms were endemic in the rivers of Vietnam. The liver flukes can produce the carcinogenic irritation. The disease can take decades to be manifested. Once the cancer is discovered and diagnosed, the overall survival is less than 6 months.[16]

6) Skin diseases – These were the single greatest cause of outpatient visits to the U.S. Army medical facilities. During the period 1965-72 there were 1,412,500 visits recorded for dermatologic disorders. Skin infection often was due to secondary insect bites.

Due to high temperatures and humidity many troops were unable to get dry for days, opportunities for bathing were infrequent and skin hygiene was poor. Bacterial and fungal infections of the feet were a major cause of temporary disability. Some of the disease conditions with not being able to stay dry have been referred to as jungle rot, jock itch, trench fever and trench foot.[13]

7) Hepatitis – There are three common types of hepatitis, A, B and C. Type A virus is spread by the fecal-oral route. It is not particularly dangerous to persons under age 30 but can be fatal at older ages. Hepatitis B is transmitted by exposure to infected blood or bodily fluids. The disease leads to liver inflammation, vomiting and jaundice. Chronic hepatitis B can lead to cirrhosis and liver cancer. Hepatitis C is spread by blood-to-blood contact. The infection can lead to liver scarring and cirrhosis. It was estimated that 10 percent of Vietnam veterans could have hepatitis C. The C form is often cured with medications and for hepatitis A and B there is a vaccination.[11]

8) Other Diseases – There were additional always health problems affecting the military including childhood diseases (e.g., measles, mumps, influenza and pneumonia). Diseases that were typical for the military or specific for Vietnam include:[12,17]

1) Venereal diseases – The military was affected by the venereal diseases (VD) of syphilis and gonorrhea. VD was a common problem, as true for all wars. This was mainly from unprotected contact with prostitutes.

2) Chikungunya – This is found where there is high humidity and mosquito population. The bite of an infected mosquito will cause fever, joint pian, fatigue and nausea, it is rarely lethal.

3) Japanese encephalitis – This is a mosquito-borne viral disease found in rural areas in Asia. Acute encephalitis can progress to paralysis, coma and death; fatality rates 30%.

4) Rabies – In Vietnam, it is very expensive to vaccinate dogs and animals that carry rabies. However, with over 900 deaths in Vietnam in the past decade caused by rabies, it is necessary to take action against this disease.

d) Prisoners of war

1) Communist Prisons As expected treatment of American Prisoners of War (POWs) was not good. Starvation was a major factor in deaths of POWs, either directly or by causing diseases incurred from a weakened immune system. Sometimes the rice received by POWs was rotten and full of bugs and rat feces. Also, polished rice removed the outer layer of the grain which contained the vitamin thiamin, thereby resulting in beriberi.[18]

Health problems included malaria, beriberi, dysentery, scurvy, eczema, osteomalacia, anemia, bleeding gums, gingivitis, lost teeth, edema, and a skin disease which caused severe itching. The itching led to scratching, which resulted in infections – all were common. The fungal disease could be so severe as to cover almost the entire body. Osteomalacia is a softening of the bones caused by long-term deficiency of calcium, digestive disorders, and poorly functioning kidneys. These came from the poor diet and lack of sunlight common to Southern camps. Weight loss could be as much as half the prisoner's body weight at capture.

American POWs had to endure torture. Locking prisoners in ankle stocks or leg irons for 4 or 5 days. This was common not to receive food or water for this time period. Weakness from starvation was the intended effect.[19]

2) Viet Cong and North Vietnam Prisoners of War (POWs) – U.S. forces would ordinarily only keep captured forces for a short time and then turn them over to the South Vietnamese service. They would not have normally killed their prisoners, though that often enough did take place.

The South Vietnam prisons were not at all friendly places and fear was used as a weapon. Fear of execution, fear of phobias, which were watched carefully, noted, and exploited to the useful degree. There was some use of tiger cages, which were a form of torture. The prisoners suffered from the same diseases as the Vietnamese population, such as malaria, dengue fever, tuberculosis, Japanese encephalitis hepatitis B and influenza.

e) Trauma and disease affect veterans following the war

1) Disease conditions associated with Agent Orange – During the Vietnam War, U.S. forces sprayed Agent Orange and other powerful defoliants over large swathes of the Vietnamese landscape. The U.S. military used over 20 million gallons of Agent Orange and other herbicides in Vietnam in order to strip the Viet Cong and North Vietnamese Army of cover and concealment and to kill off crops they depended on to feed their fighters. It was common for U.S. forces to operate in the immediate vicinity of areas that were sprayed with defoliant. Thousands of U.S. service members were directly exposed to high concentrations of Agent Orange.

As of 2020, there are many health conditions associated with Agent Orange. These are chronic B-cell leukemia, Hodgkin's disease, multiple myeloma, non-Hodgkin's lymphoma, ischemic heart disease, porphyria cutanea tarda, Parkinson's disease, type 2 diabetes, AL amyloidosis, prostate cancer, respiratory cancers and soft tissue sarcoma. Other presumptive conditions include skin disorders and neurological disorders that include tremors, rigid muscles, loss of ability to perform unconscious movements (e.g., blinking) and peripheral neuropathy. There are several conditions that appear to be strongly linked to Agent Orange but have not yet been added to the presumptive list, these include hypothyroidism and high blood pressure. Also, Agent Orange can be related to birth defects leading to increased miscarriage rates, spina bifida, and other nervous system disorders.[20]

2) Post Traumatic Stress Disorder (PTSD) – Veterans of heavy combat in Vietnam who were diagnosed with PTSD were significantly more likely to have a host of both chronic and infectious diseases as long as 20 years later, a medical researcher has found. After studying medical histories of 1,399 Vietnam veterans, Joseph A. Boscarino, found that, compared to non-PTSD veterans who saw little combat, those with PTSD who saw heavy combat were 50-150 percent more likely to have circulatory, digestive, musculoskeletal, respiratory, infectious, and other serious diseases 20 years after military service.[7] The national study was one of the first to confirm a direct link between exposure to traumatic stress and the occurrence of a broad spectrum of diseases many years later.

Of the 1,399 Vietnam veterans studied, 24 percent (332) were diagnosed with PTSD sometime after military service, and nearly all cases of PTSD in the study resulted from exposure to heavy or very heavy combat in Vietnam.[7] The research suggested that those with PTSD often have altered neuroendocrine and sympathetic nervous systems. Disturbances in these key body systems are the main reason for increases in a broad spectrum of diseases among combat veterans. The research also uncovered abnormal immune functioning and clear medical evidence of coronary artery disease among the veterans studied. Sleep disorders were also more prevalent with PTSD. PTSD and alcohol dependence are two of the most common and debilitating disorders among American military veterans. Alcohol dependence and PTSD often occur together.

D. Summary

Vietnam had been a colony of France. In May 1954 the Indochina War ended with Vietnam divided into two parts, Communist North Vietnam and Democratic South Vietnam. In 1957 Communist guerrillas, called the Viet Cong, who were supported by North Vietnam invaded South Vietnam to unite the country as a Communist country. The U.S. was the main ally of South Vietnam, along with other anti-communist allies. Highlights of the war are noted. Under President Eisenhower, the U.S. provided advisors and economic support. President Kennedy increased the training and provided troops. President Johnson greatly increased the war effort economically and by supplying ground troops with air force and navy support. The U.S. and South Vietnam forces relied on air superiority and overwhelming firepower to conduct search and destroy operations, involving ground forces, artillery, and airstrikes. North Vietnam was heavily backed by the Soviet Union and China. In all the major battles the U.S. and allies won, however, the war was very unpopular in the U.S. with many antiwar protests.

A major battle was the Tet Offensive where the Communists had large-scale attacks against more than 100 cities and outpost. Although the Tet Offensive was a massive military defeat for North Vietnam, it was a turning point in the war due to many protests in the U.S. concerning the war. President Nixon's plan to end the war was to reduce U.S. soldiers in Vietnam and to have a program of 'Vietnamization", calling on South Vietnam to do more fighting. When peace talks broke down, Nixon called for heavy bombing of North Vietnam which forced them to the bargaining table. In January 1973 there was a cease-fire agreement signed in Paris, with the last American troops leaving South Vietnam in March. South Vietnam surrendered to the Communists in April 1975.

Before World War II deaths due to infectious diseases outnumbered those due to direct combat injuries. In the Vietnam War, military preventive medicine measures such as the provisions of safe water and food and the use of vaccines, chemoprophylaxis, and vector control measures – kept the numbers of casualties from infectious disease low. There were no longer massive deaths from smallpox, typhus, typhoid fever, yellow fever, cholera and diphtheria. The Vietnam War experience focused attention on malaria, viral hepatitis, dengue, scrub typhus, murine typhus, leptospirosis and bacterial diarrheas.

Malaria was the most important disease with over 40,000 cases in U.S. troops. Diarrhea/dysentery disease has always been of major military importance due to the severe debilitating effects. Hospital admissions for diarrheal diseases outnumbered those for malaria by nearly 4 to 1. Although tuberculosis was the most fatal infectious disease in the Vietnam population, it was not a serious disease for U.S. troops. Attack rates for dengue fever often occurred in U.S. troops. Intestinal parasites were a problem for troops. One reason for this was consuming raw or undercooked fish which contained liver flukes. Skin diseases were the single greatest cause of outpatient visits. Skin infections often were due to secondary insect bites. Skin hygiene was poor due to high temperatures, humidity and less opportunity for bathing, resulting in disease conditions of jungle rot, jock itch, trench fever and trench foot. Bacterial and fungal infections of feet were a major cause of temporary disability. Other problem diseases induced venereal diseases, chikungunya, Japanese encephalitis and rabies. Following the war diseases were in evidence that were associated with Agent Orange and Post Traumatic Stress Disorder (PTSD).

For the U.S. fatal casualties of the Vietnam War are recorded as 58,220 records. Of these a total of 41,872 were killed in action or died of wounds. Only 938 of the 58,220 died of an infectious disease or some other illness; indicating unlike early U.S. wars, infectious diseases were under better control.

Table 13.1
Vietnam War Highlights[1,2]

1954	The Indochina War ended with the defeat of French forces.
1957	The Viet Cong began to attack the South.
1960-1961	President Eisenhower provided military advisors to South Vietnam to train soldiers.
1961-1963	President Kennedy provided 16,000 personnel for training and troops to South Vietnam.
1964 (Aug. 7)	President Johnson asked the U.S. Congress to pass the Gulf of Tonkin resolution, which gave the president power "to take all necessary measures to repel any armed attack against the forces of the United States and to prevent further aggression".
1965 (Feb.7)	President Johnson ordered U.S. pilots to bomb military targets in North Vietnam.
1965 (March 6)	President Johnson sent U.S. Marines to Da Nang, South Vietnam, to protect American bases there. The Marines were the first U.S. ground troops in the war.
1965 (Aug. 18)	Battle of Van Tuong – First purely American assault on the Viet Cong.
1965 (Oct.-Nov.)	Battle of la Drang - First major battle between U.S. forces and North Vietnam.
1968 (Jan.21-Apr. 9)	Battle of Khe Sanh – Heavy casualties, 205 Marines and between 10,000-15,000 North Vietnamese.
1968 (Jan. 31-Feb. 28)	Battle of Hué – One of the bloodiest battles of the war.
1968 (Jan. 30-Mar. 28)	The Communists launched the Tet Offensive, a large-scale attack against more than 100 cities and outposts across South Vietnam. The Tet Offensive was a massive military defeat for North Vietnam but was a turning point in the war due to many protests in the U.S. concerning the war.
1969 (June)	Vietnamization – New President Nixon had plans to end the war and reduce U.S. soldiers in Vietnam. The Vietnamization program called upon South Vietnam to do more of the fighting.
1969 (May 10-20)	Battle of Hamburger Hill – Despite heavy losses, a joint U.S.-South Vietnam force captured the hill.
1970 (May 4)	Violet protest – President Nixon escalated the war in Cambodia and Laos in 1970 and 1971. These actions resulted in massive protest and violence at Kent State University.
1970 (June 24)	The Senate repealed the Gulf of Tonkin resolution.
1972 (Mar. 30-Oct. 22)	Easter Offensive – a victory for South Vietnam and U.S. forces with heavy North Vietnam casualties.
1972 (Dec.	Operations Linebackers – when peace talks collapsed in 1973, Nixon

18-29)	called for heavy bombing of North Vietnam in order to force them to the bargaining table. The attacks led to severe damage to the North Vietnam infrastructure.
1973 (Jan. 27)	The United States, North and South Vietnam, and the Viet Cong signed a cease-fire agreement in Paris.
1973 (Mar. 29)	The last American troops left South Vietnam.
1975 (Apr. 30)	South Vietnam surrendered to the Communists.
Total War	The number of casualties from infectious diseases were far less starting with World War II. Vietnam War most serious diseases included malaria, diarrhea/dysentery, dengue fever, parasite, skin diseases, hepatitis, venereal diseases, Japanese encephalitis and rabies. Disease conditions were associated with Agent Orange and soldiers suffered with Post-Traumatic Stress Disorder (PTSD).
Total War	There were 58,220 U.S. military fatal casualties of the Vietnam War.

Fig. 13.1 Helicopter unloading infantrymen on a search and destroy mission at La Drang Valley.

Fig. 13.2 The Vietnam War involved jungle warfare and use of helicopters.

CHAPTER 14

The Gulf War – Iraq War and Afghanistan War

A. Gulf War (Desert Storm) – On August 2, 1990, Iraqi President Saddam Hussein ordered the invasion and occupation of Kuwait, an independent state since 1961. On the same day the United Nations Security Council adopted Resolution 660 condemning the invasion and demanding Iraq's immediate withdrawal from Kuwait. Hussein defied United Nations Security Council demands to withdraw from Kuwait by mid-January 1991, and the Persian Gulf War began (Fig.14.1).[1]

Hussein's assumption that his fellow Arab states would stand by in the face of his invasion of Kuwait, and not call in outside help to stop it, proved to be a miscalculation. Two-thirds of the 21 members of the Arab League condemned Iraq's act of aggression, and Saudi Arabia's King Fahd, along with Kuwait's government-in-exile, turned to the United States and other members of the North Atlantic Treaty Organization (NATO) for support.[2]

The coalition forces prepared to face off against Iraq numbered some 750,000 including 540,000 U.S. personnel and smaller forces from Britain, France, Germany, the Soviet Union, Japan, Egypt and Saudi Arabia, among other nations. President George H. Bush had skillfully created an international alliance sanctioned by the United Nations, which had included such unlikely allies as the Soviet Union and many Arab countries. Iraq, for its part, had the support of Jordan, Algeria, the Sudan, Yemen, Tunisia and the Palestinian Liberation Organization.[3]

Iraqi forces were defeated on February 27, 1991. The next day President George H. Bush declared a cease fire, ending the Persian Gulf War. Some referred to the war as the First Iraq War as war was resumed in 2003 with the Iraq War.

b) Background - The Gulf War was the first major foreign policy crisis for the U.S. since the end of the Cold War. Iraq, which had built up the fourth-largest army in the world with U.S. assistance, was heavily in debt after its costly eight-year war with Iran. It pressured Kuwait and Saudi Arabia to forgive its debts, but they refused. Iraq had claimed, since gaining independence from the United Kingdom in 1932, that Kuwait was rightfully Iraqi territory, and accused Kuwait of exceeding its OPEC quotas for oil production. Hussein also accused neighboring nation Kuwait of siphoning crude oil from the Ar-Rumay oil field located along their common border. Not only had Saddam Hussein invaded Kuwait, but they had also threatened to move into Saudi Arabia.[4]

c) Military Activity – On August 8, 1990, the day on which the Iraqi government formally annexed Kuwait, the first U.S. Air Force fighter planes began arriving in Saudi Arabia as part of a military buildup dubbed Operation Desert Shield. The planes were accompanied by troops sent by NATO allies as well as Egypt and several other Arab nations, designed to guard against a possible Iraqi attack on Saudi Arabia.

On January 17, 1991, Operation Desert Storm commenced with a sustained air assault against Iraq by the U.S. and allied forces that lasted 42 days. The air campaign involved nearly every type of fixed-wing aircraft in the U.S. inventory, flying about 40,000 air-to-ground and 50,000 support sorties. Approximately 1,600 U.S. combat aircraft were deployed by the end of the war. Planes struck Baghdad and B-52 bombers pounded Saddam's army, while naval ships hit targets with Tomahawk cruise missiles. The air campaigns were the largest use of U.S. air power since the Vietnam War. During Operation Desert Storm, Iraqi forces launched Scud missiles into Israel and Saudi Arabia. These were mostly intercepted by U.S. Patriot missiles.[5]

On February 24, 1991, U.S. ground forces began their assault. The main land campaign only lasted 100 hours before Iraqi forces withdrew from Kuwait. The Iraqis had been routed and Kuwait liberated. As the Iraqi forces retreated, they set fires to about 650 Kuwaiti oil wells resulting in the release of an estimated 1.5 billion barrels of oil into the environment. It took ten months and 11,450 workers from 38 countries to extinguish the fires. One problem was the Iraqi forces placed land mines around the wells to make extinguishing the fires more difficult.

The number of fatalities for Iraq were between 20,000 and 35,000 and others suggest that "at least 65,000 Iraqi soldiers were killed." The U.S. forces suffered 148 battle-related deaths, with other coalition troops killed ranging from 1 to 92.[5]

B. Iraq War

a) Introduction and Background - The Iraq War was a protracted armed conflict that began in 2003 with the invasion of Iraq by a United States-led coalition that overthrew the government of Saddam Hussein. The first war against Iraq by the U.S. led coalition that ended on February 27, 1991, was called various names including Iraq War. The new war in 2003 was a continuation against Saddam Hussein, so the previous war's name was changed by some to First Gulf War or First Iraq War.

In August 1990 Iraqi President Saddam Hussein had ordered occupation of Kuwait and threatened invasion of Saudi Arabia. The U.S. led coalition forces defeated Iraqi forces on February 27, 1991. Following the war, the U.S. and its allies tried to keep Saddam Hussein in check with a policy of containment. This policy involved numerous economic sanctions by the UN Security Council; the enforcement of Iraqi no-fly zones declared by the US and the UK to protect the Kurds in Iraqi Kurdistan and Shias in the south from aerial attacks by the Iraqi government; and ongoing inspections to ensure Iraq's compliance with United Nations resolutions concerning Iraqi weapons of mass destruction. Inspections were carried out by the UN Special Commission in cooperation with the atomic energy agency to make sure that Iraq destroyed its chemical, biological, and nuclear weapons and facilities.[4]

In the decade after the Gulf War, the UN resolutions called for the complete elimination of Iraqi weapons of mass destruction. However, Iraq ignored its disarmament obligations and harassed inspectors and obstructed their work. In August 1998 the Iraqi government suspended inspectors completely. In November 1998 the U.S. and Great Britain launched a bombardment campaign on Iraq called Operation Desert Fox. The rationale was to reduce Saddam's government's ability to produce chemical, biological and nuclear weapons. This seemed ineffective.[1]

President George W. Bush began laying the public groundwork for the invasion of Iraq. In his 2002 State of the Union Address, Bush focused attention on Iraq, which labeled the country as part of an "axis of evil" allied with terrorists and posing "a grave and growing danger" to U.S, interests. The United States of America will not permit the world's most dangerous regimes to threaten us with the world's most destructive weapons. The Bush administration began to draw worldwide attention to Iraqi President Saddam Hussein and to suspicions that Iraq possessed or was attempting to develop weapons of mass destruction in violation of the Security Council resolution. In October 2002, the U.S. Congress passed the "Iraq Resolution", which authorized the President to "use any means necessary" against Iraq. By February 2003, 64% of Americans supported taking military action to remove Saddam from power.[6]

b) Military Activity – In July 2002 the CIA and the U.S. military's elite Special Operation Command prepared for an invasion by conventional forces. These efforts consisted of persuading commander of Special Iraqi military divisions to not oppose the invasion. More importantly organizing the Kurdish Peshmerga to become the northern front of the invasion. This force defeated Ansar al-Islam in Kurdistan prior to the invasion and later defeated the Iraqi army in the north. The battle against Ansar al-Islam, known as Operation Viking Hammer, led to the death of a substantial number of militants and the uncovering of a chemical weapons facility at Sargant.[7]

Bush ordered the invasion of Iraq on March 20, 2003, when the U.S., joined by the U.K. and several coalition allies, launched a "shock and awe" bombing campaign. The 2003 invasion of Iraq was led by U.S. Army Kurdish Peshmerga forces in the north. Approximately forty other governments, the "Coalition of the Willing" participated by providing troops, equipment, services, security, and special forces, with 248,000 soldiers from the United States, 45,000 British soldiers 2,000 Australian soldiers and 194 Polish soldiers from Special Forces unit sent to Kuwait for the invasion. The invasion force was also supported by Iraqi Kurdish militia troops, estimated to a number upwards of 70,000.[5]

More than 20 nations (most notably the U.K.) joined the United States in invading Iraq. The Iraqi regime had prepared to fight both a conventional and irregular, asymmetric warfare at the same time, conceding territory when faced with superior conventional forces, largely armored, but launching smaller-scale attacks in the rear using fighters dressed in civilian and paramilitary clothes.

Coalition troops launched air and amphibious assaults on the al-Faw Peninsula to secure the oil fields there and the important ports, supported by warships of the Royal Navy, Polish Navy, and Royal Australian Navy. The U.S. Marine Corps' 15th Marine Expeditionary Unit, and the Polish Special Forces unit attacked the port of Umm Qasr, while the British Army's 16 Air Assault Brigade secured the oil fields in southern Iraq.[8]

The heavy armor of the U.S. 3rd Infantry Division moved westward and then northward through the western desert toward Baghdad, while the 1st Marine Expeditionary Force moved more easterly along Highway 1 through the center of the country, and one UK Armored Division moved northward through the eastern marshland. The U.S. 1st Marine Division fought through Nasiriyah in a battle to seize the major road junction. The United States Army 3rd Infantry Division defeated Iraqi forces entrenched in and around Talil Airfield.[9]

In the ground phase of the Iraq War, U.S. and British forces quickly overwhelmed the Iraqi army and irregular Iraqi fighters, and by mid-April they had entered Baghdad and all other major Iraqi cities and forced Saddam's regime from power. On May 1, 2003, Bush declared the end of major combat operations in Iraq (Fig.14.2). The invasion led to the collapse of the Ba'athist government; Saddam Hussein was captured during Operation Red Dawn in December of that same year and executed three years later. Battle estimates for the coalition were 214 killed, 606 wounded. There were 7,269 civilian Iraqi fatalities.[7]

In 2004 the Iraq Survey group, a fact-finding mission comprising American and British experts, concluded that Iraq did not possess weapons of mass destruction or the capacity to produce them at the time of the invasion, though it found evidence that Saddam had planned to reconstitute programs for producing such weapons once UN sanctions were lifted. When interrogated by the FBI, Saddam Hussein admitted to having kept up the appearance of possessing weapons of mass destruction in order to appear strong in front of Iran.[1]

In January 2005 free democratic elections were held in Iraq for the first time in 50 years. A referendum to approve a constitution in Iraq was held in October 2005, supported by most Shiites and many Kurds. Bush praised the event, saying that the Iraqis "have taken rightful control of their country's destiny".

Unfortunately, from 2004 until 2007, the situation in Iraq deteriorated with some observers arguing that there was a full-scale civil war in Iraq. Bush's policies met with criticism, including demands domestically to set a timetable to withdraw troops from Iraq. According to Iraq Body Count, some 251,000 Iraqis had been killed in the civil war following the U.S.-led invasion, including at least 163,841 civilians.[1]

C. Afghanistan War

a) **Introduction** – On September 11, 2001, four American commercial airplanes were hijacked by Islamic terrorists (Fig.14.3). Two of the planes were deliberately crashed into the twin towers of the World Trade Center in New York City, destroying both towers and collapsing or damaging many surrounding buildings, and the third was used to destroy part of the pentagon building outside Washington, D.C.; the fourth plane crashed outside Pittsburgh, Pennsylvania, after passengers apparently attempted to retake it.[10]

The fourth plane which crashed outside Pittsburg may have spared either the Capitol or the White House from destruction. Great heroism was displayed when passengers stormed the cockpit. President George W. Bush later stated, "Their act of courage ranks among the greatest in American History".[11]

During the attacks, 2,977 victims and 19 hijackers were killed, and more than 6,000 others were injured. The immediate deaths included 265 on the four planes, 2,606 in the World Trade Center and in the surrounding area, and 125 at the Pentagon. This was the worst terrorist incident on U.S. soil. The terrorist attack had a higher death toll than the Japanese attack at Pearl Harbor with 2,403 casualties.

The shocked and angry nation demanded action. President Bush went on national television in September 2001 to reassure the U.S public and explain what had happened. Bush referred to the deliberate and deadly attacks which were carried out against our country as more than acts of terror, they were "acts of war".[1]

The War in Afghanistan is an ongoing war following the invasion of Afghanistan that began when the U.S. and its allies successfully drove the Taliban from power in order to deny Al-Qaeda a safe base of operations in Afghanistan.

b) Background – For many years Afghanistan was involved with Civil wars and wars with Britain and Russia. Britain had three wars with Afghanistan in 1839, 1878 and 1919. The British decided to end their relationship and Afghanistan became fully independent on August 8, 1919. In the early 1950's Afghanistan developed good relations in the cold War between Communist and non-communist nations. During the Cold War Afghanistan received financial aid from both the U.S. and Russia.[12]

Soviet forces invaded Afghanistan on December 24, 1979. The soviet presence touched off a nationwide rebellion by fighters-known as the Mujahideen – who drew upon Islam as a uniting source of inspiration. These fighters won extensive covert backing from Pakistan, Sandi Arabia, and the United States and were joined in their fight by foreign volunteers (who soon formed a network, known as al-Qaeda, to coordinate their efforts). The guerrilla war against the Soviet forces led to their departure in 1989. In the Soviets' absence, the mujahideen ousted Afghanistan's Soviet-backed government and established a transitional government.[13]

In 1992-1996 various warlords come into power, next the Taliban came into power. The Taliban imposed their fundamentalist interpretation of Islam in areas under their control. Osama bin Laden, who founded Al-Qaeda in the late 1980's, came to Afghanistan in 1996 when he was forced to leave the Sudan. It was Osama bin Laden of Al-Qaeda who was responsible for the September 11, 2001, attack on the U.S.[14]

C. Military activity – Following the September 11 attacks in 2001 on the U.S., which was carried out by the Al-Qaeda terrorist organization led by Osama bin Laden, who was living or hiding in Afghanistan and had already been wanted since the 1998 United States embassy bombings, President George W. Bush demanded that the Taliban, who were de facto ruling Afghanistan, hand over Osama bin Laden, or face the consequences. The U.S. would consider any nation that harbored terrorists to be responsible for the acts of those terrorists. Nations had to choose whether they would fight the terrorists or share in their fate.[11]

Bush worked to form a multinational coalition to wage the war, and with the

Afghan government having rejected his demands, a military strike on that country began. The CIA team was soon joined by U.S. and British special forces contingents, and together they provided arms, equipment, and advice to the Afghans. They also helped coordinate targeting for the air campaign, which began on October 7, 2001, with U.S. and British war planes pounding Taliban targets, thus marketing the public start of Operation Enduring Freedom. The objectives of the attacks were to knock out Al-Qaeda training camps, eliminate the organization and its followers, and destroy the Taliban regime.

The U.S. supplied the Northern Alliance, an opposition group to Al-Qaeda, with weapons and military advisors. Slowly, the Northern Alliance conquered city after city and, in November, Kabul, the capital of Afghanistan fell.[1]

Kandahar, the largest city in southern Afghanistan and Taliban's spiritual home, fell on December 6, marking the end of Taliban power. By December 2001, the Northern Alliance with the help of U.S. ground troops had taken the rest of the country. The Taliban leadership retreated into Afghanistan's rural areas and across the border to Pakistan.

The U.S. public stood behind Bush as he rode a record wave of approval. Bush's ratings were as high as 90 percent in the winter of 2001 with the war in Afghanistan going well. In 2002, based on UNICEF figures, Nicholas Kristof reported that "our invasion of Afghanistan may end up saving one million lives over the next decade" as the result of improved healthcare and greater access to humanitarian aid.[15]

The Taliban and their Al Qaeda allies had been mostly defeated. Unfortunately, the war continued. In 2003 the Taliban was reorganized. From 2006 the Taliban made significant gains and showed an increased willingness to commit atrocities against civilians. Troop numbers fighting the Taliban and Al-Qaeda increased to 140,000, with 100,000 from the U.S. On May 1, 2011, U.S. Navy SEALS killed Osama bin Laden in Abbottabad, Pakistan. NATO troops as well as the U.S. and British forces began to be reduced. On February 29, 2020 the U.S. and the Taliban signed a conditional peace deal that has not been lived up to, and March 9, 2021 a second draft peace agreement was being considered. The Afghanistan War was the longest war, almost 20 years, with U.S. involvement, starting in September 11, 2001 and ending August 2021.

Over 100,000 people were killed in the war beginning in 2001. U.S. military deaths from war as of July 27, 2018, was 2,372, with 20,320 service members wounded. Also, there were 1,720 U.S. civilian contractor fatalities.

The U.S. withdrawal from Afghanistan turned ugly and deadly. When President Trump left office, the Taliban was not in control of major Afghanistan cities. Trump had arranged for peaceful withdraw and would have done extensive bombing if the Taliban tried to take over cities prior to the U.S. departure. When Biden became president, he lied by claiming that the Taliban was in control of half the country. The U.S military could have easily controlled the Taliban until all U.S. and support staff were evacuated. However, no attempt was made to militarily stop the advance of the Taliban by the Biden administration, and the incompetent Biden removed all the troops prior to the civilian and support workers.

Biden did make the statement "no one would be left behind"; what a lie that was. A number of deaths resulted as people tried to reach the airport. Also, many Afghans that supported the U.S. will die, because of the betrayal of the U.S. government. Biden's withdrawal plan is an embarrassment to our nation; he has a great deal of blood on his hands. Not only was there undo death but over 60 billion in sophisticated weapons and equipment were left behind. It is sad to say, but Biden is incompetent, tells lies and should be impeached.

D. Diseases during Iraqi wars (1990, 2003) and Afghanistan War (2001 – 2021) - Infectious diseases have accompanied war throughout recorded history. This is true for the military activity in Iraq and Afghanistan. Prior to World War II the major cause of death was from disease. Disease killed more people than everything else including gunshots, artillery accidents, drowning, starvation, suicide etc.… For example, there seems to be agreement that about two-thirds of Civil War deaths were from disease. Simple hand washing by troops and surgeons would have been a critical activity in preventing and controlling disease. This was not done and as a result, thousands died from disease such as typhoid and dysentery. Poor sanitation, bad hygiene and diet bred disease, infection and death.

The greatest death losses from disease in earlier wars were from typhoid fever, yellow fever, diarrhea/dysentery, pneumonia, malaria, tuberculosis, smallpox, nutritional deficient diets (e.g., scurvy, night blindness), typhus and cholera. For the Iraq and Afghanistan wars most of the deadly diseases of previous wars were not major problems. Instead, military preventive medical measures such as the provision of safe water and food and use of vaccines, chemoprophylaxis, and vector control measures – along with favorable combat conditions and rapid care of the wounded – had kept the numbers of casualties from infectious diseases low.

Historically, infectious diseases have had significant impact on the conduct of military operations, and the conflict in southwest Asia is no exception. Physicians caring for returning military personnel should be aware of the diseases prevalent for these campaigns, particularly cutaneous leishmaniasis and infections with multiple drug-resistant bacteria.

The infectious disease challenges of war include pathogens endemic to the geographic area of operations as well as wound infections with common environmental microorganisms. Infectious diseases during these wars, however, were not a major cause of sickness or lost worktime. For example, during the Gulf War only one death due to infectious disease (meningococcal meningitis) was reported. Due to the low death rate, U.S. forces were more likely to die from suicide than an infectious disease.

Although deaths were infrequent, major infectious diseases related to southwest Asia and Afghanistan during military service included the following: Gulf War Syndrome, diarrhea/dysentery, respiratory diseases, leishmaniasis, wound infections, malaria, viral hepatitis, Q fever, brucellosis and West Nile virus.

a) Gulf War Syndrome – This illness is a chronic and multi-symptomatic disorder affecting returning military veterans of the 1990-1991 Gulf War. A wide range of acute and chronic symptoms have been linked to it, including fatigue, muscle pain, cognitive problems, insomnia, rashes and diarrhea. Approximately 250,000 of the 697,000 U.S. veterans who served in the 1991 Gulf War were afflicted with enduring chronic multi-symptom illness – a condition with possible serious consequences. While Gulf War veterans are no more likely to die or be hospitalized, they complain of more symptoms than their non-Gulf War counterparts. Diversity of diagnosis among participants include, 18.6% of veterans were diagnosed with musculoskeletal disorders, 18.3% with psychiatric disorders, and 17.8% with "symptoms, signs and ill-defined condition" (e.g., fatigue, insomnia). The most common diagnosis was "pain in joints" (31%), tension headache (19%), and dysthymia (17%). Potential causes of the syndrome are illusive and may not be related to an infectious disease.[5,16]

b) Diarrhea/dysentery – Infectious diarrhea/dysentery is among the most common medical problems associated with military deployments and has been reported as a frequent problem for troops currently deployed to Iraq and Afghanistan. The diarrheas among military travelers deployed globally in conflict and peacekeeping activities remains one of the most important heath threats. With more than 140,000 U.S. military personnel currently deployed to the Middle East in support of the global war on terror, it is important for health care providers and planners to be aware of the incidence and potential impact of diarrheal disease in that region.

Overall, diarrhea was commonly reported (76.8% in Iraq and 54.4% in Afghanistan) and was frequently severe (more than six stools/d) (20.8% in Iraq and 14.0% in Afghanistan) or associated with fever (25.8%), and vomiting. Many organisms cause the diarrheas, this includes Shigella. With Shigella in addition to diarrhea, there is fever, nausea and vomiting. Of 4,348 volunteers, 76% reported at least one diarrhea episode during their deployment and more than half reported multiple episodes. In 45% of subjects, diarrhea resulted in decreased job performance for a median of 3 days. Most soldiers reported seeking care for diarrhea, but appropriate treatment, including self-treatment with over-the-counter medicines, was generally successful. Most treatments were with either loperamide or an antibiotic.[17,18]

c) **Respiratory disease** – Historically, respiratory infections have had a significant impact on U.S. military missions. About 70% of military personnel deployed to Iraq and Afghanistan in 2003 and the first quarter of 2004 contracted a respiratory infection during their tour of duty. Mild acute respiratory disease was one of the two leading infectious causes of morbidity among U.S. troops. Crowded living conditions – and for some troops, residence in tightly constructed, air-conditioned buildings-probably facilitated the transmission of respiratory pathogens among U.S. forces[19] not particularly life-threatening, but 1.8% of personnel with symptoms were for a period of time unable to perform routine duties.

More than 1,800 U.S. personnel deployed to the Persian Gulf region developed respiratory disease severe enough to require hospitalization of a day or more. Among those patients, 214 were diagnosed with pneumonia, 90 with acute sinusitis, 102 with chronic sinusitis, and 81 with bronchitis, and 678 cases were diagnosed as asthma.[20]

The most important respiratory disease worldwide is tuberculosis (TB). Despite 90 years of vaccination and 60 years of chemotherapy, TB remains the world's leading cause of death from an infectious agent. The disease affects the lungs and causes symptoms such as chest pain, persistent cough (sometimes bloody), weight loss and fever.[21]

Although respiratory disease is serious in populations of Iraq and Afghanistan, it was not a serious disease incidence for U.S. troops during the wars. Military recruits had been screened for TB prior to induction and vaccines and medications were administered for those detected during the wars. TB was negligible for each of the three wars.

d) **Leishmaniasis** – This protozoan infection is usually transmitted by the bite of an infected sand fly. Cutaneous leishmaniasis includes skin lesions that range in severity from small, dry, crusted areas to large, deep, mutilating ulcers. Mucocutaneous leishmaniasis is characterized by lesions that may lead to destruction of the nose, oral cavity, pharynx, and larynx. The visceral leishmaniasis symptoms include fever, weight loss, enlargement of the spleen and liver, and anemia.

In a survey of 15,500 troops, 2.1% of respondents were diagnosed with leishmaniasis. Extrapolating that finding to the entire force of 140,000 personnel deployed to Iraq and Afghanistan at that time suggests that 2,940 troops may have contracted the disease.[22] This may be an overestimation as overall a very low rate of infection has been attributed to several factors: use of insecticides and repellents; stationing of most combat troops in the open desert, where there is a low rate of sand flies and their rodent hosts.

One of the treatments for the disease is with parenteral sodium stibogluconate for up to 30 days. Most skin lesions for cutaneous leishmaniasis do not require treatment, as they heal spontaneously.

e) Wound infections – Nearly 18,000 members of the U.S. military had been wounded in action while serving in Iraq or Afghanistan. Soldiers can experience a wide variety of exposures to pathogens from explosives or combat (wound infections) or in hospital or other healthcare facilities. Military personnel who might have been killed in an earlier era may now live to be hospitalized because of the use of body armor, better helmets, and more rapid emergency care. Although most infections are not life-threatening, multiple drug-resistant strains were now prevalent among U.S. military troops during the wars. Extended use of combination antibiotics to which the organisms are sensitive was generally successful in curing patients.[23] Advice given was there should be a prudent use of antibiotics with an emphasis on infection-control mechanisms – particularly hand washing to limit the spread of multidrug-resistant bacteria.

f) Malaria – Both Iraq and Afghanistan had serious malaria epidemics. However, very few cases of malaria were reported for U.S. troops for these wars. A total of 52 cases were reported for U.S. troops who served in Afghanistan or Iraq.[23]

g) Viral Hepatitis

Clinicians diagnosed a few cases of hepatitis A and B among deployed U.S. troops during the Gulf War[19]. Staff at the Armed Forces Institute of Pathology diagnosed one case of hepatitis B and 15 cases of hepatitis C among Gulf War veterans from 1992 to 1997.

h) Q Fever – Q fever is a zoonotic disease endemic in southwest and south-central Asia. The clinical syndrome may be acute or chronic. The acute illness usually manifests as a nonspecific febrile illness, pneumonia (sometimes atypical pneumonia), hepatitis, or a combination of the three. Three cases of Q fever were reported in U.S. troops who participated in the Gulf War[24], and 10 cases have been diagnosed in troops deployed to Iraq.

Cattle, sheep, and goats are the main reservoirs of the disease, which is caused by the bacterium *Coxiella burnetii*. *C. burnetii* most frequently infects humans who inhale infected aerosolized body fluids of infected animals; the consumption of raw milk from *C. burnetii*-infected animals also has caused Q fever in humans.

i) Brucellosis – Brucellosis is a serious zoonotic disease endemic in many parts of the world including southwest and south-central Asia. Humans can contract the etiological agent, *Brucella* spp disease by ingesting unpasteurized dairy products, by way of infected aerosols inhaled or through direct contact between animals or their secretions and cut or abraded skin. Among all U.S. soldiers who participated in the wars, only one case of brucellosis had been diagnosed.[25]

j) West Nile Virus – A disease spread by mosquitoes characterized by symptoms such as fever, headache, muscle pain or weakness, nausea, and vomiting. Symptoms may range from mild to severe. In the military there were very few reports of the disease and no deaths.

k) Typhoid fever – The disease is a public health concern in Iraq and Afghanistan, but due to U.S. troop vaccination, no cases were reported.

E. Summary

There were two wars with Iraq in 1990 and 2003 and a war with Afghanistan started in 2001 and ended in 2021. Under Saddam Hussein, Iraq invaded Kuwait in 1990. President George H. Bush formed a coalition to free Kuwait from Iraq. Iraq was easily defeated on February 27, 1991. In 1998 a UN resolution called on Iraq to eliminate weapons of mass destruction. The UN resolution was ignored by Saddam Hussein and President George W. Bush organized a coalition to invade Iraq. Kurdish enemies of Hussein were an important fighting force. The Iraqi army was quickly overwhelmed, and the war came to an end May 1, 2003. Later Hussein was captured and executed.

On September 11, 2001, four American commercial airplanes were hijacked by Islamic terrorists which deliberately crashed into the World Trade Center and part of the Pentagon. A total of 2,997 victims and 19 hijackers were killed. This was organized by Osama bin Ladin of the Taliban which was controlling the country of Afghanistan.

President George W. Bush formed a multinational coalition, and the war began on October 7, 2001. Early in the war U.S. and British war planes destroyed Taliban targets. The U.S. supplied weapons and training to the northern alliance which slowly conquered Afghanistan cities. In December 2001 with their defeat, Taliban leadership retreated to rural areas and into Pakistan. By 2003 the Taliban was reorganized and was shown to commit atrocities against civilians. On May 1, 2001, U.S. Navy Seals killed Osama bin Laden in Pakistan. In August the war ended with the U.S. and allies leaving the country.

For the three wars very few U.S. troops died from infectious diseases. During the Gulf War an illness known as the Gulf War Syndrome affected many. This was nonfatal but included a wide range of acute and chronic symptoms. The infectious diseases giving the greatest problems were diarrhea/dysentery, respiratory diseases, leishmaniasis and wound infections not responding to drug-resistant strains of bacteria. Due to the low death rate, U.S. forces were more likely to die form a suicide than an infectious disease.

Table 14.1
The Iraqi Wars and Afghanistan War[1,2,5,7,14]

Gulf War (Desert Storm)	
Aug. 2 1990	Iraq under Saddam Hussein invasion of Kuwait.
Aug. 2 1990	United Nations condemns Iraq's invasion.
Jan. 17, 1991	U.S. Coalition formed by President George H. Bush led a massive air attack on Iraq.
Feb. 27, 1991	Iraq forces were defeated.
Iraq War	
Aug. 1998	A UN resolution called for Iraqi elimination of weapons of mass destruction which was ignored by Saddam Hussein.
March 20, 2003	War began with President George W. Bush ordering invasion of Iraq. The Kurdish were important for the northern front in fighting Saddam Hussein's attack regime.
April 2003	The ground phase of Iraq War, U.S. and British forces quickly overwhelmed the Iraqi army.
May 1, 2003	President Bush declared end of major combat in Iraq.
Dec. 2003	Saddam Hussein captured and later executed.
Afghanistan War	
Sep. 11, 2001	Four American commercial airplanes were hijacked by Islamic terrorists which deliberately crashed into the World Trade Center and part of the Pentagon. A total of 2,977 victims and 19 hijackers were killed.
Sept. 2001	President George W. Bush demanded that the Taliban, who were ruling Afghanistan, hand over terrorist organizer Osama bin Ladin.
Oct. 7, 2001	Bush had formed a multinational coalition and the war began with U.S. and British war planes destroying Taliban targets.
Oct. 2001	The U.S. supplied the Northern Alliance, an opposition group to Al Qaeda, with weapons and they slowly conquered Kabel and other Afghanistan cities.
Dec. 6, 2001	Kandahar the largest city in southern Afghanistan fell, marking the end of Taliban power.
Dec. 2001	With their defeat, Taliban leadership retreated to rural areas and into Pakistan.
2003	The Taliban was reorganized again.
2006	The Taliban showed increased willingness to commit atrocities against civilians.
May 1, 2011	U.S Navy SEALS killed Osama bin Laden in Pakistan.
Feb. 29 2021	The U.S. and Taliban signed a conditional peace deal and withdrawal of U.S. and other troops.
Mar. 9, 2021	A second draft peace agreement was being considered.

Aug. 1990 – Feb. 1991	For the Gulf War between 20,000 and 65,000 Iraqi soldiers were killed with 148 battle-related deaths for U.S. forces.
Mar. – May 2003	For Iraq War 214 from the coalition were killed with 7,269 civilian Iraqi fatalities.
Oct. 7 2001 – July 27, 2018	There were over 100,000 people from Afghanistan killed with 2,372 U.S. service members killed.
August, 2021	Withdrawal from Afghanistan was chaotic and deadly due to the incompetent Biden's decisions. He foolishly withdrew the military prior to U.S. personnel and Afghan supporters resulting in U.S. and Afghan deaths. Likewise, the Biden administration left behind over 60 billion in military weapons and equipment. Biden's withdrawal plan is a great embarrassment to our nation.
Aug. 1990 – Aug. 2021	For the three wars very few U.S. troops died from infectious diseases. The infectious diseases giving the greatest problems were diarrhea/dysentery, respiratory diseases, leishmaniasis and wound infections not responding to drug-resistant strains of bacteria.

Fig. 14.1 Desert Storm (Iraq War). The war began in Mid-January 1991 and ended February 27, 1991.

Fig. 14.2 Iraqi War: George W. Bush with sailors.

Fig. 14.3 World Trade Center attack resulted war declared on Afghanistan.

References

1. World Diseases

1. Smallman-Raynor, M. and A. Cliff. 2004. "Impact of infectious diseases on war", Infect. Dis. Clin. North Am. 18(2):341.
2. McDowell, L. 2017. "Mineral Nutrition History, The Early Years", First Edition Design, Inc., Sarasota, FL.
3. Cirillo, V. 2008. "Two Faces of Death: Fatal Ties from Disease and Combat in America's Principal Wars, 1775 to Present" Perspect. Biol. Med. 51(1):121.
4. McDowell, L. 2013. "Vitamin History, The Early Years", First Edition Design, Inc., Sarasota, FL.
5. Cartwright, F. 1972. "Disease and History", Dorset Press, New York.
6. Ritchie, H. and M. Roser. 2018. "Causes of Death", https://ourworldindata.org/causes-of-death
7. Rossel, A. 2020. "Infectious Disease", http://needtoknow.nas.edu/id/threats/global-killers/
8. Jarus, O. 2020. "20 of the Worst Epidemics and Pandemics in History, https://www.livescience.com/worst-epidemics-and-pandemics-in-history.html
9. Huremovic, D. 2019. "Brief History of Pandemics" https://www.ncbi.nlm.nih.gov/pmc/articles/PMC7123574/
10. Sabbatani, S. and S. Fiorino. 2009. The Antonine Plague and the Decline of the Roman Empire. Infez. Med. 17(4):261.
11. Timeline-History. 2020. "Pandemics that changed history", https://www.history.com/topics/middle-ages/pandemics-timeline
12. Johny, S. 2020. "Analyses, how Pandemics have Changed the World", https://www.thehindu.com/news/national/analysis-how-pandemics-have-chaged-the-world
13. Wikipedia, 2020. "Typhus" en.m.wikipedia.org/wiki/Typhus
14. Zinsser, H. 1960. "Rats, Lice and History." Bantam Classic.
15. Wikipedia, 2020. "History of smallpox", https://en.wikipedia.org/wiki/History_of_smallpox
16. Roos, D. 2020. "How 5 of History's Worst Pandemics finally ended, https://www.history.com/news/pandemics-end-plague-cholera-black-death-smallpox
17. Staples, J. 2008. "Yellow Fever: 100 years of discovery", JAMA 300(8):960.
18. World Health Organization. 2018. "Typhoid Fever", http://www.who.int/topics/typhoid_fever/en/
19. History Diseases. 2020. History's Nine Most Contagious Diseases: Where are they now? https://chippenhammed.com/blog/entry/historys-nine-most-contagious-diseases-where-are-
20. Wikipedia, 2020. "Cholera", https://en.wikipedia.org/wiki/Cholera
21. Wikipedia, 2020. "Timeline of Influenza", https://en.wikipedia.org/wiki/Timeline_of_influenza
22. Price, A. 2008. "Contagion and Chaos", MIT Press.
23. Carmosina, A. 2020. "Background and History of the Coronavirus", http://psychcentral.com/coronavirus/backgroundhistoryofcovid-19/
24. Arrow, K. C. Panosian and H. Gelband. 2004. "Saving Lives, Buying time" Economics of Malaria Drugs in an Age of Resistance", National Academies Press, Washington, D.C.
25. Wikipedia, 2020. "History of Tuberculosis", https://en.wikipedia.org/wiki/

History_of_tuberclosis

26. Barberis, I. N. Bragazzi, L. Galluzzo and M. Martini. 2017. The History of Tuberculosis: from the First Historical Records to the Isolation of Koch's Bacillus. J. Prev. Med. Hyg. 58(1):E9.

27. Wikipedia, 2020. "United States Military Casualties of War", https://en.wikipedia.org/wiki/United_States_military_casualties_of-war

2. Early Diseases in the Americas

1. Mann, H. 2011. "1491, New Revelations of the Americas before Columbus", 2nd Edition, Vintage ISBN: 978-1-4000-3025-1.

2. Calloway, C. 2003. One Vast Winter Count: The Native American West before Lewis and Clark. University of Nebraska Press, Lincoln, NE.

3. Cook, S. and W. Borah. 1979. "Royal Revenues and Indian Population in New Spain", University of California Press, Berkeley, CA.

4. Dobyns, H. 2004. "In Search of Native America" J. of the South West 46:443.

5. Cieza de León, P. 1998. "The Discovery and Conquest of Peru." Duke University Press (~ 1553), Durham, NC.

6. Dobyns, H. 1963. "An Outline of Andean Epidemic History to 1720" Bulletin History of Med. 37:493.

7. Hudson, C. 1993. "Reconstructing the De Soto Expedition Route West of the Mississippi River", Young and Hoffmann, eds. 143.

8. Galloway, P. 1997. "The Hernando De Soto Expedition: History, Historiography, and Discovery in the Southeast", Lincoln, NE.

9. Pettula, T. 1993. "The Long-Term Effects of the De Soto Entrada on aboriginal Caddoan Populations", Young and Hoffman 237.

10. Marr, J. and J. Cathey. 2020. 'New Hypothesis for Cause of Epidemic among Native New England, 1616-1619", https://www.ncbi.nim.nih.gov/pmc2957993/

11. Morton, T. 1637. "New English Canaan or New Canaan", Charles Green, London.

12. Neel, J. 2001. "The Yanomamo and the 1960s Measles Epidemic". Science 292:1836.

13. Black, F. 1992. "Why did they Die?" Science 258:1739.

14. Black, F. 2004. "Disease Susceptibility among New World Peoples," Salzano and Hurtado, 147.

15. Borah, W. 1976. "The Historical Demography of Aboriginad and Colonial America: An Attempt at Perspective", Denevan, ed., 13.

3. King Philip's War

1. Wikipedia. 2020. "Disease in Colonial America", https://en.wikipedia.org/wiki/Disease_in_colonial_America

2. Tougias, M. 2020. "King Philip's War in New England", http://www.historyplace.com/specials/writers/kingphilip.htm

3. History of Massachusetts. 2020. "History of King Philip's War", https://historyofmassachusetts.org/what-was-king-philips-war/

4. History. 2020. "King Philip's War – Definition Cause and Significance", https://www.history.com/topics/native-american-history/king-philips-war

5. Saunders, L. 2018. "First Ranger Benjamin Church", Lisa Saunders, Copyright, Mystic, Connecticut.

6. Lodi, E. 2015. "Who, When, Where in King Philip's War", Rock Village

Publishing Middleborough, MA.

7. New England Historical Society. 2020. "Exactly how New England's Indian Population was Decimated", https://www.newenglandhistoricalsociety.com/exactly-new-englands-indian-population-decimated

8. Marr, J. and J. Cathey. 2020. "New Hypothesis for Cause of Epidemic among Native Americans", New England, 1616-1619", https://www.ncbi.nlm.nih.gov/pmc/articales/PMC2957993/

9. Martin, D. and A. Goodman. 2002. Health Conditions before Columbus: Paleopathology of Native Americans. The Western J. Medicine 176: 65.

10. McDowell, L. 2013. "Vitamin History, the Early Years, University of Florida, First Edition Design Publishing, Inc., Sarasota, FL.

4. French and Indian War

1. Wikipedia. 2020. "French and Indian War", https://en.wikipedia.org/wiki/French_and_Indian_War

2. Griffith, W. "The French and Indian War (1754-1763): Causes and Outbreak" https://www.battlefields.org/learn/articles/french-and-indian-war-1753-1763-causes-and-o...

3. World Book Encyclopedia. 1979. World Book – Childcraft International, Inc., U.S.A. p. 438.

4. History, 2020. "The Seven Years' War", https://www.history.com/topics/france/seven-years-war

5. Wood, B. 1999. "A Constant Attendance on God's Alter: Death, Disease, and the Anglican Church in Colonial South Carolina", South Carolina Historical Magazine 100(3):204.

6. Bauer, J. 1940. "Yellow Fever", Vol. 55(9), March 1940

7. Becker, A. 2004. "Smallpox in Washington's Army: Strategic Implications of the Disease during the American Revolutionary War", J. Military History 68:2.

8. Nielsen, K. 2012. "A Disability History of the United States", Beacon Press, ISBN 9780807022047.

9. Portero, A. 2020. "Deaths caused by Diseases among the Native Americans in the 18th Century", Synonym.com/effect-did-participation-europeanpowers-re

10. Charters, E. 2010. "Military Medicine and the Ethics of War", CBMH/BCHM 27(2):273.

11. Fowler, W. 2005. "Empires at War: The French and Indian War and the Struggle for North America", ISBN 978-0-8027-1411-4, New York.

12. Anderson, W. and R. Wetmore. 2006. "Disease, Destruction, and Loss of Cherokee Land", https://www.ncpedia.org/cherokee/disease

13. Kiger, P. 2018. "Did Colonists Give Infected Blankets to Native Americans as Biological Warfare?", history.com/news/colonists-native-americans-smallpox-blankets

5. American Revolutionary War

1. McDowell, 2018. "The Presidents, Humor, Events and Morality", University of Florida, Xulon Press, Maitland, FL.

2. History, 2020. "French and Indian War", https://www.history.com/topics/native-american-hisotry-french-and-indian-war

3. Flexner, J. 1968. "George Washington in the American Revolution", Little Brown and Company, Boston.

4. Leckie, R. 1993. "George Washington's War: The Saga of the American Revolution", Harper Collins, New York.

5. Taylor, A. 2016. "American Revolutions a Continental History, 1750-1804", New York, ISBN 978-0-393-35476-8.

6. Washington, G. 2018. "George Washington in the American Revolution", https://www.mountvernon.org/george-washington/the-revolutionary-war/timeline/

7. Wikipedia, 2018. "George Washington", https://en.wikipedia.org/wiki/George_Washington

8. Gruber, I. 1972. "The Howe Brothers and the American Revolution", Atheneum Press, New York.

9. Hamilton, N. A. 2001. "Presidents, a Biographical Dictionary", Checkmark Books, New York.

10. Ward, C. 1952. "War of the Revolution", MacMillian, New York.

11. Alden, J. 1993. "George Washington, a Biography", Easton Press, ISBN 978-0-8071-4108-3.

12. Wikipedia, 2020. "U.S. Military Casualties of war". https://en.wikipedia.org/wiki/UNited_States_military_casualities_of_war

13. Schenawolf, H. 2014. Diseases and Epidemics During Revolutionary War, 1763-1783", https://www.revolutionarywarjounal.com/diseases-and-epidemics/

14. McCandless, P. 2007. "Revolutionary Fever Diseases and War in the Lower South", Trans. Am. Clin Ass. 118:225.

15. Fenn, E. 2001. "Pox America & the Great Smallpox Epidemic of 1775-1782", Hill and Wang, New York.

16. Gill, Jr., 2003. "Colonial Germ Warfare", https://www.history.org/foundation/journal/spring04/warfare.cfm

17. Joymer, W. 2006. "Infectious Diseases", https://www.ncpedia.org/infectious-diseases-part-11

18. Benenson, A. 1984. "Immunization and Military Medicine", Rev. Infectious Diseases 6(1), January.

19. Mann, c. 2007. "America Found & Lost", National Geographic, May p. 32

20. Yagi, Jr. 2016. "Beating the Bloody Flux, War on Dysentery", Militaryhistorynow.com/2016/03/02thebloody-flux-how-one-british-a

21. McDowell, L. 2013. "Vitamin History, The Early years", University of Florida, First Edition Design Publishing, Inc., Sarasota, FL.

22. McDowell, L. 2021. The Presidents as Officers of the Military", First Edition Design Publishing, Inc., Sarasota, FL.

23. The World Book Encyclopedia, Vol. 16, World Book -Childcraft Int., Chicago.

6. War of 1812

1. Wikipedia. 2020. "War of 1812", https://en.wikipedia.org/wiki/War_of_1812

2. Beschloss, M. 2018. "Presidents of War", Crown, New York.

3. War of 1812. 2020. "War of 1812 Facts", https://www.battlefields.org/learn/articles/war-of-1812

4. McDowell, L. 2021. "Presidents as Military Officers", University of Florida, First Edition Design Publishing, Inc., Sarasota, FL.

5. Langguth, A. 2007. "Union 1812: The Americans who Fought the Second War of Independence, New York.

6. Remini, N. 2001. "Andrew Jackson, His Indian Wars", Penguin Putnam, New York.

7. Wikipedia. 2018. "Battle of Bladensburg", http://en.wikipedia.org/wiki/

Battle_of_Blandensburg
8. Blassingame, W. 2001. "Book of Presidents", Random House, New York.
9. Walker, A. 1856. "Jackson and New Orleans", New York.
10. Burstein, A. 2003. "The Passions of Andrew Jackson", Alfred A. Knopf, New York.
11. Office of Medical History. 2020. "The War of 1812", https://history.amedd.army.mil/booksdocs/misc/evprev/ch5.htm
12. Military Medicine. 2020. "The War of 1812", https://www.pbs.org/wned/war-of-1812/essays/military-medicine/
13. National Park Service. 2020. "Wounded Soldiers Contend with Crude Treatments", https://nps.gov/articles/military-medicine.htm
14. Chapman, B. and J. McCallum. 2014. "Infectious Diseases", The Encyclopedia of Wars of the Early American Republic, Santa Barbara, Ca.
15. McDowell, L. 2013. "Vitamin History, The Early Years", University of Florida, First Edition Design Publishing, Inc. Sarasota, FL.
16. McDowell, L. 2021. "Presidents as Military Officers", University of Florida, First Edition Design Publishing Inc., Sarasota, FL.

7. Mexican – American War

1. Hamilton, N. 2001. "Presidents", Checkmark Books, New York.
2. McDowell, L. 2018. "The Presidents, Humor, Events and Morality", University of Florida, Xulon Press, Maitland, FL.
3. Leonard, T. 2001. "James K. Polk, A Clear and Unquestionable Destiny, SR Books, Wilmington, DE.
4. Stadelman, W. 2002. "U.S. Presidents for Dummies", Wiley Publishing Inc. Hoboken, N.J.
5. Minister, C. 2017. "The Battles of the Mexican – American War, https://www.thoughtco.com/battles-of-theMexican-American-War-2136200
6. Howard, O. 1892. "General Taylor", D. Appleton and Co. New York.
7. Wikipedia, 2020. Mexican – American War., https://en.wikipedia.org/wiki/Mexican%E2%80%93American_War
8. Tschanz, D. 2020. "Yellow Fever and the Strategy of the Mexican – American War", http://www.montana.edu/historybug/mexwar.html
9. Andrews, E. 2020. "10 Things You May Not Know About the Mexican – American War", https://www.history.com/news/10-things-you-may-not-know-about-the-mexican-american-war
10. Cowen, T. 2018. "How Dangerous was the Mexican – American War for American Soldiers? https://marginalrevolution.com/marginalrevolution/2018/09/dangerous-mexcian-american-war
11. Winders, R. 1997. "Mr. Polk's Army", Texas A&M University Press, College Station, TX.
12. McDowell, L. 2013. "Vitamin History, The Early Years. First Edition Design Publishing, Inc., Sarasota, FL.
13. Cirillo, V. 2020. "More Fatal Than Powder and Shot", Dysentery in the U.S. Army during the Mexican War. https://www.ncbi.nlm.nih.gov/pubmed/19684375
14. McDowell, L. 2021. "The Presidents as Military Officers", First Edition Design Publishing, Sarasota, FL.

8. American Civil War

1. McDowell, L. 2018. "The Presidents, Humor, Events and Morality", University of Florida, Xulon Press, Maitland, FL.

2. Chrastina, P. 2020. "No Plan to Free Slaves, Lincoln Assures Crowd", Old News, Landisville, PA.

3. Civil War Disease. 2020. "Statistics – Disease and the Civil War", http://civil-war-disease.leadr.msu.edu/statistics-2/

4. Wikipedia. 2020. "List of American Civil War Battles, https://en.wikipedia.org/wiki/List_of_American_Civil_War_battles

5. Newtonic, L. 2020. "10 Major battles of the American Civil War", https://learnodo-newtonic.com/american-civil-war-battles

6. McFeely, W. 1974. "Grant: A Biography", New York, ISBN 0-400-05923-2.

7. McDowell, L. 2021. "The Presidents as Military Officers", First Edition Design Publishing, Inc., Sarasota, FL.

8. Civil War Battles, 2019. "Major battles from the American Civil War", America's Civil War Magazine, https://www.historynet.com/civil-war-battles

9. Bulla, D. and G. Borchard. 2010. J. Civil War Era. Peter Lang Publishing Inc. ISBN 1-4331-0722-8.

10. Coolidge, L. 1917. "Ulysses S. Grant", Houghton Miffin Co., New York.

11. The World Book Encyclopedia. 1979. Vol. 4, p. 472, ISBN 0-7166-0079-X, Chicago.

12. Bollet, A. 2004. "The Major Infectious Epidemic Diseases of Civil War Soldiers". Infect. Dis. Clin N. Am. 18:293.

13. Goellnitz, J. 2009. "Medical Statistics", https://civilwarwiki.net/wiki/Medical_Statistics

14. Civil War Medicine. 2020. "Civil War Medicine: An Overview of Medicine", The Ohio State University, https://ehistory.osu.edu/exhibitions/cwsurgeon/cwsurgeon/introduction

15. Woodward, J. 1863. "Outlines of the Chief Camp Diseases", J. Lippincott, Philadelphia.

16. Dorwart, B. 2009. "Death is in the Breeze: Death during the American Civil War", National Museum of Civil War Medicine Press, Frederick, Maryland.

17. Dixon, I. 2020. "Modern Medicine's Civil War Legacy", https://www.battlefields.org/learn/articles/civil-war-medicine

18. Chisholm, J. 1864, "Manual of Military Surgery", Columbia, SC

19. Civil War Casualties. 2016. U.S. National Library of Medicine, https://simple.wikipedia.org/wiki/American_Civil_War-casualties

20. Burns, S. 2020. "Disease: Behind the Lens: A History in Pictures", http://www.pbs.org/mercy-street/uncover-history/behind-lens/disease/

21. National Museum of Civil War Medicine. 2020. "How Parasites Changed the American Civil War", https://www.civilwarmed.org/parasites/

22. Hopkins, D. 1983. "Princes and Peasants: Smallpox in History", University of Chicago Press.

23. Sternburg, G. 1864. "Is Yellow Fever Endemic in New Orleans", Am. Med. Times 8:197.

24. Jones, J. 1892. "Medical history of the Confederate States army and navy: South Hist Soc Papers 20:109.

25. McDowell, L. 2013. "Vitamin History, The Early Years", First Edition Design Publishing, Inc., Sarasota, FL.

26. Bollet, A. 1992. Scurvy and Chronic Diarrhea in Civil War Troops: were they both Nutritional Deficiency Syndromes? J. Hist Med Allied Sci 47:49.

27. Sauberlich, H. 1997. "Vitamin C in Health and Disease", L. Parker and J. Fuchs, eds., p. 1, Marcel Dekker, Inc., New York.

28. Bourne, G. 1944. Proc. Royal Soc. Med. 37:512.

29. Hamidullah, I. 2020. "The Impact of Disease on the Civil War", https://teachers.yale.edu/curriculum/viewer/initiative_10.06.02_u

30. Lee, R.E. 1987. The Wartime Papers of Robert E. Lee. Da Capo Press; New York.

9. Spanish-American War

1. Hamilton, N. 2001. "Presidents", Checkmark Books, New York.

2. Spanish American War,2020. "Spanish-American War", https://www.history.com/topics/early-20th-century-us/spanish-american-war

3. Trask, D. 2020. "The Spanish-American War", https://www.loc.gov/rr/hispanic/1898/trask.html

4. Hayes, M. 1998. "Naval Operations in the Spanish-American War", https://www.history.navy.mil/research/library/online-reading-room/title-list-alphabetically/

5. McDowell, L. 2018. "The Presidents, Humor, Events and Morality", Xulon Press, Maitland, FL.

6. Roosevelt, T. 1898. "111", The Rough Riders, http://www.bartleyby.com/51/bartleby, p.2

7. Brands, H. 1997. T.R.'s The Last Romantic", Basic Books, ISBN 978-0-465-06958-3, New York.

8. Wikipedia. 2020. "Spanish-American War", https://en.wikipedia.org/wiki/Spanish%E2%80%93American_War

9. Wikipedia. 2020. "United States Military of War", https://en.wikipedia.org/wiki/United_States_military_casualties_of_war

10. Cirillo, V. 2004. "The Patriotic Order: Sanitation and Typhoid Fever in the National Encampments during the Spanish-American War, https://www.jstor.org/stable/26304872?seq=1

11. McDowell, L. 2013. "Vitamin History, the Early Years", University of Florida, First Edition Design Publishing, Inc. Sarasota, FL.

12. Cirillo, V. 2000. "Fever and Reform: The Typhoid Epidemic in the Spanish-American War" J. History

13. Gibson, J. 1958. "Soldier in White, The Life of General George Miller Sternberg". Duke University, Duram.

14. Cirillo, V. 2005. "Bullets and Bacilli, The Spanish-American War and Military Medicine" J. Clin. Invest. 115:3

15. Budd, W. 1873. "Typhoid Fever: In Nature, Mode of Spreading and Prevention", Longmans, Green and Co., London.

16. Sternberg, G. 1912. "Sanitary Lessons of the War and Other Papers", B. Adams, ed., p. 8, Washington, D.C.

17. Reed, W., V. Vaughan and E. Shakespeare. 1900. "Abstract of Report on the Origin and of Typhoid Fever in Spanish War of 1898" Government Printing Office, Washington, D.C.

18. Woodhull, A. 1909. Military Hygiene for Officers of the Line", 4th ed. John Wiley & Sons, New York.

19. American Experience. 2020. "Scourge of the Spanish American War, http://www.shoppbs.pbs.org/wgbh/amex/fever/peopleevents/e_cuba.html

20. Bollet, A. 1987. Plagues and Poxes: The Rise and Fall of Epidemic Disease", Demos Publications, New York.

21. Feng, P. 2020. "Major Walter Reed and the Eradication of Yellow Fever", https://armyhistory.org/major-walter-reed-and-the-eradication-of-yellow-fever/

22. Jones, G. 1963. "The First Epidemic in English America", The Virginia Magazine of History and Biography vol. 71, No. 1
23. McDowell, L. R. 2021. "The Presidents as Military Officers, University of Florida, First Edition Design Publishing, Sarasota, FL.

10. World War I

1. World Book Encyclopedia. 1979. "World War I", Vol. W. World Book – Childcraft International, Inc., Chicago
2. Karuga, J. 2019. "Major Battles of World War I", https://www.worldatlas.com/articles/major-battles-of-the-war-I-ww1.html
3. Norwich University Online 2017. "Important Battles of World War I", https://online.norwich.edu/academic-programs/resources/6-important-battles-of-world-war...
4. World War I Battles. 2020. "10 significant battles of the First World War" https://www.iwm.org.uk/history/10-significnat-battles-of-the-first-world-war
5. McDowell, L. 2021. "The Presidents as Military Officers", First Edition Design Publishing, Inc., Sarasota, FL.
6. Wikipedia. 2019. United States Campaigns in World War I https://en.wikipedia.org/wiki/UnitedStatescampaigns
7. Annin, R. 1924 "Woodrow Wilson", Dodd, Mead and Co. New York
8. Pennington, H. 2019. "The Impact of Infectious Diseases in Wartime, a look back at WWI https://www.futuremedicine.com/doi/full/10.2217/fmb-2018-0323
9. Ayers, L. 1919. "The War with Germany: A Statistical Summary", Government Printing Office, Washington, D.C.
10. Gabriel, R. and K. Motz. 1992. "A History of Military Medicine, Vol. 2, Greenwood Press, New York.
11. Byerly, C. 2010. "The U.S. Military and the Influenza Pandemic of 1918-1919. https://www.ncbi.nlm.nih.gov/pmc/articles/PMC2862337/
12. Adhikari, S. 2019. "Top 10 Diseases that were Common in World War I. https://www.ancienthistorylists.com/world-war-1/top-10-diseases-that-were-spread-in-world-war-1
13. Viewpoint. 2014. "The Deadly Disease that Killed more People than WWI", https;//www.bbc.com/news/magazine-29541235
14. Byerly, C. 2005. "Fever of War", New York University Press, New York
15. MacDonald, P. 2020. "When the 1918-19 Influenza Pandemic Came to Gainesville." Gainesville Magazine, The Gainesville Sun, p. 18, Gainesville, FL.
16. Noymer, A. and M. Garenne. 2003. "The Spanish Influenza Pandemic of 1918-1919." New Perspectives Rootledge Press, New York.
17. Bollet, A. 1987. "Plaques and Poxes: The Rise and Fall of Epidemic Disease". Demos Publishing, New York.
18. Crosby, A. 1989. "American's Forgotten Pandemic, The Influenza of 1918", Cambridge University Press, New York.
19. Van Way, C. W. Martile and G. Thompson. 2020. "World World I Diseases" https://www.worldwarIcentennial.org/index.php/diseases-in-world-war-I.html
20. World War I. 2020. "Diseases in World War I, Infectious Diseases" https://www.worldwarIcenternnial.org/index/php/diseases-in-world-war-I.html

11. World War II

1. World Book Encyclopedia. 1979. "World War II, Vol. W. World Book-Childcraft International, Inc., Chicago

2. Hambling, D. 2020. "The Most Important Battles of World War II", https://www.popularmechanics.com/militar/g2652/most-important-battles-world-war-ii/

3. Adhikan, S. 2019. "The 10 Major Battles of World War II, https://www.ancienthistorylists.com/world-war-2/10-major-battles-of-world-war-2/

4. McDowell, L. 2018. 'The Presidents, Humor, Events and Mortality", Xulon Press, Maitland, FL.

5. Hamilton, N. 2001. "Presidents", Checkmark Books, New York.

6. Wikipedia, 2019. "Franklin D. Roosevelt", http://en.wikipedia.org/wiki/FranklinD.Roosevelt

7. Beschloss, M. 2018. "Presidents of War", Crown, New York.

8. World War II, 2020. "World War II: Summary, Combatants & Facts", https://www.history.com/topics/world-war-ii/world-war-ii-history

9. CQ Researcher. 2020. "Disease in Wartime", https://library.cqpress.com/cqresearcher/document.php?id=cqresrre1942021000

10. Hoyt, K. 2018. "More Soldiers used to Die of Disease than Battle Injuries", https://www.businessinsider.com/how-world-war-ii-and-the-us-army-spurred-vaccine-inno...

11. WHV.2020 "We Honor Veterans" https://www.wehonorveterans.org/working-for-veterans/by-conflict/wwii/

12. Moore, A. 1952. "Malaria Chemotherapy", Encyclopedia of Chemical Technology, R. Kirk and D. Othmer, eds., New York.

13. Packard, R. 2007. "A Short History of Malaria", Johns Hopkins University Press, Baltimore.

14. Zinsser, H. 1996. "Rats, Lice and History: A Chronicle of Pestilence and Plagues", Black Dog & Leventhal, ISBN 978-1-884822-47-6

15. Wikipedia. 2020. "Epidemic Typhus", https://en.wikipedia.org/wiki/Epidemic_typhus

16. Hepatitis Outbreak. 1987. "World War II Hepatitis Outbreak was biggest in History".

17. Mancuso, J. 2017. "Tuberculosis Screening and Control in the U.S. Military in War and Peace", https://www.ncbi.nlm.nih.gov/pmc/articles/PMC5308149/

18. Vonderiehr, G. 1938. "Control of Venereal Diseases", E.R.R., Vol. 11, p.281.

19. Office of Medical History. 2020. "Army Experience with Diarrheal Disorders during World War II", https://history.amedd.army.mil/booksdocs/wwii/PM4/CH17-2.htm

20. McDowell, L. 2013. "Vitamin History, The Early Years, University of Florida, First Edition Design Publishing, Sarasota, FL.

21. Brinson, F. 2020. "Soldiers Battled Enemies, Filth Conditions, Foreign Disease, and Wounds that Linger in the Aftermath", https://www.aapc.com/blog/26557-wwii-military-health-in-the-pacific/

22. Camp Hospitals. 2020. "Sickness and Epidemics", http://auschwitz.org/en/history/camp-hosptials/sickness-and-epidemics/

23. Holocaust Museum. 2018. "Search Results-Starvation and Disease", https://www.ushmm.org/wlc/search/index.php?query=Starvation+and+Disease&langcode=.

24. LaMay, C. 2014. "Strategist and Tactician", Warren Kozak, Barnes & Noble

25. Robson, D., E. Welch, N. Beeching and G. Hill. 2009. "Consequences of Captivity: Health Effects of Far East Imprisonment in World War II, Inter. J. Medicine 102:87.

26. McDowell, L. 2021. "The Presidents as Officers in the Military", University of

Florida, First Edition Design Publishing, Inc. Sarasota, FL.

12. Korean War

1. Wikipedia, 2021. "Korean War", https://en.wikipedia.org/wiki/Korean_War
2. The World Book Encyclopedia. 1979. Vol. 11, p. 299. ISBN 0-7166-0079-X, Chicago.
3. CBS Interactive Inc., 2018. "The Korean War: Timeline", https://www.cbsnews.com/news/the-korean-war-timeline/
4. Korean War Battles. 2019. "List of Korean War battles", https://www.ranker.com/list/a-list-of-all-korean-war-battles/reference
5. Misachi, J., 2017. "Major Battles of the Korean War", https://www.worldatlas.com/articles/major-battles-of-the-korean-war.html
6. Grabenstein, J., P. Pittman, J. Greenwood, and R. Engler. 2006. "Immunization to Protect the U.S. Armed Forces: Heritage, current practice and prospects" Epidemiologic Rev. 28:3.
7. Knowledge Sharing Program. 2013. "Establishment of Korea's Infectious Disease Surveillance System", Ministry of Health and Welfare, Republic of Korea.
8. Malaria Korea History. 2011. "A History of Malaria in Modern Korea, 1876-1945" Uisahak Jun. 30:20(1):53.
9. Long, A. 1954. General Aspects of Preventative Medicine in the Far East Command. P. 248, Washington, D.C.
10. Lee, H. "Korean Hemorrhagic Fever, http://www.enivd.de/EBOLA/ebola-53.htm
11. Cook, G. 2001. "Influence of Diarrheal Disease on Military and Naval Campaigns", J.R. Soc. Med. 94:95.
12. Pond, W. and J. Smadel. 1954. "Neurotropic Viral Diseases in the Far East during the Korean War", https://history.amedd.army.mil/booksdocs/korea/recad2/ch5-3.html
13. Greenberg, J. 1972. "Venereal Disease in the Armed Forces". Med. Aspects Human Sexual 6:165
14. Korean War Educator. 2021. "Cold Weather Injuries in Korean War", http://www.koreanwar-educator.org/topics/homefront/p_cold_injury.htm
15. Lee, M., M. Kang and S. Huh. 2013. "Causes of Death of Prisoners of War during the Korean War" Yonsei Med. J. 54(2):480.
16. Cowdry, A. 1986. "The Medics' War: U.S. Government Center for Military History.
17. Ritchie, E. 2002. "Psychiatry in the Korean War: Perils, PIES and Prisoners of War" Military Medicine 167:(11):898.
18. McDowell, L. 2021. "Presidents as Military Officers", University of Florida, First Edition Design Publishing Inc., Sarasota, FL.

13. Vietnam War

1. The World Book Encyclopedia. 1979. Vol. 20, p. 292g ISBN 0-7166-0079-X, Chicago.
2. McDowell, L. 2021. "Presidents as Military Officers", University of Florida, First Edition Design Publishing Inc., Sarasota, FL.
3. Wikipedia. 2021. "Vietnam War", https://en.wikipedia.org/wiki/Vietnam_War
4. Russell, S. 2016. "The Vietnam War: II Major Battles", War History Online, https://www.warhistoryonline.com/vietnam-war/top-11-battles-vietnam-war-x.html
5. Battlefield Vietnam. 2021. "The Black Church, PBS, https://www.pbs.org/battlefieldvietnam/timeline/index1.html
6. Key Battles. 2021. "Vietnam War", https://www.pritzkermilitary.org/explore/

vietnam-war/key-battles

7. Center For the Advancement of Health. 1997. "Vietnam Combat Linked to Many Diseases 20 Years Later" Science Daily 26, November

8. Lemon, S., S. Thaul and S. Fisseha 2002. "Protecting our Forces: Improving Vaccine Acquisition and Availability in the U.S. Military. National Academies Press, Washington, D.C.

9. Fatal Casualty Statistics. 2008. "Vitamin War U.S. Military Fatal Casualty Statistics", https://www.archives.gov/research/military/vietnam-war/casualty-statistics

10. Diseases in Vietnam. 2021. "Diseases in Vietnam, Facts and Details", https://factsanddetails.com/southeast-asia/Vietnam/sub5_9f/entry-3462.html

11. Health. 2019. "Common Diseases in Ho Chi Minh City", https://www.citypassguide.com/forum/what-are-the-most-common-diseases-and-sicknesses

12. Kelley, P. 2021. "Did U.S. Soldiers Contact Diseases during The Vietnam War?" https://quora.com/Did-U-S-soldiers-contract-diseases-during-the-Vietnam-War

13. Office of Academic Affiliations. 2021. "Military Health History, Vietnam", https://www.va.gov/oaa/pocketcard/vietnam.asp

14. Lloyd, S. 2002. "U.S. Vietnam. War Soldiers and Malaria", Vietnam Magazine, June.

15. Cook, G. 2001. "Influence of Diarrheal Diseases on Military and Naval Campaigns." J.R. Soc. Med. 94:95.

16. Reno, J. 2017. "Parasite Reportedly Killing Vietnam Veterans, 40 years after War", https;//www.healthline.com/health-news/parasite-killing-vietnam-veterans

17. The Borgen Project. 2021. "Five of the most common diseases in Vietnam", https://borgenproject.org/5-of-the-most-common-diseases-in-vietnam/

18. McDowell, L. 2013. "Vitamin History, The Early Years", University of Florida, First Edition Design Pub., Sarasota, FL.

19. Hubbell, J. 1976. "P.O.W., A definitive history of the American Prisoner-of-war Experience in Vietnam, 1963-1973. New York: Reader's Digest Press.

20. Hill & Ponton P.A. 2020. "Agent Orange Diseases and Symptoms breakdown", https://www.hillandponton.com/agent-orange-and-your-body-symptoms/

14. Iraq and Afghanistan Wars

1. McDowell, L. 2021. "Presidents as Military Officers", University of Florida, First Edition Design Publishing Inc., Sarasota, FL.

2. History.com Editors. 2009. "Persian Gulf War", https://www.history.com/topics/middle-east/persian-gulf-war

3. Brangwin, N. 2021. "Anzac Day 2020: 30th Anniversary of the Gulf War", https:///www.aph.gov.au/About_Parliament/Parliamentary_Departments/Parliamentary_Library/p

4. Hamilton, N. 2001. "Presidents", Checkmark Books, New York.

5. Wikipedia: 2021. "Gulf War", https://en.wikipedia.org/wiki/Gulf_War

6. Schifferus, S. 2013. "U.S. Names Coalition of the Willing", BBC News Retrieved Spt. 1, 2008.

7. Wikipedia. 2021. "Iraq War", https://en.wikipedia.org/wiki/Iraq_War

8. Garamone, J. 2002. "Iraq part of Global War on Terrorism, Rumsfeld" http://www.defenselink.mil/news/Sep2002/n09192002_200209194.html

9. Sengupta, K. 2006. "Occupation Made World less Safe, Pro War Institute. https://web.archive.org/web/20060920050852/http://www.commond05htm

10. Britannica 2018. "George W. Bush", https://www.britannicacom/biography/George-W-Bush

11. Bush, G. 2010. "Decision Points", Crown Publishers, New York

12. The World Book Encyclopedia. 1979. Vol. 1, p. 82, ISBN 0-7166-0079-X, Chicago

13. Witte, G. 2021. "Afghanistan war", https://www.britannica.com/event/Afghanistan-War

14. Wikipedia. 2021. "War in Afghanistan", https://en.wikipedia.org/wiki/War_in_Afghanistan_(2001%E2%80%93present)

15. Kristof, N. 2002. "A Merciful War", https://www.nytimes.com/2002/02/01/opinion/a-merciful-war.html

16. Sartin, J. 2000. "Gulf War Illnesses: Causes and Controversies" Mayo Clinic Proceedings Vol. 75(8):811.

17. Putnam, S., J. Sanders, R. French, M. Monteville. 2006. J. Travel Med. 13:92

18. Sanders, J., S. Putnam, M. Riddle and D. Tribble. 2005. "Military Importance of Diarrhea: Lessons from the Middle East" Curr. Opin. Gastroenterol 21:14

19. Hyams KC. 1999. Gulf War Syndrome: Potential Role of Infectious Diseases. Current Opinion in Infectious Diseases 12(5):439

20. Smith TC, T. Corbeil, M. Ryan, J. Heller and G. Gray. 2004. In-theater Hospitalizations of U.S. and Allied Personnel during the 1991 Gulf War. Am. Of Epidemiology 159(11):1064.

21. Bloom, B., R. Atun, and T. Cohen. 2017. "Tuberculosis", Major Infectious Diseases", 3rd Ed., Washington, D.C.

22. Sanders, J., S. Putonam, and C. Frankart 2005. Impact of illness and Non-Combat Injury during Iraq and Afghanistan Wars. J. Trep. Med. And Hygiene 73:713.

23. Aronson, N., J. Sanders and K. Moran. 2006. "In Harm's War: Infectious in Deployed American Military Forces". Clinical Infectious Diseases 43(8)15.

24. Hyams, K., K. Hanson, and J. Wignall. 1995. "The Impact of Infectious Diseases on the Health of US Troops Deployed to the Persian Gulf during Operations Desert Shield and Desert Storm." Clinical Infectious Dis. 20(6):1497

25. Andrews, R.B. 2004. "Brucellosis in a Soldier who recently Returned from Iraq". Medical Surveillance Monthly Report 10(4):30.

ABOUT THE AUTHOR

Dr. Lee R. Mcdowell

The author of the book, Dr. Lee R. McDowell, is an emeritus professor of nutrition at the University of Florida. In nutrition research he has published over 1500 scientific articles and has taught five different nutrition courses. He has written a total of 16 books. This is the 3rd book written by the author dealing with American History.

Why is a nutrition professor writing books on history? Although his major work is nutrition, he has taken college American History courses and is particularly familiar with presidential history.

The first history book was "The Presidents, Humor, Events and Morality" (2018). The second book was "Presidents as Military Officers" (2021). The present, War and Disease" book emphasizes disease incidences during U.S. wars. For this publication the president's role as Commander-in-Chief will be noted. The book has two major sections: 1) Major battles for each war and 2) Incidence of major diseases and treatments.

Dr. McDowell has given many talks on history and nutrition in the U.S. and many countries, to include 6 continents.
He is a "Fellow" of two International Societies and has won many awards in teaching and research. From one society he won the highest award available for research (Morrison Award).

His other books include Latin American Tables of Feed Composition (1974), Latin American Symposium of Mineral Nutrition for Grazing Ruminants (1978), Minerals for Grazing Ruminants in Tropical Regions (4 editions, 1985-2005). Nutrition of grazing Ruminants in Warm Climates (1985); Vitamins in Animal and Human Nutrition (1989, 2000); Minerals in Animal and Human Nutrition (1992, 2003); Vitamin History, The Early Years (2013); Mineral Nutrition History, The Early Years (2017).

The McDowells have a great interest and appreciation of American history. Both the author and his wife (Lorraine) are direct descendants of Mayflower passengers in 1620. Lee is the 13th descendant of both Richard Warren and James and Suzannah Chilton. Lorraine is the 12th direct descendant of both Isaac Allerton and William Brewster.

Made in the USA
Coppell, TX
20 November 2024

40624776R00131